NARCISSISTIC CONFRONTATIONS

A BIBLICAL GUIDE TO YOUR ABUSIVE FAMILY AND CHURCH FAMILY'S BATTLE TACTICS, COVERT OPERATIONS, AND NUCLEAR MELTDOWNS

SISTER RENEE PITTELLI

outskirtspress
DENVER, COLORADO

Narcissistic Confrontations
A Biblical Guide To Your Abusive Family And Church Family's Battle Tactics,
Covert Operations, And Nuclear Meltdowns

v3.0

Outskirts Press, Inc.
http://www.outskirtspress.com

ISBN: 978-1-4787-0707-3

Library of Congress Control Number: 2013907819

PRINTED IN THE UNITED STATES OF AMERICA

Disclaimer

By reading this book, you certify that you understand and agree that the author is not a professional counselor, but just an ordinary woman who loves the Lord and hopes that her experiences and testimonies can be used to help others. Professional counseling with your pastor or therapist and prayer for wisdom from the Lord is strongly urged before making any decisions concerning your own personal relationships. Whatever the author writes is strictly her own personal opinion and testimony and not intended to give or offer any advice. The ideas in this book are not intended to take the place of professional counseling. The testimonies discussed in this book are composites of many different testimonies. All names and identifying details mentioned have been changed, and any resemblance to any locations, organizations, persons or characters, real or fictional, living or deceased, is entirely coincidental and unintentional. Therefore, the author and the publisher accept no responsibility for any inaccuracies or omissions and specifically disclaim any liability, loss, risk, damage, or injury, personal or otherwise, caused directly or indirectly, by the contents of this book.

Dedicated with Love and Gratitude to
My Inspiration and Role Model for Ideal Motherhood
My Cousin Rose
Beloved Family Matriarch
Who Raised Her Beautiful Family With Love, Devotion and Selflessness
And Who Always Had Some Love, Encouragement and Thoughtful Advice Left Over For Me
Who Was Treasured All The Days Of Her Long and Wonderful Life
By Her Children, Grandchildren, Great-Grandchildren
And All Who Knew Her
Thank You, Rose
You Were Too Humble To Realize How Much You Blessed Me
I Miss You Every Day

TABLE OF CONTENTS

PART 4: VICTORY FOR THE CHILDREN OF THE KING

ALSO BY SISTER RENEE PITTELLI

INTRODUCTION

THE ABUSER'S REACTIONS TO REBUKE OR DIVORCE

BETTER A POOR BUT WISE YOUTH THAN AN OLD BUT FOOLISH KING WHO NO LONGER KNOWS HOW TO TAKE WARNING.....Ecclesiastes 4:13 NIV.

AS A DOG RETURNETH TO HIS VOMIT, SO A FOOL RETURNETH TO HIS FOLLY.....Proverbs 26:11 KJV.

BUT BECAUSE OF YOUR STUBBORNNESS AND YOUR UNREPENTANT HEART, YOU ARE STORING UP WRATH AGAINST YOURSELF FOR THE DAY OF GOD'S WRATH, WHEN HIS RIGHTEOUS JUDGMENT WILL BE REVEALED. GOD WILL GIVE TO EACH PERSON ACCORDING TO WHAT HE HAS DONE....Romans 2:5-6 NIV.

It is truly a wonder to behold the amount of time, energy, and creativity that abusers and their Silent Partners put into inventing an infinite variety of lame excuses to justify why they should be allowed to keep on hurting other people. It's disturbing and creepy to realize the amount of thought spent on advance planning, manipulation, scheming and conniving, moves and countermoves~ all just to be able to maintain control and dominance over us. And also to make sure that we have no support system, by turning other people against us. How much easier and more constructive it would be to just redirect and devote all of that effort into simply changing their behavior.

But they don't want to. So, whether you are confronting your abuser, reading about all of her ridiculous excuses, or just beginning to realize all the convoluted manipulations she is capable of, keep in mind that all you're really asking of her, and all she really has to do, is *just stop it!*

I have addressed some of these inappropriate responses and lame excuses in my previous books, *"Breaking the Bonds of Adult Child Abuse: A Biblical Textbook on Abusive Narcissistic Families, How They Operate, And How To Deal With Them"* and *"Narcissistic Predicaments: A Biblical Guide to Navigating the Schemes, Snares, and No-Win Situations Unique to Abusive Families."* Here are some more improper and unacceptable reactions that many of us have experienced when we began to set limits on our controlling or abusive relatives, and the chapters in this book which deal with a selected variety of them. An abuser's repertoire is virtually unlimited, so this list is by no means all-inclusive:

- **"I have no idea why you're mad at me!"**~ (See Chapter 10: "Selective Amnesia: 'I Have No Idea What I Did Wrong!', or 'I Don't Know What Happened~ She Just Stopped Speaking to Me!'").
- **Denial**~ "That never happened!", "I did not!"~ (See Chapter 10: "Selective Amnesia: 'I Have No Idea What I Did Wrong!', or 'I Don't Know What Happened~ She Just Stopped Speaking to Me!'").
- **Accusing you of trying to start an argument**, yelling or screaming at her, or deliberately trying to upset her by confronting her.
- **Becoming vindictive or vaguely threatening**~"You'd better be sorry for what you said!"~ as if you had no right to confront her.

- **Crying or laying on a guilt trip**~"I can't believe you would say such a thing to me", "You don't love me", "How can you be so mean to your own mother?"
- **Inappropriate, juvenile, or overly dramatic displays of anger**~ Gritting teeth, screaming, speeding up the car, name-calling, hanging up the phone, putting the phone down and walking away, making faces at you, mimicking, imitating, making fun of you when you complain or confront her, etc.
- **"I can't help it!"**~ "That's just the way I am", "I can't control myself", "It's subconscious, I don't realize I'm doing it", "You know I don't mean it", "I have trouble expressing myself," and various other mental defects she has~ (See Chapter 11: "She Can't Help The Way She Acts~ So You'll Just Have to Accept It, Forgive Her Anyway, and Not Expect Her to Change").
- "**You misunderstood me**", "You don't know what you're talking about", "You took it the wrong way," and various other mental defects *you* have~ (See Chapter 14: "The Mystery Excuse for Abuse: Various Versions of 'You Don't Know What You're Talking About' With No Further Explanation Given").
- **Refusing to take responsibility** or be accountable for her own actions.
- **She's old,** so you should let her get away with murder~ (See Chapter 12: "The Old Age Excuses: 'She's Old~ and That's How They Get,' or, 'He's Old~ So He's Entitled'").
- **Blaming you**~ (See Chapter 16: "Desperate Measures: When They Sense They're Losing Their Grip on You, Five Surprising Ways of Keeping You Attached").
- **Blaming someone else.**
- **"I did it for your own good."**~ (See Chapter 8: "Spin Control: Making Abuse Sound Like a *Good* Thing").
- **"We were *both* wrong,"** or, "We *both* hurt each other," when in reality the victim did nothing wrong at all~ (See Chapter 14:

"The Mystery Excuse for Abuse: Various Versions of 'You Don't Know What You're Talking About' With No Further Explanation Given," and Chapter 15: "The 'Christian' Abuser: Twisting God's Word to Justify Abuse").

- **Triangling** ~ Enlisting someone else against you.
- **Sarcasm.**
- **"I *said* I was sorry,"** with no change in behavior.
- Telling you that **you have "no idea what *she's* been going through"** or "What's going on in *her* life," as if *whatever* might be happening in her life would make it okay for her to abuse you~ (See Chapter 14: "The Mystery Excuse for Abuse: Various Versions of 'You Don't Know What You're Talking About' With No Further Explanation Given").
- Telling you that **she has repented to God** for what she did to *you*, **so her conscience is now clear**~ (See Chapter 15: "The 'Christian' Abuser: Twisting God's Word to Justify Abuse").
- Telling you that she has repented to God, **so she doesn't have to make any amends to *you***~ (See Chapter 15: "The 'Christian' Abuser: Twisting God's Word to Justify Abuse").
- Telling you that **God forgave her so she doesn't have to explain herself to you** or "relive the past."
- Telling you that **God forgives her, whether *you* do or not.**
- Telling you that **God forgives her, *so you have to* also.**
- **Telling you not to "judge" her** when you are confronting her~ (See Chapter 13: "'You're Not Supposed to Judge Me': The Difference Between Judging and Rebuking").
- **Trying to make *you* feel guilty**~ (See Chapter 16: "Desperate Measures: When They Sense They're Losing Their Grip on You, Five Surprising Ways of Keeping You Attached" and Chapter 18: "'My Days Are Numbered!' (And You're Speeding It Up by Confronting Me) or, 'I'm Sick, So You Can't Hold Me Accountable'").

- **"After all I've done for you!"**~ (See Chapter 9: "'After All I've Done For You': Trotting Out the 'You Owe Me' Excuse for Abuse").
- **"You're too sensitive."**
- **"You take everything the wrong way."**~ (See Chapter 14: "The Mystery Excuse for Abuse: Various Versions of 'You Don't Know What You're Talking About' With No Further Explanation Given").
- **Refusing to hear you out**~ "I'm leaving if you continue to speak to me like this."
- **Turning it around**~ Getting huffy or angry at *you* for letting him know that he upset you or for setting limits. Trying to make *you* apologize to *him!*
- **Feigned helplessness**~ "I did the best I could."
- **"*You're* the one with the problem!"**- (See Chapter 16: "Desperate Measures: When They Sense They're Losing Their Grip on You, Five Surprising Ways of Keeping You Attached," and Chapter 17: "Let's Go to Counseling Together and Work On *Our* Problem").
- Telling you that ***other people*** **think you're the one with the problem**.
- Telling you that ***you are "the only person*** **who has a problem with her."** Everybody else loves her!
- **Pretending to be insulted** when you confront him.
- **"You're always complaining!"**
- **"Nothing I do is ever good enough!"**
- **Disowning you**, "I have no daughter!"~ (See Chapter 16: "Desperate Measures: When They Sense They're Losing Their Grip on You, Five Surprising Ways of Keeping You Attached," and Chapter 29: "Getting Disowned: The Best Punishment Ever").
- **"You deserved it!"** or, "You were asking for it!"

- **Escalating the abuse,** now that she knows it's getting to you~ (See Chapter 16: "Desperate Measures: When They Sense They're Losing Their Grip on You, Five Surprising Ways of Keeping You Attached").
- **"Let's keep this between us"**, "Don't tell ________." Abusers and their Silent Partners are only able to continue their abuse if there is secrecy. They count on others being too intimidated or embarrassed to expose them~ (See Chapter 8: "Spin Control: Making Abuse Sound Like a *Good* Thing").
- **Pretending to lose his patience** with your complaints~ "Just forget it!", "Get over it!", "I said I was sorry! What more do you want from me?"~ (See Chapter 14: "The Mystery Excuse for Abuse: Various Versions of 'You Don't Know What You're Talking About' With No Further Explanation Given").
- **Minimizing** the offense or **invalidating** your feelings, telling you you're "making a big deal out of it" or "making a mountain out of a molehill."

In this book, we will study some of the abuser's most popular inappropriate responses to our attempts to resolve our conflicts or to our decision to distance ourselves or disown him. We will also talk about some of the craziness that happens when a narcissist goes ballistic and confronts *us*.

Fear of exposure is a big motivating factor in the behavior most narcissists display when confronted. Besides Nonsense Statements and other insanity they spew at us, narcissists are liars and gossips, and discrediting us so no one will believe us is one of their prime offensive tactics. Abusers isolate their victims, and they do this by eliminating or neutralizing anyone who might offer support. Narcissists are known to contact people in our lives whom *they* barely know, or don't know at all, like our in-laws, neighbors, friends, bosses or coworkers, pretending to be "upset" or "concerned" about us, and then filling their heads with how mean or mentally ill *we* are. Isolating you by going around behind your back, lying and bad-mouthing you, is a powerful weapon in your abuser's arsenal. It's often subtle, sneaky and confusing, and can be hard to recognize and counteract. You might not realize what's going on until the damage has been done. *Most people tend to retain and believe the first story they hear, regardless of all future evidence to the contrary, so beating our abusers to the punch and confiding in the people we care about* ***before*** *the narcissist can becomes an important defensive strategy in* ***our*** *arsenals.*

Many family abusers bide their time for years until our children are young adults, and then contact them, pretending to love and miss them so much, and turning our own naïve kids against us. After insinuating themselves into their lives, they then start using and abusing our kids. This is why I strongly suggest being honest with your children and raising them to know the facts about abusive estranged relatives, so they can be armed with the truth and protect themselves in the future. We need to be educated about this sneaky strategy as well as all the others, so we can protect ourselves and our loved ones from unscrupulous and manipulative relatives.

Although it's impossible to cover every excuse your narcissistic and psychopathic relatives or church family members might use for why you should allow them to continue abusing you, it is possible to learn, by these examples, something about their thought processes. You aren't a narcissist, so you don't think like one. You aren't an abuser, so you don't think like one. You aren't a psychopath, so you don't think like one. *But* ***they are****, so they do.* If you have ever wasted your time wondering "Why do they *act* this way?" the simple answer is, "Because it works." And as long as it keeps working, they will keep doing it. All of their thought processes are oriented toward enabling them to keep doing it, just like all of a predator's thought processes are focused on being able to hunt and catch prey.

We need to understand these thought processes. We need to know our enemies and how they think, just as if we were fighting a war. It's the only hope we have of protecting ourselves and the people we love who trust us and depend upon us to protect them. If you know how your abusive family thinks, then you will be able to anticipate a lot of what they are going to do next, or what they might already be doing behind the scenes, and take the necessary steps to thwart it. My prayer is that this book will help you understand some of the battle tactics and maneuvers in your abuser's arsenal.

Like my previous books, this one started out being about narcissistic and abusive birth-families and extended families. But as I was writing it, the Lord kept bringing me testimonies about abusive and narcissistic church families, as well. I began to realize that there are many similarities between our birth-families and our church families~ relationships, hierarchies, narcissists, psychopaths, bullies and abusers, cliques,"Golden Children" and Scapegoats, power-struggles, control-freakiness, jealousy, envy, battle strategies, domination, the claiming of "authority" over other people where there is no right to it, dysfunction versus healthiness, good versus evil, and on and on. In many ways, birth-families and church families are interchangeable, and we can learn valuable lessons about either one from studying the other. So after much prayerful consideration, the Lord has led me to include these testimonies and examples of abusive church families in this book along with examples of birth-family abuse, and to change the focus of the book to include both types of family structures. I pray this will be a blessing to a wider range of abuse victims caught in a variety of different situations, while still being helpful to those of us who have abusive birth-families, extended families and in-laws. Additionally, I'd like to expand the definition of "church family" to include not only those who actually attend church with us, but all of those who claim to be brothers and sisters in Christ, and yet act like anything *but*. No matter which "family" our bullies and abusers belong to, their attacks and tactics, and the defensive maneuvers and counter-strategies we will need to protect ourselves and our loved ones, are pretty much the same.

FOOLS HAVE NO INTEREST IN UNDERSTANDING;
THEY ONLY WANT TO AIR THEIR OWN OPINIONS...
Proverbs 18:2 NLT.

FOOLS MAKE FUN OF GUILT, BUT THE GODLY
ACKNOWLEDGE IT AND SEEK RECONCILIATION....
Proverbs 14:9 NLT.

PART 1

PREPARING FOR WAR: GETTING TO KNOW YOUR ENEMY AND FIGURING OUT WHAT YOU'RE UP AGAINST

CHAPTER 1

THE NARCISSIST'S 35 RULES OF ENGAGEMENT, AND SOME CLARIFICATION ON WHAT "LACKING EMPATHY" MEANS

THE NARCISSIST'S 35 RULES OF ENGAGEMENT

1. I can say anything I like, and you also can say anything I like. You are not allowed to say anything unless you are sure it will not offend me. (Hint: Praise/ compliments).
2. I can do anything I want. You are not allowed to do anything unless you are sure I will like it.
3. You must call me regularly to see how I am and give me attention. I never have to call you, unless I need something. And when I do call you, you'd better take my call or call me back immediately.
4. You have to respect me. I do not have to respect you. And I don't.
5. I am allowed to lie about you. You are not allowed to tell the truth about me.
6. I am allowed to lie about you, to make you look bad. You *must* lie about me, to make me look *good.*
7. I am the only one allowed to get angry. You are not allowed to get angry.
8. I am the only one allowed to have "hurt feelings." You are not allowed to have hurt feelings.

9. I am the only one allowed to feel "insulted." You are not allowed to feel insulted.
10. I can falsely accuse you of doing things you never did, and you are not allowed to make a liar out of me by defending yourself.
11. You are not allowed to expose me and reveal the things I really *did* do. You must cover up my misbehavior and keep it a secret.
12. You are never allowed to complain. That's *my* job.
13. You are never allowed to confront me. I'm the only one who is allowed to confront anybody.
14. I can make faces at you, scowl, roll my eyes and sneer, but you'd better not look at me "funny," or even smile at me.
15. I can stop speaking to you, but you are not allowed to stop speaking to me. If you do, I am allowed to stalk and harass you until you respond to me.
16. I can disown you, but you do not have the right to walk away from me.
17. When I'm ready *un*-disown you, you have to take me back and start talking to me again, with no further discussion of whatever caused our "rift." You have no choice in the matter. I am the only one who has a choice.
18. Everything I've ever done to hurt you is "all in the past," even if it was only five minutes ago. So you need to get over it and quit holding a grudge.
19. I can "vent" to other people about you, but you must suffer in silence.
20. I can tell everybody the things you "did to" me, but you are not allowed to tell anybody the things I did to you.
21. You are not allowed to have any opinion that differs from mine.

22. You must agree with everything I say, but I am allowed to criticize, ridicule and degrade the things you say.
23. You are not allowed to have any privacy. I can ask you any personal question I want to and you'd better answer me. I can also snoop and pry and ask other people for information about you. It is always open season on your thoughts, feelings, opinions and decisions. But don't you dare ever question *me.*
24. I have no sense of humor when it comes to me. You must take me very seriously, but I am allowed to mock you and even laugh in your face.
25. If you don't know why I'm mad, you'd better figure it out, because I'm not going to tell you.
26. If another person upsets me, you'd *better* take my side and confront and shun them. If another person upsets *you,* good for them. You deserve it.
27. I know everything, you know nothing.
28. You are weak and inferior. I am a superior being, a Special Person, and you must always acknowledge that and never forget your place.
29. You have no freedom to even think independently. I have all the freedoms in our relationship.
30. Your job is to take care of my needs and my feelings. You are not allowed to have needs or feelings of your own. If you do, then take care of them yourself and don't expect anything from me.
31. *Every interaction we have is a competition, and I am the only one who is allowed to win.* You must never "show me up," be better than me at anything, know something I don't know, or be having a nice time and enjoying yourself when I am not. And don't you dare ever feel good about yourself either, because, as far as I'm concerned, you are so far beneath me that

you can have nothing to feel good about. If you do feel good about yourself, it means that you are challenging me and my opinion of you, and that you are starting to believe you are as good as I am.

32. I can accuse you of manipulation, dishonesty and having a hidden agenda, and you are not allowed to protest or set the record straight. *People like me, who typically have ulterior motives for everything they do, assume that everybody else has ulterior motives, too.* You're not fooling me. You're just as bad as I am. You think you're so good, but you're no better than me. You try to make people think you're such an innocent little goodie-two-shoes. But I know you're just like me, only dumber.
33. You have no rights. I have all the rights.
34. If I am ever forced to "eat crow" (apologize, admit I was wrong, or change my bad behavior), don't think it's over. I will get you back at the first opportunity.
35. You are here to do for me. I am not here to do for you. You are only here for my convenience. When you are no longer useful or become too much trouble, I will kick you to the curb. Until I want something from you again.

SOME CLARIFICATION ON WHAT "LACKING EMPATHY" MEANS

Just because I'm a narcissist or a psychopath and you have heard I have no empathy, do not misinterpret this to mean that I do not understand your pain, I cannot comprehend what pain and suffering and sorrow are, or I lack the ability to know I'm hurting you. I comprehend pain just fine. I know what "feelings" are, and how to produce them in *you*. I understand exquisitely, I just don't care. I know all about pain and sorrow~ from the *giving* end, not the *receiving* end. In fact, I'm an expert. I *love* hurting you. It's what I live for. So of course I understand when you're hurt and know when I've hurt you~ it means I succeeded, I won, and it makes my day. *Just because I don't feel bad* ***for*** *you doesn't mean I don't know* ***you*** *feel bad.* Just because I don't feel any guilt or remorse doesn't mean I don't know what those feelings are. After all, one of my favorite hobbies is making *you* feel guilty. You cannot feel the pain of someone who just broke their arm, but you *do* know they're in pain. Likewise, I cannot feel your pain, but I *do* know you're in pain, and ten points for me if I'm the cause of it! I'm cold-blooded, cruel and ruthless, but I'm not stupid.

CHAPTER 2

CONVERSATIONS WITH NARCISSISTS

WHAT IS WRONG WITH THIS PICTURE?

Ever wonder just how oblivious, self-absorbed, insensitive, callous and lacking in empathy a narcissist or psychopath can be? What can you see in this post from a social networking site, written not by a child, but by a forty-something "devout, loving Christian" church leader:

"This has been the nuttiest month of *my* life ever. The loss of my uncle, and watching my parents and aunt go through a very tough time because of this, breaking up with my boyfriend *again,* and then watching as a very dear friend went through an unbearably hard situation in her life. All in a month, it was just crazy! But having said all that, I believe that *I* have grown as a friend and a person more than ever, and I am SO happy about that!!!!!! ☺ God is still great!"

Wow. The perfect example of how narcissists highjack other people's news to get attention for themselves. Her, as an observer, *watching* the disasters in other people's lives makes it the nuttiest month *she's* ever had in *her* life, because narcissists do not acknowledge boundaries and see others as separate individuals in their own right apart from the center-of-the-universe narcissist. As appalling as it is that this woman managed to make *other people's* tragedies all about her, and even made it sound as if their heartbreaks and sorrows wound up being *beneficial* to her by making her "grow as a person" and be a better "friend," what really gave me the heebie-jeebies was the inappropriate cheerfulness, right down to lighthearted words like "nuttiest" and "crazy" instead of empathetic words like "sad," the multiple exclamation points, and the smiley face. This is why I warned you up front that this was not written by a child, who might not know any better. I can almost imagine the writer grinning in delight as she posted that smiley face to let you know *she's smiling.* That's what the smiley face *means*. Yikes.

Cold-blooded, demented, chilling and creepy though it is, this post is merely an extreme example of how narcissists and psychopaths "normally" communicate. Their demeanor, facial expressions and words often fail to match the subject matter or the gravity of the situation. They tend to smile and even laugh at totally inappropriate times. There is frequently a tone in even sorrowful or tragic statements that makes it sound as if they are happy, gloating, or even bragging, like this woman bragged about her personal growth and becoming an even *better* person, thanks to her "loved ones'" heartaches. Narcissists see nothing wrong or abnormal with any of this, which you will find out by their reaction if you point it out to them.

Not all conversations with narcissists are confrontations. Some are just "normal" conversations, although I use the term loosely. Unfortunately, what qualifies as a "normal" conversation with normal people is a different animal when we're chatting with the self-centered narcissist. There is never any give-and-take, caring about us or interest in our lives or what we have to say, and no matter what the subject, the conversation always gets turned back to the narcissist. Good news or bad news, this is how it goes:

You: I had my mammogram and they found a lump.
Narcissist: I have a lump too! I felt it for six months and finally got up the courage to go. They told me it's nothing, but I'm still worried. You know how they make mistakes! What if they're wrong? What if I have cancer? I don't want to die!

You: I'm so happy. I found a lovely blue dress for my daughter's wedding.
Narcissist: It sounds just like the dress I wore for my son's wedding.

You: I think I'm getting a cold.
Narcissist: Oh, I've been sick for *weeks*. I just can't shake this cold, plus the coughing keeps giving me headaches. I feel like hell. It's horrible. I wish it would just *stop*, already.

You: I have wonderful news. We're having a baby!
Narcissist: So are we! Well, we're not pregnant yet, but we're going to start trying right now. Isn't that great? Then we'll *both* have babies!

You: We got engaged last night! We're getting married!
Narcissist: Well, when *we* got married, we had three hundred people at our wedding, it was so big but that was all our friends and family and of course business associates too, we had to book the cathedral to fit everybody, we wanted to make it a destination wedding in Hawaii but not everyone could come, I was really annoyed at that, they should have taken off from work and flown out, but some people are just so selfish, so anyway we had it at a big catering hall, we served filet mignon with a white wine reduction and cream of mushroom soup and asparagus, and oh my, we had twelve different appetizers, and you should have seen our cake, it was so gorgeous! People were talking about it for years afterwards! All the girls had orchids in their bouquets, my colors were pink and grey, blah, blah, blah, blah.....

If we told a narcissist our house got blown away by a tornado, he wouldn't even bat an eye. He'd just answer that he's been worried about *his* house getting hit for years! It never ceases to amaze me that no matter what the subject is, even if there is absolutely no connection, a narcissist will still manage to change the subject back to *him.* Usually there will not even be an acknowledgment or reply to whatever we said, much less any expression of concern or congratulations. They're just off and running.

I remember being at a party and happily telling a group of friends and acquaintances, which included the narcissist wife of one of my husband's old school chums, that we had bought a retirement home and were moving to the mountains in a few months. The narcissist showed no interest at all, and didn't even ask one question. Without a single word of congratulations or even an "Oh, how nice," the very next words out of her mouth were that *she* was retiring *in five years* and *they* wanted to move too. Then she proceeded to talk my ear off about her distant-future plans, until I excused myself in mid-sentence and walked away. She turned to the person who had been standing next to me and continued yakking about herself without missing a beat. Note that whatever is *definitely and currently* happening in our lives is ignored in favor of some vague thing that might possibly happen sometime in the future in the narcissist's life. Because, like I mentioned before, *every interaction with a narcissist is a competition,* whether *we* realize it or not.

Sisters and Brothers, it's not worth our breath trying to have a nice, two-way, give-and-take conversation with a narcissist. Why not stop worrying about being polite to people who treat us rudely, and start running the other way as soon as we see one coming, before we get stuck in their "me, me, me, I, and me" black hole?

If this is how useless trying to have a "nice, normal" conversation with a narcissist is, imagine what it takes to get through their thick skulls during a *confrontation,* and get them to actually *hear* or care about what we're saying! This is one of the main reasons why it's pretty much impossible to ever resolve a conflict with a narcissist. If it isn't about them, and something flattering to boot, it doesn't even penetrate.

CHAPTER 3

NARCISSISTIC MANIPULATION

Manipulation is *devious control*~ getting you to do something the narcissist wants in a sneaky, underhanded, roundabout or passive-aggressive way, instead of just coming right out and asking you directly, openly and honestly.

Narcissists manipulate us for two reasons~

1. By *tricking us* into doing what they want without ever actually *asking*, they are robbing us of the opportunity and our right to say no. They are forcing us to do their bidding, making sure they get what they want, and also taking away our freedom of choice.

2. If they ask us to do what they want, and we do it, then *they owe us*. But if they can *trick* us into doing it, then they get what they want without being obligated to return any favors, or even to be nice to us. They also don't have to swallow their pride and thank us, like they would if we said yes to an actual request. When we remind a narcissist of favors or nice things we've done for him (usually while protesting his abuse), he will often throw his manipulation in our faces and come right out and say "I never asked you to do that for me!" Don't expect a shred of gratitude, or even an admission that you did something he wanted you to do.

How to handle manipulation attempts? My borderline grandmother and narcissistic mother were master manipulators. I learned around the age of seven or eight that things were never as they seemed, and the stuff they pretended they wanted was rarely their true goal. As a young child, I made up a game with myself, and I played it for the rest of my life when dealing with them. Whenever I got that weird vibe that told me I was being manipulated, I would make myself stop and think before doing or saying whatever it *seemed like* they wanted from me, try to figure out what they *really* wanted~ and then do everything *but.* Whatever they were trying to get me to do in an underhanded, devious way, I would do just the opposite. Eventually, they would be forced to come right out and state whatever they wanted truthfully, and then I could decide whether I wanted to do it or not, without being *fooled* into doing it. It drove them batty, and it also forced them to be honest if they ever hoped to have a chance of getting me to do their bidding.

This has become a lifelong reaction to manipulation for me. I still do it when someone tries to manipulate me, but now that I'm a lot older and grumpier, I also get bored with the game sometimes. Then I just say no, and add something along the lines of "It seems like I'm being manipulated into doing ______, and I don't like being manipulated, so I'm not doing it," or, "I have no intentions of doing _____ and I'm not going to be manipulated into it." No one has the right to take away our freedom of choice and our right to say no. So when a narcissist is being devious and underhanded about his desires, stop and think first about what he *really* wants, and then outmaneuver him. Have a little fun with it, and *then* say no.

CHAPTER 4

PROJECTION AND THE NARCISSIST/FREELOADER/CON-ARTIST

If you want your reputation ruined, do a favor for a narcissist/freeloader/con-artist. When an N/F/C tells you a story that makes someone else look bad and makes *him* look like a hero, what you're seeing is some narcissistic *projection.* When he says that someone else wronged him, failed, or screwed up and needed *his* help, *what really happened is exactly the opposite.* If you do a favor for a narcissist, note that not only will you not get any appreciation, but you will also get embarrassed by the narcissist making you look bad to other people. The story will always get twisted. For example:

N/F/C~ My son ruined my credit/stole from me/cheated me.
Truth~ She ruined her son's credit/stole from him/cheated him.

N/F/C~ He's lying about me.
Truth~ N/F/C is lying. Not just now, but pretty much whenever she opens her mouth.

N/F/C~ I need to borrow $50. My sister charges me $1000 a month to share her house and I have nothing left.
Truth~ Sister, who is made to look like she is ripping off her own (freeloading) brother by ridiculously overcharging him for rent, in reality lets him live there for free in exchange for chores and babysitting, which most of the time he doesn't do.

N/F/C~ I want to move to Florida but I can't. The kids need me~ they're always calling me to help them out or give them money.
Truth~ N/F/C is an unemployed alcoholic who can't get his act together long enough to move and is constantly calling his adult children, who have good jobs and work hard, for money and favors.

N/F/C~ We moved in with our daughter to help her out.
Truth~ Narcissistic parents lost their house after living above their means all their lives, and the daughter helped *them* out by taking them in.

N/F/C~ My ex kicked me out and left me homeless.
Truth~ He was cheating on his ex and walked out on her and their two little kids to be with the other woman. Then his extramarital affair broke up, so now he's "homeless."

N/F/C~ I quit my job, followed by some accusation against coworkers or employer of mistreatment, dishonest business ethics, or criminal behavior the narcissist is too good to "be a part of."
Truth~ He got fired, or quit when he was disciplined. If he's an alcoholic, he quit because work was interfering with his drinking.

With narcissists, freeloaders and con-artists, no good deed goes unpunished. When we do something nice for a narcissist, it always comes back and bites us. For instance, if an N/F/C lives with us, she has to come up with an explanation for not having a place of her own that will make *her* look good, something to tell the rest of the family, friends, neighbors, people in church, local storekeepers, and anyone else she happens to run across ~ and it won't be anything that is flattering to *us*. N/F/Cs take advantage of us, and then make themselves look like big-shot heroes at our expense. We may never find out half the rumors and false gossip the narcissist is passing around about us, but we might just notice an odd coolness toward us from other people who have been led to believe that *we* are the ones who are ripping off the narcissist and taking advantage of *his* generosity and kind heart. Narcissists, freeloaders, and con-artists all have their sob stories~ but remember, *it's a con.*

CHAPTER 5

NARCISSISTIC GROUP DYNAMICS, AND ONE WAY TO TELL IF A FAMILY OR CHURCH IS TOXIC: LOOK FOR THE ONE WHO STAYS AWAY

NARCISSISTIC GROUP DYNAMICS

I once worked in an office with a narcissist named Faye. Faye was an arrogant and prudish woman who fancied herself to be classy, cultured, and better than everyone else, often bragging about attending the ballet or opera. Although plain and overweight, she was well-groomed and dressed nicely, but because of her attitude of superiority and other personality deficits, she had no luck in the dating world, and was unhappily single in middle age.

Whenever a new woman would come into the office, either as a new hire or as someone interested in doing business with us, Faye would be aloof and stand-offish. You could usually catch her surreptitiously giving the newcomer the once-over and looking her up and down with an expression of disapproval. Later on, she would make sure you knew she didn't think much of the new person, and invariably have something critical to say about her.

Once, we were at a business luncheon with several new people, including one lovely young woman with an engaging and outgoing personality. Faye sat quietly observing her for most of the time. Afterwards, she wrinkled her nose at the mention of this woman's name and told us she didn't like her. Everyone else liked her just fine and we were surprised to hear that Faye didn't. When I asked her why, she replied that the young woman had terrible table manners.

It was one of those Twilight Zone moments, because no one else had noticed any bad manners on the part of this lovely young woman; in fact, she was very ladylike.

Now, here's the punchline. Although most folks kept their distance from Faye, she did have two women in our office who were her closest friends. They often chatted together and sat together, and they socialized after work. The thing was, these two middle-aged women acted like ten-year olds who were raised by chimpanzees. They were low-class, uncouth loudmouths whose behavior was often totally inappropriate for the situation and setting, and they frequently embarrassed our colleagues in front of clients. ***Their** manners were downright atrocious, and yet **they** were Faye's best friends.* What the heck?

Narcissistic families, church families and many other groups are usually made up of an Alpha narcissist, and a bunch of secondary narcissists or little narcissist wanna-bes, who act as the Alpha's enablers, supporters and defenders, vicariously sucking narcissistic supply from her by association. They're *all* narcissists, but some are more powerful than others. One is usually the head narcissist, and it isn't always the one you think it is. Sometimes the Alpha is manipulating and pulling the strings behind the scenes, like Ahab did with Jezebel in 1 Kings 21.

The primary narcissist in a group might assume the Alpha role by virtue of holding a position which is normally associated with authority, such as parent, church leader, or boss. But just as often he has become the Alpha simply because he is the most volatile, unpredictable and mentally unstable narcissist in the bunch, and everybody else gives him narcissistic supply, like attention and admiration, for fear of setting him off and having him turn on them. Even fellow narcissists have enough sense not to antagonize the crazy person.

Most narcissists who hold positions of power in a group surround themselves with minions whom they consider to be their inferiors and "lesser beings," and snub, ignore or eliminate those who are "equal" to them or "better" than they are in status, education, profession, social class, culture, intelligence, money, looks, abilities, self-confidence, knowledge, and any other traits the narcissist values. A narcissist with a college degree will often surround herself with "friends" who didn't continue their educations past high school. A narcissist who owns her own house will only be happy with "friends" who rent apartments or live in trailers. A narcissist who sucks supply out of being able to play the piano won't want another person around who can also play the piano, because she's afraid comparisons will be made and she will come up short, or attention will be siphoned away from *her.*

Faye was best friends with women who possessed the very shortcomings she imagined and criticized in other women. But the thing was, *they* weren't competition for the attention of the men in the office, and they made her look good by comparison. They were goofy, older than she was, frumpier, and didn't know how to act professionally or appropriately. They were also already married. So to Faye, they weren't a threat, whereas a pretty young newcomer with a modicum of class might be.

Since narcissists have no loyalty, they don't hesitate to turn on one another. If, at some point, a "lesser" narcissist in the group somehow betters her station in life, all of her past support of the Alpha will be forgotten, she will become the "enemy," and eventually she will be kicked to the curb, no matter how faithful a fan of the Alpha she always was. *If we play our cards right, this little secret can sometimes be used to our advantage when dealing with a group of narcissists. They are really quite easy to pit against one another. Often all it takes is a well-timed and public compliment to a lesser narcissist to get her on the Alpha's blacklist. Divide and conquer, as they say.*

Being on the same level as the narcissist is a bad enough sin, but if you happen to be *better* than her in one of her deranged competitions (think bigger house, more advanced degree, more popular, more talented in some way), you're history! Narcissistic vanity and envy are the biggest reasons behind Narcissistic Nuclear Meltdowns~ insane, irrational, unprovoked attacks, followed by ostracizing you, which are used as an excuse to eliminate you from the picture. Then the narcissist will lie and badmouth you as well, just to take you down another peg or two, make herself seem superior, and cover up the *real* reason you and she are no longer friends~ *her* personal shortcomings, character deficits, lunacy and jealousy.

So if you're "friends" with a narcissist now, or a narcissist "likes you," don't kid yourself. It's not really a compliment. *You were only chosen to be in her inner circle because she considers you a loser.* And most likely, it's only temporary, until you inadvertently challenge her "superiority" in some way.

ONE WAY TO TELL IF A FAMILY OR CHURCH IS TOXIC: LOOK FOR THE ONE WHO STAYS AWAY

Almost every toxic family or church group has someone who stays away and keeps the group at arm's length, showing up only every now and then or for special occasions. In narcissistic families, this is usually one or more of the children, and in toxic churches, it's usually one or more of the pastor's children.

The Red Flag that will bring this "lone wolf" to your attention is the family, church members, or pastor and his wife and other children making excuses for the Prodigal Son's absence, and thinking that they have to explain it to you even though you haven't asked. They will usually take you aside "in confidence" (although everyone in the group already knows because they have done the same with them) and sadly and with great concern explain their version of why the lone wolf is almost never there, and it's always that something is wrong with *him,* never them. He's upset about something, he's irresponsible, he's questioning the faith, etc. If it's the pastor's child, you will likely be told they are very saddened that he's not a believer or doesn't come to church, and asked to pray for him.

This is a pre-emptive strike on the part of the narcissists, to undermine and discredit their MIA relative, so that you won't believe any complaints he might have about them should you ever have a chance to get into a conversation with him.

This is also your cue to not believe everything you hear and to look a little deeper. There is often a good reason why an Adult Child stays away from her family or a pastor's child does not come to church, and the narcissists in the group are too embarrassed to admit the truth about what it is, so they lie. I have met many of these Prodigals, only to find that they were wonderful folks, and in many cases they were also devout believers although they did not attend their parents' churches. While it's not all that unusual for a pastor's child to rebel, explore other religions, or even claim to be an atheist at some point and then come back to the fold later on (Proverbs 22:6), it *is* strange for a pastor's child to be a Christian, live nearby and yet not attend his family's church. This usually means there's something going on behind the scenes. Either way, it pays to keep your antennae up and take whatever you're being told about him with a grain of salt.

No matter what you are being told by a toxic family or church, remember that the one who stays away is almost always the healthiest one in the group. And when you realize what an evil bunch they are and start making yourself scarce, the narcissists are going to explain your absence by gossiping and lying about *you,* too.

CHAPTER 6

WHAT HAPPENS WHEN TWO NARCISSISTS PAIR UP, WHAT HAPPENS WHEN A NARCISSIST PAIRS UP WITH A PSYCHOPATH, AND WHICH COMBINATION IS "BETTER" FOR US?

Ever wonder what happens when two narcissists start dating, and maybe even marry? Or what you get when you cross a narcissist with a psychopath? I'm not necessarily talking about romantic couples here, although that seems to be the most common match-up between the dysfunctional and crazy and the just plain evil. A pair of narcissists or a narcissist enmeshed with a psychopath might also be a mother and daughter, a father and son, or another type of toxic duo. Either way, both the narcissist-narcissist and narcissist-psychopath combinations can present different challenges and wind up being very interesting to the unfortunate souls who cross their paths. And God help us all if they actually reproduce. As many of us know from firsthand experience, their pitiful offspring don't stand a chance of a normal life.

WHEN TWO NARCISSISTS FIND EACH OTHER

You would think that two narcissists, each a selfish, self-centered egomaniac vying for narcissistic supply from other people, would never get along because they would always be competing with one another. But surprisingly, many times the exact opposite is true, and two narcissists together turn out to be a match made in heaven. This happens when, instead of competing with each other, they join forces and team up against everybody else.

Two narcissists bring two sets of potential sources of narcissistic supply into the relationship. Each contributes an already-trained family of perfect targets accustomed to overlooking and making excuses for narcissistic abuse, a group of friends already used to paying attention to and kissing a narcissistic butt, as well as peripheral connections like tolerant or sympathetic co-workers, neighbors, and church families. By teaming up, two narcissists double the "gene pool" of potential targets. Each one can now farm his partner's associates for attention, respect, admiration, sympathy, favors or money, as well as his own.

A pair of narcissists will often lend credibility to one another, each one repeating the same tall tales, sob stories, lies and excuses the other one already told to potential sources of supply, knowing that a potential target is more likely to believe their baloney if she hears it from more than one person.

Two narcissists working together double their ability to keep an eye on their friends and family for anyone who might be wising up to them or getting annoyed with them. One might overhear a remark the other missed, or be warned by one of her Flying Monkeys that someone in their social circle is questioning something they did or might be getting ready to rebel. They can then use two sets of Flying Monkeys and Silent Partners to help them quash any rebellion and stay in control.

A pair of narcissists will also voraciously defend one another against anyone who protests their abuse. They are each other's biggest fans, and will happily use all the narcissistic weapons they possess for justifying their own behavior (lies, denial, blaming someone else, tears, rage, etc.) to justify the behavior of their partner as well. They act as extensions of one another rather than two separate individuals. If you complain about one, it's as if you complained about them both. If you "offend" one, you offended them both. If you turn down a request from one, the other one will get just as mad at you, if not madder, as the one you didn't agree to help. If one gets angry at you and disowns you, the other one will disown you as well. And when one ups and decides to un-punish you by talking to you again, the other one will start talking to you too, just like nothing ever happened between you. *Uniting against a "common enemy,"* even an imaginary one, is a tactic that keeps them from focusing on the insanity in each other and their own relationship, and has been known to keep many a dysfunctional couple together for many years.

A partnership between two narcissists is usually very beneficial to both of them, but can be much worse for their victims, who will now be double-teamed by a pair of users and abusers.

YEA, AND ALL THAT WILL LIVE GODLY IN CHRIST JESUS SHALL SUFFER PERSECUTION. BUT EVIL MEN AND SEDUCERS SHALL WAX WORSE AND WORSE, DECEIVING, AND BEING DECEIVED…2 Timothy 3:12-13 KJV.

WHAT DO YOU GET WHEN YOU CROSS A NARCISSIST AND A PSYCHOPATH?

Now here's where things get even more interesting, and can actually become quite entertaining. What you get when these two find each other, and decide to start dating or marry, is usually complete chaos, and little, if any, cooperation between the couple.

It helps to think of narcissism and psychopathy as being on a continuum, with many degrees of dysfunction and evil along the line.

Psychopaths are like narcissists on steroids. They have all the narcissistic traits, and then some, only to a much greater degree. Hence, they are able to take the narcissistic Idealization and Devaluation/Discard Cycle (see Chapter 25) to a whole new level, and use it very successfully against the narcissistic partner herself.

Psychopaths also do not differentiate between their narcissistic partner and the rest of the world. They have no love or empathy for the narcissist (or anybody else), and view their partner as extremely inferior to them, and weak and foolish to boot. Unfortunately for the not-too-bright narcissist, she thinks *she's* the superior one here, and the psychopath uses that against her. Psychopaths are much more cold-blooded, clever and cunning than narcissists, whose greatest weaknesses are that they *think* they're more clever and cunning than other people, and that they *think* they are more important, special and superior than all the common folk out there. The psychopath knows the weaknesses of the narcissist, and her greatest weakness is her arrogance and conceit. He is able to use her ego and her other weaknesses against her to toy with her, just for amusement. But the narcissist, who believes she truly *is* so wonderful and better than everyone else, never sees this. When he flatters her, she is blinded and falls for his trickery time and again. This leads to a volatile, chaotic relationship punctuated by cruel, go-for-the-jugular fights, which usually cycles between breaking up and getting back together repeatedly, each partner thriving on the drama and turmoil, although for different reasons.

Psychopaths take pleasure in hurting other people. They do it for fun and to keep themselves entertained, since they have a very low boredom threshold, and it thrills them to see the pain they can cause. They love having so much power over someone that they can play her like a puppet on a string. They especially love humbling and humiliating the egomaniacal narcissist. It's typical for a psychopath to tell a narcissist anything he knows she wants to hear~ how great she is, how he can't believe his good fortune in having her, how beautiful or talented she is, and that she is everything he's been looking for in a woman. He reflects her own ego back to her, and the narcissist just eats this up. *She thinks he's wonderful, because he "thinks"* ***she's*** *wonderful.*

Then, when he has her where he wants her~ smitten with him~ he turns on her and starts criticizing, belittling and insulting her, hitting her where it hurts the most, right in her gigantic ego. They break up, usually with him dumping her. Then, a few weeks or months later, he's back. He tells her that he's changed, and realizes what a mistake he made. Her pride is now vindicated, because when he says he "made a mistake" by leaving, she reads that as an admission on his part that he has come to his senses and finally realized how awesome she is.

The narcissist plays hard-to-get for a while, until she has milked enough attention and admiration from the psychopath to satisfy her wounded ego and hunger for supply. Her ego now fed, she smugly takes him back. The power has now temporarily shifted to her, and she keeps him squirming for a little while before allowing him back into her good graces, thus feeding her ego even more.

A few weeks later, as she starts to relax and let down her guard, he starts demeaning and degrading her again, and they break up again. And a few weeks after that, he's back *again,* assuring her that he "changed" *again,* and that he now realizes that *she is everything he's ever wanted in a woman.* Once again, her ego kicks in, and she takes him back so she can bask in more of his flattery. A few weeks later, they break up again, and the cycle starts all over. As the old saying goes, "Fool me once, shame on you; fool me twice, shame on me." What can you say about somebody you can fool four, six, ten or more times, and who is *still* too proud to admit the truth?

This is the all-too-familiar Cycle of Abuse which is common between abusers and their non-narcissistic victims, taken up a notch or two because the victim here is a narcissist, not an innocent. ***She** preys on people too, and is in fact preying on the psychopath in return. He's just preying on her **better.***

I personally know of several couples who have gone through this drama repeatedly, and the narcissist never got it. She (or he) was so blinded by ego and flattery from the crafty psychopath that she never realized she was just being played. One narcissist took the psychopath back four times and counting, another six times and counting, another seven times and counting, and with the other couples it happened so many times I lost count. A normal person would think you'd have to be a fool, and a desperate one at that, to take someone who treats you like this back so many times, but this can continue for years with no sign of the oblivious narcissist ever wising up. The psychopaths involved had lots of fun with it, mocking and laughing at the narcissists behind their backs. One enterprising psychopath placed bets with his friends on whether he could get the narcissist to take him back and how long it would take him to succeed. He managed to repeat the pattern so many times that he was able to finance a nice trip with the money he won.

AS A DOG RETURNETH TO HIS VOMIT, SO A FOOL RETURNETH TO HIS FOLLY...Proverbs 26:11 KJV.

WHICH COMBINATION IS BETTER OR WORSE FOR US?

As far as we, the potential targets, are concerned, the narcissist-psychopath combination is better than two narcissists working together. Instead of focusing on conning and abusing other people, the narcissist-psychopath couple is too toxically enmeshed in their own conflicts and drama, and too busy conning and abusing one another, to do much damage to outsiders. They become very dependent on one another, and very addicted to the thrills that the other provides and the ups-and-downs of their relationship. Each one is high-maintenance, and the dynamic between them requires constant vigilance, alertness and attention, moves and counter-moves. It can be quite draining, and they rarely have the energy left over to bring third parties into their little pas de deux. They only get that adrenaline rush with one another, as they alternate between taking on the roles of predator and prey, never knowing for sure where they stand or if they're going to get back together or if they will be able to win this time around.

The most dangerous time for outsiders is when the narcissist and psychopath have just recently broken up, and the bitter, angry narcissist has once again been mortified and has no one to take her rage out on. This is when she is most likely to attack us for no discernable reason other than to have a temper tantrum and vent. The psychopath, on the other hand, *has* no rage over the break up. *He's* laughing about it.

Two narcissists working as a team are usually more of a threat to the people around them than a narcissist and a psychopath who don't work together, but are constantly at each other's throats or trying desperately to make up with one another, and pretty much ignore everyone else. Like a pack of hyenas who turn on each other, they are too distracted to do much damage to the other available prey.

Of course which pair is "better for us" or "worse for us" is a rhetorical question. Certainly neither combination would ever be *beneficial* to us to associate with. Normal people are better off avoiding *all* narcissists and psychopaths, regardless of who they climb into bed with.

CHAPTER 7

ALL NARCISSISTS ARE LIARS

AND ALL LIARS, SHALL HAVE THEIR PART IN THE LAKE WHICH BURNETH WITH FIRE AND BRIMSTONE... *Revelation 21:8 KJV.*

YE SHALL NOT STEAL, NEITHER DEAL FALSELY, NEITHER LIE TO ONE ANOTHER...Leviticus 19:11 KJV.

We can never protect ourselves and our loved ones if we don't study and *know* our enemy. The number one rule of understanding a narcissist is very simple~ *all narcissists are notorious liars.* It is not possible to have an open, honest, trusting relationship with a narcissist because *all narcissists are liars.* If you find yourself wondering whether to believe your narcissist or not, it's because you've learned from experience (although you might not want to admit it yet) that you have good reason *not* to believe him. Narcissists will~

- Brag and boast to make themselves look good
- Invent phony credentials, experiences, connections, education, and non-existent achievements
- Make up tall tales to impress you
- Tell sob stories to con you into giving them money or attention, feeling sorry for them, doing them favors, and overlooking their bad behavior
- Deny it when they do wrong, even if they were caught red-handed

- Deny saying what they said to you, even if it was thirty seconds ago
- Lie or make up stories about people they've hurt to discredit them so no one will believe them
- Hide and cover-up what they do
- Twist conversations
- Lie just to keep you off-balance and confused
- Betray and backstab people who help them
- Gossip about people who are nice to them, using any information they got while "being nice" against their victim
- Lie by omission. When the tales they tell just don't add up, it's because they are leaving something out that they don't want you to know. When you find out what they were hiding, the missing puzzle piece will fall into place and suddenly it will all make sense. Except that the truth won't be what they told you it was…
- Punish you in passive-aggressive ways instead of having an honest discussion
- Not ask directly for something they want (because that would give you the opportunity to say no, and if you said yes, then they'd owe you one), but rather manipulate and connive, tricking or forcing you to do it in sneaky, underhanded ways
- Falsely accuse other people
- Accuse other people of doing what *they* did
- Ruin the reputations of honest people, and call those who tell the truth (and expose them) liars
- Lie just for the fun of it, when there is no discernable reason to, just to yank your chain

Narcissists will lie behind your back, and lie boldly while looking you dead in the eye. They lie to you, they lie about you, they lie about themselves, and they lie about other people. It is human nature to give those we love the benefit of the doubt and to believe what they say, especially when there is no logical reason *not* to tell the truth. But narcissists don't need a logical reason to lie~ they lie because they're the children of the devil and it's *their* nature. In John 8:44, Jesus teaches us about liars: "*YE ARE OF YOUR FATHER THE DEVIL, AND THE LUSTS OF YOUR FATHER YE WILL DO. HE WAS A MURDERER FROM THE BEGINNING, AND ABODE NOT IN THE TRUTH, BECAUSE THERE IS NO TRUTH IN HIM. WHEN HE SPEAKETH A LIE, HE SPEAKETH OF HIS OWN: FOR HE IS A LIAR, AND THE FATHER OF IT*" *(KJV).*

How can we know what the truth is? *It is usually the opposite of what the narcissist says it is.* If he says he didn't do it, he did. If he says someone else did something bad, *he*'s the one who did it. If he says he helped someone out, *they* really helped *him* out. If he says he picked up that loaf of bread you asked him to, he didn't. If he says he put gas in the car, he didn't. If he says he called the bank about that discrepancy on your statement, he didn't (and the reason there's a discrepancy is that he took money out of your account without telling you). And when he gets caught in a lie, even red-handed, he will never admit it. He will insist he's telling the truth and stick to his story no matter how preposterous, until he gets *you* to give up. If a narcissist says it, don't believe it. If his lips are moving, he's lying. When you think of every word out of his mouth as a lie, suddenly things will start making sense, those missing puzzle pieces will fall into place, and you will be better able to protect yourself.

THESE SIX THINGS DOTH THE LORD HATE: YEA, SEVEN ARE AN ABOMINATION UNTO HIM: A PROUD LOOK, A LYING TONGUE, AND HANDS THAT SHED INNOCENT BLOOD, AN HEART THAT DEVISETH WICKED IMAGINATIONS, FEET THAT BE SWIFT IN RUNNING TO MISCHIEF, A FALSE WITNESS THAT SPEAKETH LIES, AND HE THAT SOWETH DISCORD AMONG BRETHREN…Proverbs 6:16-19 KJV.

PART 2

NARCISSISTIC BATTLE TACTICS: NONSENSE STATEMENTS, SNEAKY STRATEGIES, AND LOTS OF REASONS WHY YOU SHOULD JUST KEEP YOUR MOUTH SHUT AND LET THEM DO ANYTHING THEY WANT

CHAPTER 8

SPIN CONTROL: MAKING ABUSE SOUND LIKE A *GOOD* THING

WOE UNTO THEM THAT CALL EVIL GOOD, AND GOOD EVIL; THAT PUT DARKNESS FOR LIGHT, AND LIGHT FOR DARKNESS; THAT PUT BITTER FOR SWEET, AND SWEET FOR BITTER!....Isaiah 5:20 KJV.

ALL A MAN'S WAYS SEEM INNOCENT TO HIM, BUT MOTIVES ARE WEIGHED BY THE LORD....Proverbs 16:2 NIV.

MOMMY'S LITTLE HELPER

A GOOD MAN OBTAINS FAVOR FROM THE LORD, BUT THE LORD CONDEMNS A CRAFTY MAN....Proverbs 12:2 NIV.

When I was a little girl of three years old, my mother taught me how to make coffee. In a little four-cup perk pot. On a gas stove. With an open flame. That had to be lit with a match. Not a safety match, but the kind you strike on the brick wall. She made a game of teaching me how to measure the water and the coffee, how to put the pot together, how to turn on the gas and strike the match and hold it near the gas till the flame popped on, how to wait for the coffee to perk, then lower the flame, and set the timer for five minutes. She smiled and told me what a big girl I was and how smart I was and how well I was doing. And from then on, she had me make her coffee every morning, completely unsupervised, while she remained in bed, two stories above me. By the way, children's pajamas weren't flame retardant in those days (1950s). Once in a while I would singe a sleeve, but Mommy Darling had already taught me how to put it out with water or smother it. Thank God it never actually burst into flames.

By the time I was five, I had been taught to make pancakes and eggs, scrambled or sunny-side up, in hot melted butter in a heavy cast-iron frying pan on the same gas stove, and also waffles in a waffle iron. On the weekends, I made my parents breakfast in bed, and carefully carried it all up the two flights of stairs to their room.

At six, I was standing on a stool to iron flat items such as handkerchiefs, scarves, and bed linens. By age seven, I was ironing shirts, my mother having taught me how to very carefully do the sleeves and collars. These items were made of cotton and linen, and the iron had to be on the hottest setting.

At age seven I was also cooking dinner every night, and my younger birth-sister and I were doing all the dishes and cleaning up. This entailed using the stove and oven, as well as a "rotisserie" broiler that my mother liked meats cooked to death in, and various other kitchen items, such as knives, can and bottle openers, mixers, ice picks, and vegetable peelers.

Sounds like a lot of difficult work for a small child to learn and accomplish every night. But really, my mother was doing *me* a big favor! She never tired of telling everyone how my grandmother had "never taught her to cook," and "how hard it was for her to learn" after she got married. So it was very important that she teach me (at five years old!), so that I "wouldn't have to go through the same problems she did" when I got married and had to cook for my own family, two decades down the road.

In addition to the cooking and ironing, by the time I was six, birth-mother had also done me the favor of teaching me how to make beds (*hers*, of course, as well as my own), wash and dry dishes (standing on a chair to put them away), load the clothes dryer, fold and put away clothes, vacuum, dust, and clean the bathrooms. By age ten, I was given money and a list and sent to walk the several blocks to the supermarket, down the creek bed behind our house and the neighbors' houses, for food shopping, carrying three or four heavy bags home by myself. I spent many hours of my early childhood scrubbing the black heel marks off the wood floors with steel wool, and then applying paste wax with a big waxing machine that dragged *me* around the floor. What a lucky little girl I was! I could pretend I was Cinderella~ although, unfortunately, there was never any Ball!

My birth-sister did some of these chores as well, but I did the lion's share because I was three years older, and I guess a six-year-old is a little more capable than a three-year-old. On weekends and during the summers, we were not allowed to leave the house until everything was done, and we usually did not get to go out and play until mid-afternoon or later. My mother would not take us to the beach or anywhere else unless the whole house was cleaned first. We never got to the beach before three in the afternoon. We'd get to stay a whole hour, and then pack up and go home, because by then it was time to start making supper.

The only thing my mother didn't let me do was load the washing machine, because she was afraid I would turn the dial the wrong way and break the machine. So that was the one thing she actually did herself. As a teenager, I remember thinking that I couldn't wait to see her do her own housework after I got old enough to leave home. But of course when I married and moved out, my lazy mother hired a housekeeper. She was always so proud of herself for being well known as a fanatic about keeping a clean house, as long as she didn't have to clean it herself.

From the age of six on, I was responsible for "watching" my younger sister. I had to take her everywhere with me and had the full responsibility for her safety as well as her behavior. If she did anything naughty, *I* was yelled at and punished, because I was responsible for her. I was not allowed to hit her or discipline her, but neither was I told what to do to get her to listen to me. Mommy Darling took afternoon naps for as long as I can remember. We were put outside during the day and told not to come home until dinnertime (or more precisely, until it was time for *me* to cook dinner), because our mother did not want to be disturbed. So I was responsible for keeping my birth-sister safe, entertained, and out of trouble for many hours at a time.

Of course, I was chastised and even punished if I failed to do any of these things well. But mostly I was praised and complimented. I was made to feel special. Birth-mother often bragged about me to others. I remember her proudly telling my aunt how I made entire breakfasts all by myself when I was only five years old. Obviously, Mommy Darling was certifiable, but it is also interesting to note that my aunt wasn't even horrified by any of this. Instead, she was suitably impressed.

I was so happy and proud of myself. Never mind that I burned myself on the stove, oven and iron on a regular basis. Never mind that I splattered hot grease and spilled boiling liquids on myself from pots too heavy for me to lift properly. For most of my life, I had the scars up and down my arms to prove it, and some are still visible. In fact, I can tell you just how long it takes for these burn scars to finally disappear. Fifty years. Half a century before you couldn't see them anymore unless you really knew where to look. I learned what Unguentine (burn salve) was at a very early age. I never cried~ I just sucked it up. None of that mattered. I was pleasing my mommy. She thought I was such a big girl! I wouldn't want her to think I was messing up and couldn't do a good job. I wouldn't want her to be disappointed in me. Plus it was an investment in my future! I was so lucky that she cared enough about me to "teach" me all these skills for when I'd be a married woman, twenty years in the future!

Naturally all of this early indoctrination morphed into me becoming the family "cook" who hosted all the holidays and family events for decades. That's a whole other story, which I have talked about in more detail in my previous books. In my forties, I noticed something interesting while going through our old family photographs. Out of all my childhood pictures, there is not a single one in which I am smiling. In every shot, my face is somber, serious, nervous, anxious, and sometimes sad~ even in photos of my own birthday parties. And at the age of eleven, I was hospitalized for chronic diarrhea due to "nerves." The solution was to put me on Valium for the next three years, but I was still expected to get straight A's and keep up with all of my "responsibilities," even though I was now drugged on tranquilizers every day. Hmmm...maybe I wasn't such a happy child after all.

It wasn't until I had my own children that I began to understand just what kids are capable of at certain ages. Before that, I really didn't know much about children and their development. With this revelation I realized exactly how abusive, neglectful and careless my birth-mother had been when I was a child. Instead of protecting me and being vigilant about my safety, the fact was that my own mother endangered me just about every day of my life, throughout my entire childhood!

What parent in their right mind would remain in bed sleeping while a three-year-old lit a gas stove with a match and made coffee, or while a five-year-old cooked pancakes or scrambled eggs in a frying pan with hot melted butter on the same stove? What kind of lunatic would let a child so young near an open flame, with the sleeves of her non-flame-retardant bedclothes dangling over the burners?

What normal mother lets a seven-year-old cut up slippery tomatoes and fruit with a sharp knife? No problem~ she taught me how to paint iodine or mercurochrome on my cuts and put on my own Band-Aid. Who lets a child try to lift heavy pots full of boiling water or hot grease? Or maneuver a hot iron that is so heavy she can barely lift it? Remember, in the old days, irons were made of heavy metal, not lightweight plastic. If I didn't get burned from the iron, I usually got burned from the steam.

What loving parent would make a six-year-old solely responsible for a three-year-old, locking both of them out of the house all afternoon to ride their bikes many blocks away? What good, responsible parent would leave a six-year-old unsupervised for that long, even without the younger child?

After having my own children, I wondered what Child Protective Services would have to say these days about such things if a parent was reported. I'll bet the "mother"~ and I use the term loosely~ would be taken away in handcuffs. But nobody reported my mother. Nobody helped me. The cowardly lowlifes who knew what she was doing just looked the other way and "minded their own business."

As an adult, I have read about the "parentification" of children~ a type of abuse in which the parent switches roles with the child, and forces the child to nurture or take care of the parent, or to take on adult physical, mental or emotional responsibilities. Five-year-olds are not miniature adults. A child who is forced to accomplish things far beyond her capabilities is being abused and endangered. It is the parent's job to do her own housekeeping. It is the parent's job to feed her children and care for her children, not the other way around.

My mother made no effort to hide what she was doing. She wasn't the least bit ashamed of herself. She made no secret of my "capabilities" and all the things she had managed to teach me. She bragged about them. She seemed to take great pride in me. She made it seem perfectly fine, all good, even admirable, and the other adults she told seemed to agree. So all those years, she managed to keep a spotless house, serve home-cooked meals every night, entertain (when she entertained, I was dressed up and made to pass around trays of hors d'oeuvres among her guests, just like hired help, except that *I* wasn't paid), and raise her children, all while taking her daily nap and hardly lifting a finger. And all that time, her little trained slave did just about everything, happily being thrown a crumb of a compliment and given a hug for a good job. To me, and to everyone else, my mother came off smelling like a rose. She had succeeded in making my abuse sound like a *good* thing, and it served her well until I left home for good at the age of nineteen.

CHILDREN ARE CHATTEL

HERE IS A DESCRIPTION OF WORTHLESS AND WICKED PEOPLE: THEY ARE CONSTANT LIARS, SIGNALING THEIR TRUE INTENTIONS TO THEIR FRIENDS BY MAKING SIGNS WITH THEIR EYES AND FEET AND FINGERS. THEIR PERVERTED HEARTS PLOT EVIL. THEY STIR UP TROUBLE CONSTANTLY. BUT THEY WILL BE DESTROYED SUDDENLY, BROKEN BEYOND ALL HOPE OF HEALING. …Proverbs 6:12-15 NLT.

Another interesting aspect of living with my narcissistic/psychopathic parents was that both of them regularly tried to pimp me out. Mommy Darling would arrange for me to meet the sons of women she wanted to impress or whose social circles she aspired to join, and instruct me on how to flirt with them. When I was sixteen, she arranged a date for me with a twenty-eight-year-old Russian Broadway musician and music store owner~ the perfect catch in her eyes, and someone she could boast about her daughter dating. The only problem was he was far too old and sophisticated for me, on a totally different sexual level than the typical American "boy" at the time, and way too much for me to handle. I was expected to stay "pure" and a "virgin" under penalty of severe consequences, but then I was put in the position of having to fend off the sexual advances of a much older and quite aggressive man.

Daddy Darling was no better, openly pressuring me when I was in my twenties to date his business associates, dirty old men in their forties and fifties who were attracted to me. They were "nice guys" and it would have been "good for business" according to him, but I refused anyway~ and he was offended and angry when I did. It was "disloyal" of me not to do something that would help his business, after he supported me with it when I was a child.

To outsiders, this blatant pimping was innocently portrayed by my birth-parents as innocuous matchmaking for their daughter with eligible, well-to-do bachelors. Harmless at worst, doing *me* a favor at best, by setting me up with a "good catch." But what it *really* would have been, had I cooperated, was prostitution. Me, as a teenager or young adult, dating inappropriate men I wasn't attracted to, and God forbid getting raped, all to help Daddy Darling close a business deal or Mommy Darling impress her friends or be accepted into the right cliques. I was always popular with the guys, usually had a boyfriend, and didn't need their help getting a date or attracting boys my own age. Although it was presented as them doing *me* a favor, it was really evil manipulation aimed at getting me to do *them* a favor. Dangerous, disgusting and despicable, all disguised as innocent, well-meaning and helpful to their victim.

A narcissist's children are not people, human beings who need care and protection. They are *possessions*, to be used for the narcissist's benefit and whims. It's common for an abuser to hurt or kill the children to spite his or her husband or wife. Narcissistic parents also believe that their adult children should allow themselves to be exploited because they *owe* their parents for feeding them and putting a roof over their heads when they were kids. *Narcissistic parents think they are **special** for doing what every other parent does and what society requires of them. They do the very least they can get away with when raising their children, and then expect a gold medal, undying gratitude and payback, including self-sacrifice, when the kids are adults.*

or paying for college

DADDY'S LITTLE (?) GIRL

A SCOUNDREL PLOTS EVIL, AND HIS SPEECH IS LIKE A SCORCHING FIRE. A PERVERSE MAN STIRS UP DISSENSION, AND A GOSSIP SEPARATES CLOSE FRIENDS....HE WHO WINKS WITH HIS EYE IS PLOTTING PERVERSITY; HE WHO PURSES HIS LIPS IS BENT ON EVIL....Proverbs 16:27-28, 30 NIV.

My birth-sister had what some would consider a hazardous job, and a nice life insurance policy through work. Our birth-father thought he was the beneficiary on this policy. Sis was a "mature" woman in her mid-forties, who had traveled the world and was already divorced once when she met her second husband-to-be~ a perfectly nice, respectable, responsible man. After they moved in together, he and she began to combine their finances and make joint financial decisions.

At this point, our conniving, greedy seventy-five-year-old birth-father could practically feel that life insurance policy slipping through his fingers! If sis remarried, surely her new husband would be the beneficiary and not her father. Ditto for her will, her house, and anything else she owned. So dear old dad placed a phone call to new fiancé~ to grill him, "man to man," about what his "intentions" were toward my divorced, mid-forties, fully grown, perfectly capable sister. He wanted to discuss my future brother-in-law's influence over my sister's finances. Never quite grasping the concept of "none of your business," he decided to exercise what he believed was *his right* to pry into their joint financial business.

He also told her husband-to-be not to tell anyone, and to "keep this just between us." Now obviously, if his intentions were truly honorable, he would not have been concerned with keeping this little discussion a secret. If he wasn't doing anything wrong, then he wouldn't have cared *who* knew about it. My future brother-in-law refused to keep Daddy Darling's phone call a secret, reported it to sis, and spoke openly about it to my husband and me as well. He was not doing anything underhanded and he wasn't going to start sneaking around discussing their finances with his father-in-law-to-be. He had nothing to hide.

Now, most normal adults would have felt violated and mortified by this incident. You would think that birth-sis would have been outraged by her father's interference, and by his going behind her back to interrogate her boyfriend as if she had no brains or judgment of her own. His blatant distrust of her fiancé's motives, and butting into their lives, was insulting to both her fiancé and herself. Lucky for her that her husband-to-be was not easily intimidated or angered. After all, another man might have thought that if this was the kind of garbage he was going to be putting up with for the next twenty years, who needs it? Another man might have broken up with her. Daddy Darling could have caused her to lose the man she loved, and most likely that was the intention.

Yet her reaction when she discussed this episode with me? "He was just trying to be a good father. He was looking out for me." Oy! What can you say to that? Remember, this is coming from a middle-aged woman, not a twelve-year-old. Apparently she still wanted a "daddy" to protect her, even if it meant having "man to man" talks *about her* that *didn't include her*~ because, of course, she's "just a woman" and not competent to make these choices or think for herself. She's just a naïve little girl (in her forties!) who has to be protected from all the big, bad men out there who would take advantage of her, by her elderly father interrogating them! Ugh! Stuff like this sets women back fifty years!

Usually it's the abuser who justifies his behavior by pretending it was for the victim's "own good." This story is noteworthy because *both the abuser and the victim are in complete agreement*~ that the abuse was necessary, acceptable, and even admirable, because it was for the victim's "own good." In fact, one of my birth-father's favorite sayings was "You don't know what's good for you." None of us ever knew what was good for us--~only *he* knew! Birth-sis "didn't know what was good for her," so her father had to check things out, get to the bottom of whatever paranoid plot was going on, and take care of it for her.

This is a classic example of a victim who is an enabler. Our birth-father never had any boundaries, and had no concept of overstepping his bounds, and birth-sis didn't feel that her daddy had overstepped his bounds, either. Most people would realize that someone who is sneaking around behind their backs and keeping secrets from them does not have good intentions. If he truly had her best interests at heart, Daddy Darling would have had nothing to hide. A mature, adult woman would have defended her fiancé, instead of her father. She would have set boundaries on questioning an honorable man's intentions, not trusting her judgment as a fully grown adult, prying into her personal business, and sneaking around behind her back for any reason.

But instead, it looked like birth-sis now had the father she always wanted~ a daddy to take care of her and have "man to man" talks with her boyfriends, just like she was fifteen again. It's a *good* thing that daddy cares so much about her ("No, no~ it's not really my life insurance policy, or my estate! It's *me!*"). It's a *good* thing that he interferes in her life. He can interfere all he wants, as long as he's "looking out for her."

So both the abuser and the victim have managed to spin this abuse into a good thing. And everybody's happy. Except possibly the husband-to-be. He didn't seem too thrilled~ but, oh well. Who cares? As long as my daddy loves me! For years, whenever birth-sis defended one of our birth-father's outrageous and humiliating stunts, the rest of us would laughingly recall Bette Davis in "Hush, Hush, Sweet Charlotte" and "Whatever Happened to Baby Jane?"

Anything daddy does is fine with me because he says he's doing it for my own good! *He* knows what's best for me. Demented and creepy, perhaps, but as long as both the abuser and the abused are okay with the abuse, then who are *we* to complain?

"IT'S FOR YOUR OWN GOOD/ I WAS ONLY TRYING TO HELP"

LIKE A MADMAN WHO THROWS FIREBRANDS, ARROWS, AND DEATH, IS THE MAN WHO DECEIVES HIS NEIGHBOR, AND SAYS, "I WAS ONLY JOKING!"...Proverbs 26:18 NKJV.

Abusers who are really just trying to manipulate, control, degrade or demean their victims often claim "it's for your own good" when discovered or challenged. Nobody has the right to decide what is or is not for someone else's "own good." A variation on this, designed to make the victim feel guilty, is "I was only trying to help." *But the truth is that the abuser's words or behavior did not accomplish anything helpful at all.* Adults do not need that kind of help from other adults.

When the victim is an Adult Child, "constructive criticism" is often used to justify cruelty or control. Many times, "helpful" comments concern something you *can't* help~ like my birth-father pointing out a new pimple on my face, or my birth-mother telling me I looked much better without my eyeglasses, even though I couldn't walk across the room without them. I have seen "helpful" relatives embarrass their victim by "pointing out" her shyness or introversion in front of others, loudly and publicly warning her that she is gaining a lot of weight, or announcing that she "looks terrible" for some reason.

Remarks about someone's appearance or harmless personality traits such as shyness are never called for, are not in reality the least bit helpful, and are just thinly disguised cruelty. And according to the etiquette books, they are also very bad manners. Most such abusers would never dream of making these kinds of comments to an employer, coworker, neighbor, or stranger on line at the bank. *Why not, if they only have good intentions?*

Part of the problem is that some people don't think they need to treat their family members with the same courtesy, manners and respect that they give to total strangers. Another factor is that many abusers have no boundaries whatsoever when it comes to family members. They *know* their behavior is unacceptable, but they think they can get away with it with relatives, whereas a stranger or a casual acquaintance might just let them have it!

"I DID IT OUT OF LOVE"

This is pretty much the same as saying "I know I abused you", "I know I betrayed you," or "I know I snuck around behind your back to deceive you," *but that's okay,* because I did it for the purest of motives~ *love!* For example, it is common for controlling grandparents to ignore the wishes of the parents when dealing with their grandchildren. Often, they will give unwanted "helpful suggestions" on child-rearing. Many times they will not follow the parent's instructions, perhaps giving the grandchildren snacks they are not normally allowed, or indulging them in other ways contrary to how their parents want them raised. This confuses the kids and teaches them to sneak around.

Some grandparents go so far as to *tell the kids not to tell Mommy or Daddy.* Teaching children to disobey, sneak around, lie, and hide things from their parents is certainly not doing the children, or their parents, any good. But it *is* doing *the grandparents* good. By bribing their grandchildren, these grandparents are blatantly trying to get the kids to prefer them to their rightful parents.

Again, the excuse is that this is done "out of love." But in reality, such grandparents are undermining their children's authority as parents, and often end up causing the grandkids to challenge their parents' rules, causing discord in their families. This, just like all narcissistic interactions, is a competition. Grandparents who do this are trying to *compete* with the parents for their grandchildren's love. *They want the children to favor them.* This is *not* an unselfish motive. *It is very selfish.* It is not a grandparent's place to sabotage their children's child-rearing efforts, or to interfere in their children's families.

TAKE MY ADVICE~ *OR ELSE!*

In normal families, it is common and beneficial for the younger generation to go to the older generation for advice, especially when it comes to big decisions like buying a house or other areas where the older folks might have more experience or knowledge, and expensive mistakes can be avoided. Thoughts and opinions are asked for and given and discussions are held with respect and love on both sides, and private details are not passed around to other people in or out of the family. However, this is not possible in abusive families, where control-freaks and envious relatives do not have the best interests of their family members at heart, but instead are looking to forward their own agendas.

My birth-parents were famous for giving unsolicited advice, and then demanding that you take it. This always concerned some issue in my own adult life that was basically none of their business. I never asked for their advice, because I already knew that their judgment was faulty, and I had learned early on that it was much safer to guard my privacy and keep my abusers in the dark about my life, because revealing just about anything was an open invitation to abuse, demeaning and criticism. I was a perfectly competent adult, capable of figuring out things like which house or furniture to buy, where to go on vacation, what to say on a job interview, or how to give my children a balanced diet, all on my own. If for some reason I felt that I needed someone else's opinion, the Lord had always blessed me with good friends and other loving relatives of the older generation. These other folks *waited* to be asked for advice, and then gave it respectfully and lovingly.

My birth-parents, on the other hand, viewed "giving advice" as just another excuse to interfere where they weren't welcome, and to undermine my self-confidence. "*THE PLANS OF THE RIGHTEOUS ARE JUST, BUT THE ADVICE OF THE WICKED IS DECEITFUL*"... *Proverbs 12:5 NIV.* Their opinions were always given with disdain, contempt, and a sarcastic sneer. My birth-father often called me "stupid" right to my face, and constantly told me that I "didn't know what I was talking about", "didn't know what I was doing," and "didn't know what was good for me."

Know-it-alls crave attention. Often the only way they can stay center-stage is to shut everyone else up. Daddy Darling's tactic for doing this was to demean the opinions of others, become insulting and nasty, and argue forcefully and rudely with anything they said. This resulted in other people giving up, keeping silent, and not expressing their thoughts in his presence, which was just what he wanted because it allowed him to continue spouting off his own opinions uninterrupted. He really loved doing this when he had a "captive audience" at holidays or family dinners.

I always politely listened, and then did what I felt was best anyway. But ignoring their advice was not something my parents let you get away with easily. If I did not do what they "advised," I would never hear the end of it. They would bring it up again and again. They would pry and ask questions about what I had decided to do. They would continually defend their opinion and become more and more demanding to know if I was going to follow it or not.

Mommy Darling turned this into an art form. No matter what subject we were talking about, she would find a way to segue into whatever "advice" of hers I hadn't yet acted on, sometimes days or weeks later. It was amazing how the subject would always get turned back to her opinion of a personal issue which I thought had been long settled or forgotten. But because I had not revealed my decision to her, discussed it with her, or taken her advice, it was never a closed issue in her mind. Neither she nor my birth-father would be satisfied unless I did what they told me to do. Keep in mind that I was a grown woman, and this was always *unasked for and unwelcome* advice.

Under the guise of being "helpful," my birth-parents thought they had the right to *force* their opinions on me. *When someone **demands** that you take their "helpful suggestions," they are not really trying to help you. They are trying to **control** you.* You can be sure that anyone who takes offense when you fail to follow his "helpful" advice has an ulterior motive or a hidden agenda.

"I DIDN'T THINK YOU'D MIND"

Probably the worst type of manipulation and control is sneaking around behind someone's back, like Daddy Darling did with birth-sis. Gathering information, grilling, interrogating, and asking questions that are none of their business, is not acceptable behavior. Trying to intimidate, warn, or "put on notice" a prospective spouse, or anyone else in an adult child's life, is completely out of line. Adults do not need to have their choices "investigated" behind the scenes by their relatives.

Telling someone to keep a secret, "keep this between us," or not tell the victim about this "little discussion" is also totally unacceptable. "*HE WHO CONCEALS HIS TRANSGRESSIONS WILL NOT PROSPER, BUT HE WHO CONFESSES AND FORSAKES THEM WILL FIND COMPASSION*" ....*Proverbs 28:13 NASB.* People with honorable motives don't need to be secretive about them. Interfering in someone else's life with the intention of influencing it without their knowledge is outrageous. No one needs other people pulling the strings behind their back.

Adults do not need other people to make their decisions for them, meddle in their lives, manipulate, or control them. This cannot be justified by pretending it is an attempt to be helpful. An adult does not need another person telling him something cruel or hurtful "for his own good." Adults can figure out what is "for their own good" all by themselves. To suggest that they need help in running their own lives is insulting, degrading, and demeaning. It is an attempt to undermine the victim's confidence and self-esteem, make him feel stupid and incompetent, and keep him in an "inferior" position and dependent upon the advice-giver. Calling the shots in *your* life makes your abuser feel powerful.

TIME TO SINK OR SWIM

Such abusers have not yet gotten with the program. Often these parents still expect their grown children to run everything by them before they do it. If they could, they would have you ask their permission to breathe! They don't want to see that you are all grown up now and don't need or want their interference. They do not see you as a mature adult. They do not see you as an individual, with your own personality, opinions, experiences, knowledge, wants, likes and dislikes. They don't trust your judgment. And most importantly, they do not *respect* you.

A parent's job is to raise their children to be independent and successful as mature, responsible adults, not to stay tied to the parents' apron strings forever. Eventually every child will be out on her own (one can only hope), and good parents prepare her for this. It is not "for the child's own good" to still need mommy or daddy's meddling and influence in her thirties, forties, and beyond. That is just not normal. It is to the child's detriment not to be able to stand on her own two feet. If she still needs her parents to make decisions for her at that stage, then they didn't do a very good job of raising her in the first place. With that in mind, it would seem foolish to give them even *more* opportunities to mess up her life.

So what to do if you have such a "helpful" control freak in your life? The common denominator in this type of abuse is a lack of boundaries and limits. When you were a child, you were unable to set and enforce limits that your abusive parents would respect. Many children, like me, accepted abuse because it was normal to us, and there was nothing we could do about it anyway. As children we had little choice in the matter. And if the mistreatment was presented as a "good thing," seemed to make our parents proud of us, and earned us their approval and love, then we might actually have *felt good* about it, while we were in reality being abused.

However, this situation changes when we become adults. Now we *do* have a choice. If your parents have done a good job in undermining your self-confidence, then you may really believe that you still need their advice before you can make any decisions. You may not be able to believe that you are indeed capable of handling your own life. You may only feel comfortable being dependent on them for their opinions. But that is not true. With the Lord's help, you can overcome your birth-family's brainwashing and develop the self-confidence you need to take care of yourself.

SOME SIGNS OF REAL MATURITY

One key to perceiving whether this is a healthy or unhealthy pattern for you is to ask yourself if relying on each other for advice is a two-way street. After all, *you* are now a competent, equal adult, *so does your parent ever ask for* ***your*** *opinion, and take* ***your*** *advice before making a decision?* Do you feel free to speak *your* mind and offer *your* suggestions and guidance to your parent? Do you have mutually respectful conversations in which you genuinely try to help each other? Or is your parent still the "I know what's best for you" "parent," and you still the dependent "child?"

One boundary that we learn as mature adults is what is appropriate to discuss with our relatives, and what is not. Many times, *we* are at fault for simply revealing too much personal information. If you let your life be an open book, some people will take advantage of that. They will view your candor as an invitation to butt in. A good friend or therapist is a much better confidante, and will truly "have your best interests at heart."

As mature Christians, we need to rely on the Lord in all things, not other people. The Holy Spirit is our Counselor and Comforter. No man or woman should take the place of God in this function. We need to earnestly pray about every decision we are considering, and turn our lives over to our Father. One thing I have learned is that no matter how much you *think* you can trust another person~ even a close relative~ the only one you can *really* trust is the Lord! God never has any ulterior motives or secret agendas. He is the only one who truly acts "for our own good," and has absolutely no selfish motivations at all.

"WHY DO YOU ASK ME ABOUT WHAT IS GOOD?" JESUS REPLIED. "THERE IS ONLY ONE WHO IS GOOD"....
Matthew 19:17 NIV.

"FOR I KNOW THE THOUGHTS THAT I THINK TOWARD YOU, SAYS THE LORD, THOUGHTS OF PEACE AND NOT OF EVIL, TO GIVE YOU A FUTURE AND A HOPE. THEN YOU WILL CALL UPON ME AND GO AND PRAY TO ME, WHEN YOU SEARCH FOR ME WITH ALL YOUR HEART. I WILL BE FOUND BY YOU, SAYS THE LORD, AND I WILL BRING YOU BACK FROM YOUR CAPTIVITY....Jeremiah 29:11-14 NKJV.

CHAPTER 9

"AFTER ALL I'VE DONE FOR YOU": TROTTING OUT THE "YOU OWE ME" EXCUSE FOR ABUSE

IT WAS FOR FREEDOM THAT CHRIST SET US FREE; THEREFORE KEEP STANDING FIRM AND DO NOT BE SUBJECT AGAIN TO A YOKE OF SLAVERY...
Galatians 5:1 NASB.

We've all heard it in one way or another. "After all I've *done* for you.......," it begins. And then, "This is the thanks I get", "How could you do this to me?", "How can you say that to me?", "How dare you speak to me like that!", "Have you no gratitude?", "You should be ashamed of yourself", "How could you even think such a thing?", and on and on.........

Another version of this narcissistic guilt-trip is the one they won't say to our faces, but will use to badmouth us behind our backs. It goes like this: "After all I've done for her...," followed by, "How could she think that about me?", "How could she be so ungrateful?", "Doesn't she know I only have her best interests at heart?", yada, yada, yada.....

Many times the topper will be one of the two ultimate cry-me-a-river lines~ "*What* have I ever done to deserve this?" and "*Where* did I go wrong?" Which, occasionally, to add to the aura of sincerity, will be accompanied by, "No, *really*. Tell me! Was I *wrong* to do so much for her? Did I spoil her? Was I *really* such a terrible parent?"

Aaah, the guilt. So thick you could cut it with a knife. Along with denial and blaming someone or something else for their own bad behavior, trying to lay on a guilt trip is probably one of the most common responses an abuser will have when he is rebuked. Guilt tactics are many and varied. There are dozens, if not hundreds, of possibilities, and abusive or controlling relatives usually have quite a repertoire.

In this chapter, we will talk about one of the most popular~ the "After All I've Done for You" excuse for why an abuser thinks he should be allowed to continue unchallenged in his efforts to control, manipulate, interfere and abuse. The idea is to make you seem like an ingrate for even *suggesting* that something he's doing is unrighteous, hurtful or selfish. Because, of course, he has nothing but the best of intentions, which he's proven to you already by *all he's done for you.* You should be ashamed of yourself. And never bring up the subject again.

DOING YOU A FAVOR ENTITLES ME TO PRY, MAKE DEMANDS, AND RUN YOUR LIFE

Although any relative or friend could be guilty of manipulating you and keeping score for the sole purpose of obligating you to them, the one who uses this tactic most frequently will usually be a parent. No surprise there. Parents are just so good at it. I remember when I was a kid hearing one woman tell her child that he "owed her" because of all she had done for him. The child innocently asked his mother *what* she had done, and she replied that if it wasn't for her, he wouldn't have even been born. I'm not sure if she was joking or serious. It seems like a strange response now, but since I was a child myself at the time, I couldn't get a read on it. But the boy had the perfect comeback. He just shrugged and replied, "I didn't ask to be born!"

As family members, we *all* do favors for one another. You don't even have to be related to someone~ friends do favors for each other all the time. That's what families are for, and that's what friends are for. Many kind folks even do favors for strangers. *But that does not entitle **any** of us to have a say in the other person's life.*

Many times, favors are unasked for by the adult child. A parent offers, and the child accepts, not knowing that there are strings attached, as there are with *all* narcissists. The price to pay may be allowing the parent control over the child's choices, decisions, or life, giving the parent personal information, having to answer questions about things the child may prefer to keep private or would rather not discuss, or giving in to the parent's demands. Some parents feel that if they help their child out, that obligates the child to them. Such favors are *not* done out of love, but done for an ulterior motive~ to allow the parent to remain in a controlling position. And some parents can be very pushy about insisting that their child accept their help, whether she asked for it or not.

THE BUSINESS DEAL WITH THE HIDDEN CLAUSES

IT IS BETTER TO TAKE REFUGE IN THE LORD THAN TO TRUST IN MAN...Psalms 118:8 NASB.

Such a situation is not really a loving or caring thing. It is a business deal. But it is a business deal in which one party has not been informed of the price she will have to pay, which is giving up her independence. If this was laid out on the table openly, right from the beginning, and the parent was honest about the payback he expected, then the child would have the opportunity to turn down the deal. She would be able to choose *not to accept the favor* from her parent, and *not to owe* something in return.

But the parent wants to deprive the child of this opportunity to refuse the favor, so he does not let her know that there are strings attached. He misrepresents his intentions. *What the parent leaves unsaid is the most important part of the bargain.* He sets a trap, so to speak, which she will fall into without understanding what the consequences will be. By his deception, he takes away his adult child's freedom of choice.

In some parents' minds, if you accept their help, it just goes to prove what they have known about you all along~ that you can't really make it without them. In their minds, if you need help from them, then you are still a dependent child. They will lose respect for you, assuming they ever had any in the first place. They will not see you as an equal. Some families will help you out, and then feel they have the "right to protect their investment" in you by prying, making demands, or being controlling.

Sometimes we innocently accept an offer of help, never thinking of it as something that will obligate us. It never enters our heads that our relative expects something from us in return, because many of us are used to our families helping us out. Still others of us are always helping out our families, or doing plenty of favors for them in return for what they do for us. We figure, well, we always do for them, how nice, now they're doing something for us as well. One hand washes the other. *What we don't realize is that somehow all of the nice things we've done for them in the past will either be conveniently forgotten or just not count once they've done something for us.* The only way they will see it is that *now we owe them.*

This is not to say that all relatives consciously keep score, although some do. But our willingness to accept help from a relative often subconsciously puts us in a one-down position of inferiority, in their minds and sometimes even in our own. It keeps us dependent on them, and makes it imperative that we stay in their good graces, even if that means accepting abuse, control or interference.

FINANCIAL HELP~ THE GIFT THAT KEEPS ON GIVING (AGGRAVATION, THAT IS)

THEREFORE I TELL YOU, DO NOT WORRY ABOUT YOUR LIFE, WHAT YOU WILL EAT OR DRINK; OR ABOUT YOUR BODY, WHAT YOU WILL WEAR. IS NOT LIFE MORE IMPORTANT THAN FOOD, AND THE BODY MORE IMPORTANT THAN CLOTHES? LOOK AT THE BIRDS OF THE AIR; THEY DO NOT SOW OR REAP OR STORE AWAY IN BARNS, AND YET YOUR HEAVENLY FATHER FEEDS THEM. ARE YOU NOT MUCH MORE VALUABLE THAN THEY? WHO OF YOU BY WORRYING CAN ADD A SINGLE HOUR TO HIS LIFE? AND WHY DO YOU WORRY ABOUT CLOTHES? SEE HOW THE LILIES OF THE FIELD GROW. THEY DO NOT LABOR OR SPIN. YET I TELL YOU THAT NOT EVEN SOLOMON IN ALL HIS SPLENDOR WAS DRESSED LIKE ONE OF THESE. IF THAT IS HOW GOD CLOTHES THE GRASS OF THE FIELD, WHICH IS HERE TODAY AND TOMORROW IS THROWN INTO THE FIRE, WILL HE NOT MUCH MORE CLOTHE YOU, O YOU OF LITTLE FAITH? SO DO NOT WORRY, SAYING, "WHAT SHALL WE EAT?" OR "WHAT SHALL WE DRINK?" OR "WHAT SHALL WE WEAR?" FOR THE PAGANS RUN AFTER ALL THESE THINGS, AND YOUR HEAVENLY FATHER KNOWS THAT YOU NEED THEM. BUT SEEK FIRST HIS KINGDOM AND HIS RIGHTEOUSNESS AND ALL THESE THINGS WILL BE GIVEN TO YOU AS WELL. THEREFORE DO NOT WORRY ABOUT TOMORROW, FOR TOMORROW WILL WORRY ABOUT ITSELF. EACH DAY HAS ENOUGH TROUBLE OF ITS OWN....Matthew 6:25-34 NIV.

Monetary help in making large purchases is often misrepresented by the giver as a "gift," and the recipient foolishly believes that, and fails to realize that there are strings attached.

Parents who help foot the bill for their child's wedding often expect to run the show, and the bride and groom suddenly find their wishes taking a back seat to those of a parent who now considers it to be "*my* wedding."

Many young adults have accepted parental financial help for the down payment on their first home, only to find out that their parents now thought they had the right to tell them where to live, how many bedrooms and bathrooms they needed, which house to buy, and how to decorate~ and to supervise any future remodeling projects as well.

I was a realtor for many years. Many times, "helpful" parents tagged along with their adult children to look at houses, often dictating what town, school district, type of house, or even which exact house to buy. They believed that contributing money gave them the right to choose the house *for* their child, or to nix the one their child liked. They believed they had bought the right to make this decision for their child, in the name of "protecting their investment." And because, after all, if the child wasn't grown up enough to pay for it, then she obviously was too immature and incompetent to make a good choice for herself. Contributing to such a purchase gives some parents a sense of ownership or entitlement. They view their child's house as really being *theirs,* or at least partly theirs, because they helped buy it.

If we were talking about normal parents, it can often be quite helpful to have them come along on real estate outings. They are usually experienced homebuyers and homeowners who will see and ask about things the younger generation might not notice. But when the parents are narcissists, it's a different story altogether. Like every other narcissistic encounter, it soon becomes all about the narcissist. I've met narcissistic parents who accompanied their adult children on real estate excursions and did all the talking, interrupted their children, spoke for their children, and wouldn't even give the younger adult(s) a chance to have all of their questions answered. Sometimes, the younger person caught on before the process went any further, and left mom and dad at home the next time he went house-hunting. But if he didn't, the situation usually deteriorated from there.

Other parents who have given their children a "gift" to help buy a house want even more control. They insist on attending meetings with realtors, mortgage companies and attorneys, and prying into their child's and his or her spouses' private financial business until they have found out every personal detail. Some have even gone so far as to attend the closing. Their presence can be awkward and intrusive and make everyone else feel uncomfortable.

The personal information they manage to find out about their child and his or her spouse by intruding on these meetings is incredibly detailed, and includes exactly how much money their adult child and his or her spouse makes, how much they owe, how much they have saved (and~ do the math~ how much they must be spending. Foolishly, of course), what the younger couple's credit rating is, and other private facts that are none of their business. One set of parents caused a scene at the closing after finding out about their son-in-law's previous marriage, which their daughter had chosen not to reveal to them previously, precisely because she knew how they would react.

Another couple I know who accepted a financial "gift" for their down payment were devastated when their parents "withdrew" their "gift," because the younger couple would not use it to buy a house two doors down from the parents. Apparently the gift only applied to that particular house, so that the parents could keep the kids under their thumbs and only two doors away. But this was not a requirement that had been mentioned up front. The younger couple then had to back out of a deal on the house they really wanted, because they suddenly found themselves without the anticipated funds.

Yet another unhealthily enmeshed mother insisted on "helping" her fortyish daughter select a house and negotiate the deal because many years ago the mother had been a realtor and both she and her child apparently considered her an expert in the field. In this case, the parent was not contributing money, just time and interference. At first, the mother carried on as if someone had died when the daughter was getting ready to move out, but suddenly she decided to pitch in and help. I should have been cued in by the about-face, but I wasn't. For weeks, we heard how great the house they chose was and how helpful the mother had been.

At one point this mother looked at me knowingly, because she knew that I, too, had been a realtor, smiled like the cat that ate the canary, and said, "*You* know what the most important thing is. Location, location, location." So imagine my shock when I finally saw the house the daughter bought, and it was on a main drag surrounded by motels and other commercial establishments, had a construction business across the street with chain saws and other heavy equipment going most of the day from early morning on, and had railroad tracks and trains going through the land adjacent to the backyard. It could not have been a worse location. In my opinion, it needed updating in almost every room, she grossly overpaid for it, and reselling it would be a nightmare. I would never have advised one of my children to buy that house.

My husband and I were astounded after seeing it, since we had been led to expect something completely different. On the way home, it was the topic of conversation in our car, and I, shaking my head in disbelief, repeated the mother's comment to me about "location" being the most important thing. With a laugh, my husband solved the mystery for me. He said, "Yeah, location, location, location. It's right down the road from her mother's!" And the light bulb went off! Of course, he was right. It certainly seemed like the mother must have had *her* best interests in mind when she "helped" her daughter buy this house. In my opinion, the daughter wound up paying a steep price for her mother's "help."

"HELPING WITH THE GRANDKIDS"

Another "favor" that often comes with an expected payback is "helping" with the grandkids. Many grandparents think that babysitting their grandchildren automatically gives them the right to interfere in the grandchildren's upbringing. They think they have the right to feed the grandkids what they want them to eat, instead of what the parent says. Or that they have the right to discipline, or spoil, their grandkids, contrary to the parents' wishes. Some grandparents think that "helping out with the grandkids" entitles them to have a say in whom their child (the grandkids' parent) dates, or where their child lives.

I know of more than one set of grandparents who, without being asked to by their adult child, *sold their house and moved to the same town where their child and her family lived, much to the horror of the child, who had moved away to escape her controlling parents.* To hear them tell it, these parents had "previously discussed" their move with their daughter, so they "couldn't understand" why she now wasn't happy about it. But in reality, there was no "discussion." They had simply *informed* their child of a decision they had already made. This unasked for and totally unwelcome gesture was done under the guise of "being able to help out more with the grandchildren." But the grandparents' *real* motive for moving was *to be able to continue to interfere in their daughter's life* and exert inappropriate control, which the previous long distance had hindered.

A typical scenario was illustrated by one set of grandparents, who continued to force themselves on their adult child, criticizing her decisions, and disapproving of how she raised her kids, the men she dated, and other aspects of her life. Then, when the inevitable conflict occurred, the first thing they said was, "After all we've done for her….. helping her out, watching her kids…..why, *we even sold our house and moved so we could be closer to her in case she needed us….*"

But the thing is, *she didn't need them*. She, and her children, were doing just fine and were perfectly happy without them. Knowing that their adult child was independent and competent was a blow to the egos of these controlling parents. They went to the extreme of selling their house and *moving* to their daughter's new town because they had to get themselves back in the picture. Then they needed to make up an excuse to cover their true motives, so they *used their grandchildren* as their excuse, for their own selfish purposes.

Grandparents like these are not interested in, or grateful for, the opportunity to develop a nice relationship with their grandchildren, which in itself would be a wonderful pay-off for truly loving and considerate grandparents. They do not genuinely care about what is best for the grandkids whom they pretend to love so much. Instead, *they are using their grandchildren to benefit themselves* and for their own selfish motivations~ *to help them maintain a toxic connection to their daughter*, so that they will be able to continue to control her and to interfere in her life. The grandkids are just pawns in their game.

MALEVOLENT CONTROL IN A BENEVOLENT DISGUISE

DO NOT EAT THE FOOD OF A STINGY MAN, DO NOT CRAVE HIS DELICACIES; FOR HE IS THE KIND OF MAN WHO IS ALWAYS THINKING ABOUT THE COST. "EAT AND DRINK," HE SAYS TO YOU, BUT HIS HEART IS NOT WITH YOU. YOU WILL VOMIT UP THE LITTLE YOU HAVE EATEN AND WILL HAVE WASTED YOUR COMPLIMENTS….Proverbs 23: 6-8 NIV.

Normal families rarely wind up in these situations, but those of us from abusive families deal with them all the time. Abusive people keep score and manipulate situations to their advantage. They don't do favors out of love. *They do favors because there is a benefit to* ***them,*** and they expect a payback. They don't do things out of the goodness of their hearts. There is always an ulterior motive. The challenge to us is figuring out what it is and what is really going on.

Many times this dynamic is able to occur because our eyes are veiled and we are blinded to the true nature of our relative. In our lifelong quest for a family who really loves us, we are often in denial about these traits when they are present in someone we love. We don't want to think that our parent or sibling isn't really trying to help us, but is in fact setting us up. It seems completely contradictory that a kindness actually has its roots in dishonesty and selfishness instead of love.

Unfortunately, our wishful thinking doesn't change what is, and we need to take off the rose-colored glasses and see our relative as he truly is before we put ourselves in the position of being obligated to him. If we think back, we will often recognize many past instances in our relative's dealings with us, or with other people, where this behavior was present. The key is to learn from the past and not keep repeating history.

We may not care much about money, but we make a grave error in underestimating its importance to an abuser. *Money is always a very significant commodity to a control freak.* It is a very important issue to him, because he believes he can use it to "buy" you or others. Especially if he has spent years mistreating you, he knows that he has precious little else to offer that might get you to do what he wants. Once you are grown, you are free from his direct control, so manipulation is now the order of the day. As an adult, you are not likely to feel kindly and cooperative toward someone who has always behaved hatefully towards you. He will need to "sweeten the pot" (one of my controlling birth-father's favorite phrases) to buy your cooperation. Money will often be all he can think of. He will either use it directly, as a bribe, or indirectly, as in threatening to cut you out of the will.

Daddy Darling occasionally offered me token amounts of money in return for "doing something his way." Sometimes, he offered a small sum for no apparent reason, or tried to insist that I accept some other "favor" which I didn't want and had never asked for. But I knew his true nature, and I knew he never did anything for anyone without expecting something in return. I didn't want to be obligated to him. I didn't want to give him the satisfaction of being able to say I "owed him" something. I didn't want to give him any control or rights over my life. So, no matter how much I might have needed it, I never took a dime.

When I was a young adult, out on my own for the first time, money was very tight, to say the least. I could not afford health insurance, dentist or doctor's visits, a reliable car, clothes, or even food, sometimes. But I would have slept in the streets before I would have taken anything from him. It would not have been worth it. The price would have just been too high.

The interesting thing was, when I was *really* poverty-stricken, he never offered anything~ and I was bound and determined not to ask. Smug and sadistic as he was, he liked seeing me suffer. To him, I deserved it for trying to be independent. He was just itching to see me "come crawling back" to him, to prove to himself, me, and everybody else that I couldn't make it without him. But there was no way that was going to happen. I knew I would never have heard the end of it. I refused to ask, and he did not offer.

But he *did* start offering his "bribes" after I had gotten on my feet, was doing well financially, and didn't need them anymore. His previous manipulations and attempts to control hadn't worked, so now he figured he might as well bring out what he considered to be "the big guns," and give money a try. I have heard him say that "every man has his price." But the only thing he learned from his scheming is that I couldn't be bought. Every man might have his price, but *I* didn't. He wound up right back where he had started, with nothing to hold over my head. And I wound up with my independence, self-respect and dignity. I could spend the rest of my adult life being able to look him in the eye as an equal. He knew he couldn't get the better of me. He resented it, but he also respected it.

CLARIFY THE TERMS OF THE DEAL BEFORE YOU SIGN ON THE DOTTED LINE

When you accept a favor from a controller or a manipulator, *you are "signing" an unwritten contract.* To an abuser, his "generosity" is his half of The Deal. Now the question is, what is *your* half of The Deal? The best way to handle an offer of help is to ask right up front what will be expected of you in return. Most manipulative relatives will deny that they expect any payback, and insist that there are no strings attached and that they are doing it "because they love you" and "are only trying to help." They will act insulted and offended that you could even think such a thing. At which point, you can apologize and accept their "kind" offer, "knowing" that it is free and clear.

Of course, it really isn't. But at least now, down the road when they throw it in your face to make you feel guilty, you can remind them that you clarified what the deal was before accepting it, and they told you there were no strings attached. If those are the circumstances under which you agreed to accept their offer, then you are free to choose whether to agree to or deny their future demands for "payback," and your conscience can be perfectly clear.

You wouldn't enter into any other business agreement without knowing what you were agreeing to, so don't be shy about this one. Be direct and clarify the terms. Ask what the conditions are on this offer. Know what you're getting into. If your manipulative control freak still chooses to be dishonest about his true motives and mislead you by telling you that he wants nothing in return, then you have absolutely no reason to feel guilty in the future. You owe him nothing. One party doesn't have the unilateral right to change the terms weeks, months, or years after it's a done deal.

PUTTING AN END TO THE MYTH OF THE "LOVING" ABUSER

GIVE US HELP FROM TROUBLE, FOR THE HELP OF MAN IS USELESS...Psalms 108:12 NKJV.

Abusers and control freaks never do anything out of love. There is simply no such thing. This is because they do not love anyone but themselves. They do not have love in their hearts to begin with, so they cannot act out of love. Sometimes we confuse other traits with love, such as possessiveness, ownership, dominance, entitlement or enmeshment. We may view such traits as a sign that an abuser really cares about us. But she does not. We are misinterpreting what is really going on.

Abusers, controllers and manipulators are accomplished liars. They are not persons of honor or integrity, so it would be very foolish to take whatever they might say at face value. They can be very convincing when they try to steamroll us into accepting their "offers of help." But no matter what she says, we are deluding ourselves if we think that an abusive, controlling relative really wants to help us because she loves us.

Abusers do not serve the Lord, and they do not live to help others. The only people they are interested in helping are themselves. They never do anything for anybody else without first calculating what is in it for them. Those are the sorry facts, plain and simple. Forewarned is forearmed.

Although it is sad that we need to think first before accepting a favor from a loved one, unfortunately that is the case for many of us. With some people, we *do* need to think first. We need to avoid asking for favors. We need to buy time if an offer is made, and not give a quick answer. We need to consider our relative's personality and true nature. We need to recall if this person has a history of trying to obligate others to him, or of putting them in the position of "owing him one." We need to think carefully about what strings are attached and whether accepting favors from certain people is worth the price we are going to have to pay.

THE SECRET TO GETTING ALONG JUST FINE, MINUS THE GUILT TRIP

COME UNTO ME, ALL YE THAT LABOUR AND ARE HEAVY LADEN, AND I WILL GIVE YOU REST. TAKE MY YOKE UPON YOU, AND LEARN OF ME; FOR I AM MEEK AND LOWLY IN HEART: AND YE SHALL FIND REST UNTO YOUR SOULS. FOR MY YOKE IS EASY, AND MY BURDEN IS LIGHT....
Matthew 11:28-30 KJV.

Above all, we need to learn to turn all our problems over to our real Father. We need to trust completely in him, and know beyond a doubt that he will always provide for all of our needs. We do not need to put ourselves in the position of "owing" any man. The Lord will always take care of his children. God's grace is *unmerited favor.* We do not "earn it" or "owe" the Lord for it. His grace is *a free gift* to us! Thank you, Father God! Your grace is sufficient for us! We give you all the honor and glory!

MAY THE LORD ANSWER YOU IN THE DAY OF TROUBLE! MAY THE NAME OF THE GOD OF JACOB SET YOU SECURELY ON HIGH! MAY HE SEND YOU HELP FROM THE SANCTUARY AND SUPPORT YOU FROM ZION! MAY HE REMEMBER ALL YOUR MEAL OFFERINGS AND FIND YOUR BURNT OFFERING ACCEPTABLE! SELAH. MAY HE GRANT YOU YOUR HEART'S

DESIRE AND FULFILL ALL YOUR COUNSEL! WE WILL SING FOR JOY OVER YOUR VICTORY, AND IN THE NAME OF OUR GOD WE WILL SET UP OUR BANNERS. MAY THE LORD FULFILL ALL YOUR PETITIONS. NOW I KNOW THAT THE LORD SAVES HIS ANOINTED; HE WILL ANSWER HIM FROM HIS HOLY HEAVEN WITH THE SAVING STRENGTH OF HIS RIGHT HAND. SOME BOAST IN CHARIOTS AND SOME IN HORSES, BUT WE WILL BOAST IN THE NAME OF THE LORD, OUR GOD. THEY HAVE BOWED DOWN AND FALLEN, BUT WE HAVE RISEN AND STOOD UPRIGHT. SAVE, O LORD; MAY THE KING ANSWER US IN THE DAY WE CALL.....Psalm 20:1-9 NASB.

CHAPTER 10

SELECTIVE AMNESIA: "I HAVE NO IDEA WHAT I DID WRONG!" OR, "I DON'T KNOW WHAT HAPPENED~ SHE JUST STOPPED SPEAKING TO ME!"

AND HE SAID TO THEM, "YOU ARE THOSE WHO JUSTIFY YOURSELVES BEFORE MEN, BUT GOD KNOWS YOUR HEARTS. FOR WHAT IS HIGHLY ESTEEMED AMONG MEN IS AN ABOMINATION IN THE SIGHT OF GOD"....Luke 16:15 NKJV.

THE HEART IS DECEITFUL ABOVE ALL THINGS, AND DESPERATELY WICKED: WHO CAN KNOW IT? I THE LORD SEARCH THE HEART, I TRY THE REINS, EVEN TO GIVE EVERY MAN ACCORDING TO HIS WAYS, AND ACCORDING TO THE FRUIT OF HIS DOINGS...Jeremiah 17:9-10 KJV.

ALL THE WAYS OF A MAN ARE PURE IN HIS OWN EYES, BUT THE LORD WEIGHS THE SPIRITS....Proverbs 16:2 NKJV.

A couple of months before we were to move a few hundred miles away, my psychopathic birth-father, who had spent seven years slowly driving by, watching our house, parking across the street and stalking us, finally accosted my husband in our front yard. He requested to meet in secret with my husband, and told him not to tell me. Never mind that my son and I were standing on the porch in plain sight watching him. *Evil people assume that everyone else is as sneaky and secretive as they are.* As I've mentioned before, they assume that everyone else is just like them in every way, only dumber. My husband, of course, proceeded to tell me everything, and never did contact Daddy Darling for their clandestine meeting.

A few weeks later, I wrote birth-father a letter. A ten-page letter, to be exact, detailing a couple of dozen of the literally hundreds of episodes of abuse he had inflicted upon me and my family in the course of over fifty years. I told him very plainly that none of us wanted anything further to do with him, and that he was to quit stalking us and not to contact me, my husband, or my children again. Anticipating the possibility of needing evidence for a future restraining order or stalking charges, I sent this letter certified mail and still have the signed return receipt proving that he received it.

We moved to our new home and two and a half peaceful years passed. Then one morning, the Friday after Thanksgiving to be exact, the phone rang. It seems that one of my evil ex-cousins, who had disowned me when I finally began setting limits on my parents, got my unlisted phone number online for my internet-ignorant birth-father. So dear old dad finally found us, and decided to give me a call.

He started out with a few seconds of crying about how it was good to hear my voice again after ten years, and that he wanted to be back in the family. I thought it had only been eight years, but after doing the math, I realized that he was right about it being ten. It was very creepy to learn that after all this time, he was still obsessed enough to keep track of how long it had been, instead of moving on with his life. Control freaks who lose control of you in round one are always looking for an opportunity to start round two. They just never get over it. And it is interesting and relevant to note that, when it suited his purposes, dear old dad's memory was perfectly fine~ remarkably accurate, in fact. No amnesia problem here!

I don't know what I was thinking, but on the odd chance that he was genuinely remorseful and might have actually changed, I told him that I was willing to listen to what he had to say. About thirty seconds of dead silence ensued, followed by his statement that *he had no idea what he had done wrong!*

A bit taken aback, I inquired as to what was unclear about that ten-page certified letter he had signed for, and no doubt read repeatedly~ and which was still only the tip of the iceberg. That letter was sent only a couple of years earlier. Surely he remembered it, since he had no problem recalling ten years ago. In fact, it was probably sitting on the desk right in front of him, even as we spoke.

His reply was a typical abuser tactic~ that it was "all in the past" and I should let bygones be bygones. I told him no, not without an apology and some proof that he had changed. He continued to insist that he had no idea what he did wrong. But in so doing, he was actually contradicting himself and getting caught in a lie. When he had just said that the things he did wrong were "all in the past," that proved that he *did* know perfectly well what he did wrong. *Otherwise, what exactly was he talking about that was "all in the past?"*

DEJA-VU~ OR, JUST LIKE OLD TIMES

Because his ploy was to deny any knowledge of anything he had done wrong, I decided to test the waters by reminding him of just one example of his evil behavior, and see what his reaction would be. I pointed out his final act of treachery and abuse before I had cut ties with him altogether~ stealing the money that my mother had put in a trust account for me. She had inherited this money from her mother. It did not come from him or his side of the family, and was never his in any way.

As soon as I mentioned what he had done to me, all pretense of niceness and wanting to make amends and be back in the family vanished. He immediately began ranting, raving and screaming that he *fed* my mother all the years they were married and so was entitled to any money she inherited from her parents, and that she had no right to leave it to anyone else. (I know, I know. Now you have an idea of what it's like to deal with a psychopath, if you didn't already…)

I asked if he didn't even think that *that* episode merited an apology, since it was *me* he had stolen from, and not my mother. He thought for a minute, and then slowly and slyly offered, "I'm sorry the relationship went bad. Is that *good* enough for you?" This is typical satanic conniving and "bargaining." Of course I said no, that I wanted a specific apology for his evil behavior and all the things he had done to me and my family.

He then arrogantly stated that he had "nothing to apologize for." I replied that, in that case, we had nothing further to say to each other. Whereupon he again became enraged and abusive, just like he always was, began screaming at me and demanding information about my children, called me "pig-headed" when I wouldn't give it to him, and slammed the phone down in my ear. At warp speed, I was transported back in time forty years! Even more amazing is that this entire conversation, all the way from Dr. Jekyll to Mr. Hyde, took place in under three minutes!

There is much more creepy evil to this story, including the totally psycho "Christmas presents" he sent my kids two weeks later, which I have detailed in Chapter 25, "*Some Things Just Never Change,*" in my book *"Breaking the Bonds Of Adult Child Abuse,"* but for now this brief account will give you an idea of the point I'm trying to make.

HOW QUICKLY THEY FORGET

Selective Amnesia is a classic damage-control tactic, the abuser's phony defense of very conveniently "forgetting" anything that does not support his case. Suddenly he can't recall anything he ever did wrong, only whatever he can manage to twist to make himself look innocent and make *you* look like the villain. If he can put on a convincing enough act, pretending that he doesn't remember doing what you say he did, then maybe he can convince you, and everyone else, that it never really happened.

Many of us have had our abusers claim innocence and pretend they have no idea what we're talking about when we rebuke them for their behavior. When we are finally driven to cut ties with our abusers, or, strangely enough, even if *they* are the ones who disowned *us*, sooner or later they will claim to have no clue what they did wrong that brought about the end of the relationship.

The main characteristic of Selective Amnesia is that it only goes one way. Rest assured that your abuser will have no problem at all recalling how you threw a ball in the house when you were seven years old and broke her favorite lamp, or how you tripped on the sidewalk when you were four and bled all over your new white blouse on the way to church, causing the whole family to be ten minutes late. You were "always a problem," and she will miraculously have an infinite variety of detailed memories at her instant disposal to prove it.

In order to avoid accountability whenever you confront her about her behavior, your abuser will deflect the conversation and attention away from what *she* did, and focus it on *you*. She will have a photographic memory of every childhood or adolescent mistake you made, total recall of every time from the moment you were born right up until the present day that you sassed her, embarrassed her, talked back, or stood up to her, although she will conveniently not remember what she was doing to you that forced you to stand up to her. Of course, she will twist and embellish these incidents to make you look even worse. And she'll also throw in a few completely fictitious episodes just for good measure.

But remind her of anything that *she* did wrong, and she will suddenly develop brain damage. A look of bewilderment and hurt may cross her face as she tearfully denies what you are saying. Or her head may turn a shade of purple you've never seen on human skin before, as she screams that she never did any such thing and you are a liar. Either way, it will be an Oscar-worthy performance. How *could* you? And how *dare* you accuse her of mistreating you, *after all she's done for you?*

You may be momentarily confused, thinking that perhaps since the abusive incident you mentioned was a few weeks or months ago, maybe she really doesn't remember. This is because of a normal person's natural tendency to give others the benefit of the doubt and not assume malice.

However, if you test her, you will no doubt discover that she doesn't remember anything she did to you *yesterday,* either. She might not even recall torturing you in some way just a few minutes ago. And if by some chance she does remember, a lot will get lost in the translation. She is not going to remember it the same way you do. It will get twisted, denied, and added to until it sounds like either you're completely delusional, or *you* are the one who wronged *her.*

If that tactic fails, and you persist in holding her accountable, her last ditch strategy will be to tell you it was all "in the past," and *you* are wrong for not getting over it by now. *Aha!* ~ so she admits there was an "it!" If "it" was all in the past, then *what* ***is*** *"it?" What exactly* is "in the past?" How can she say "it" was in the past, if she denies remembering "it?" She will try this even if "the past" was five minutes ago. *Of course, technically,* ***everything*** *we've already done is "in the past."* So by this logic, you will have no right to rebuke her for *anything* she's *ever* done without being accused of carrying a grudge, because it's *all* "in the past." How convenient. You just can't win.

BEATING YOU TO THE PUNCH AND DRAGGING YOU THROUGH THE MUD

Most estranged abusers will then take it a step further, and go running to the rest of the family, friends or church, like the juvenile little crybabies they are, with lies about how you ditched them for absolutely no reason, when they never did anything wrong. This is part of the smear campaign an abuser will wage against her victim, getting to other people first, before the shell-shocked victim can pull herself together, and lying about everything that happened between you to make herself look like a saint and *you* look like the one who is at fault.

I speak from experience, because this is what my birth-mother did to me. After *she* ended our relationship, leaving me stunned and brokenhearted, and before I could gather my wits about me, she went crying to the other relatives that, *after forty-seven years of loving and caring for her, **I** had just upped and stopped talking to **her** for no good reason.*

Now to my normal relatives with half a brain, this didn't even make sense, and they did not believe her lies. But the jealous, holier-than-thou phonies, who were just looking for any excuse to judge and disapprove of me, chose to believe her and disown me and my family. "Punishment by Proxy" is typical in a Lord of The Flies dysfunctional family or church.

The truth about why my relationship with my mother broke up is that I had finally begun setting limits on my birth-parents' abuse. So Mommy Darling decided to stop speaking to me, rather than stop abusing me and exposing me and my children to her husband's abuse. But somehow my ex-mother neglected to mention this little detail when she was busy trashing me and lying about me to the few gullible relatives who could be easily influenced into taking her seriously. She took full advantage of the knowledge that her audience was too ignorant to question the fact that her accusations against me just didn't add up, and that it was obvious she must have been leaving something out. This is another example of an abuser's Selective Amnesia. Whether she is angrily badmouthing you, or tearfully lying about you to other people, she will conveniently "forget" to mention anything and everything that *she* did to contribute to the demise of your relationship. It really is quite a show.

Another illustration of Selective Amnesia is the abuser who will look you dead in the eye and claim to have no clue what he did to upset you, *even though he has been plainly and clearly told, in no uncertain terms, **exactly** what he did.* This was my birth-father's tactic. My ten-page letter spelled out in minute detail abuse after abuse, he signed a receipt for the letter, which I still have, and yet he still claimed to be clueless. *This is because he was lying.* The only reason he "doesn't remember" is that he *chooses* not to remember, because it is not to his advantage to admit the truth.

THE DEVIL'S ADVOCATE, OR SICCING THE FAMILY MEDDLER ON YOU

Some abusers will confront their victims in person and claim innocence. Then, when you give them specific examples, they deny, lie, blame you or someone else, and in general refuse to take responsibility, apologize, or make amends. They are just looking for an excuse to keep you talking and interacting with them, so they can argue with everything you say instead of showing any remorse. Once again, you will be the one put on the defensive, trying to justify and explain your position, while they tell you it never happened, they don't remember a thing, or it's all in the past and you need to get over it.

Other abusers, however, either can't handle a direct confrontation with you, or realize that you will refuse to speak with them. So they will enlist a third party to do their dirty work for them. I like to refer to this bit player as the Devil's Advocate, also known in Abuse-Recovery circles as a Flying Monkey, sent to do the evil witch's bidding. Your abuser may point-blank ask another relative to contact you on her behalf. Or, she will go on and on, crying a river to anyone who will listen, pretending that she loves and misses you so much and has no idea why you won't have anything to do with her, and in general acting as pathetic as possible. She will keep this performance up until some meddling busybody takes pity on her and decides to "intervene" (translate: butt in), by calling you and either volunteering to "help" you patch things up or criticizing *you* for hurting your abuser.

When this happens, the family budinski may pretend that she just can't stand to see the family having problems, and took it upon herself to call you without your abuser's knowledge. *This is a lie,* told to make you think the "well-intentioned" budinski is neutral and is not taking sides, and that you can trust her not to repeat whatever you might say. But make no mistake, the Devil's Advocate's real purpose is just that~ *to advocate for the devil in your family or in your church,* ***not you.*** She is on *his* side, the dark side, the evil side. She is not on the side of truth and goodness and light. She will gain your trust, get you to confide in her, and then she will report every detail back to your abuser, *who knows perfectly well that she is calling you* because he either put her up to it directly or manipulated her into doing it.

Almost every abusive family or church has at least one attention-grabbing narcissist who will be more than happy to exploit your situation so that she can take the credit for trying to "make peace" between you and your estranged relative. She will just soak it up as others praise her for having the courage to get involved and trying to "help." It makes her feel important to have everyone know about the noble and selfless thing she did. She will pry and ask you all kinds of nosy questions that are none of her business, in a sham attempt at "finding a compromise." Then she will be the big shot with the inside information that everyone else wants to hear. So she will be sure to announce it at every family gathering or church fellowship, discussing your conversations, in appropriately hushed tones and with a look of somber concern, with anyone who seems interested, and repeating everything you said, whether in confidence or not. *She will use your pain to get attention and make herself look like a hero.* A meddler is not the family "peacemaker." She is the family *gossip.* Of course she has to broadcast her "selfless" act. Because after all, if no one knows about it, then what's the point?

Trust me on this. I guarantee that if you confide in the meddling budinski, you will be a topic of conversation at every get-together for at least the next five years, and probably much longer. The best defense against this abuse by proxy is to refuse to discuss the relationship between you and your abuser with any third parties who have any kind of connection to him. Remember that just because the donkey brays, doesn't mean you have to answer her. Just say "Thanks for your concern, but my situation with my mother (or whoever else you might have a "situation" with) is between her and me, and I'm not going to discuss it with you. It's private."

You can also say "Despite what he's told you, my father knows exactly what he did, and when he's ready to make amends, he'll have to call me himself. My advice to you is don't get involved and don't believe everything you hear." Hopefully, your meddling go-between will take the hint and back off before you have to tell her point blank to mind her own business.

THREE BASIC PRINCIPLES OF SELECTIVE AMNESIA

1. Abusers will only choose to "remember" whatever will make them look innocent, and make you look bad. Anything they

don't want to remember will be conveniently forgotten, except for the things they will claim are "in the past, and you need to get over it and let bygones be bygones." However, be aware that, by the abuser's definition, "in the past" includes abuses she inflicted upon you yesterday, an hour ago, and five minutes ago. *Everything* she even halfway admits to will be "in the past," and therefore off-limits for you to confront her on.

2. When your abuser claims to have "no idea what he did wrong," ***he is lying.*** He knows perfectly well what he did. He will try this ploy even if you have told him point blank and in no uncertain terms exactly what he did wrong, argued with him and protested his mistreatment for years, and repeated your complaints dozens of times. And yes, even if you have written him a detailed, ten-page letter listing a few decades worth of examples, which he has no doubt read and re-read a couple of hundred times. He has seen your distress every time he hurt you. In fact, that was his *reward* for hurting you and the reason he continued to hurt you. Because he loved knowing that he *could.* You probably complained, rebuked, confronted, cried in front of him, fought with him, and tried in vain to set limits for years, if not your entire life. And nothing worked, leaving you no choice but to end it for your own survival. There is no way he does not know what he did. That is a lie. He only has Selective Amnesia because it serves his purposes to "forget."

3. If you take the bait, *again,* and tell him what he did, *again,* he will only use it to involve you in a lengthy, pointless discussion *again,* in which he will lie and deny, *again.* He does not really want to know the answer to this question. He is not going to respectfully listen to your complaint, carefully consider what you have to say, admit guilt, and try to make amends.

> He is only going to argue with everything you say, just like he always has. It will be the same old pattern it always was, and *you* will be the one who winds up aggravated, stressed out, upset, and on the defensive. You will just be wasting your breath. And your abuser will use the fact that you're even talking to him at all as a golden opportunity to manipulate, con you, bicker, criticize, rant and rave, vent his spleen, get things off *his* chest, and upset and abuse you all over again. Who knows when he'll get another opportunity to tell *you* a thing or two? After all, that is what he *really* missed~ not you as a person and a loved one, but you as *a target.*

It does not pay to attempt any nice, reasonable discussion (on any subject) with an abuser. You are deluding yourself if you think you can ever make him understand, admit to anything, or be accountable in any way. No matter what he claims, *he has no interest in resolving your issues.* He only wants to bait you into another endless argument, so he can pick up where he left off when you rebuked or disowned him and abuse you some more. Reconciliation is not his goal. Upsetting you some more, just like old times, is his goal. It's a power thing. He just loves pulling your strings, claiming amnesia, lying and denying everything you say, watching you get all worked up, and knowing that he still has the ability to do that to you. If you answer an abuser who claims he doesn't know what he did wrong, you will be playing right into his hands. The best response is to refer him back to whatever letter or e-mail you sent in the past, and say, "You have already been told what you did. I'm not going to repeat it," or to simply state, "If you really don't know what you did, then we have nothing more to say to each other," and end the conversation.

IT WOULD TAKE FOREVER TO TELL YOU WHAT YOU DID WRONG, AND I JUST DON'T HAVE THE TIME

How do you chronicle fifty years of abuse? How do you put it into words? Abusers want to know "what they did wrong" as if it was merely one or two incidents which could be discussed and settled in a few minutes. But it's not. *It's a lifetime of incidents*~ twenty, thirty, fifty or more years. Hundreds, if not thousands, of times. It's overwhelming. It's not one or two obnoxious behaviors or hurtful episodes. It's a *pattern* of ongoing, continuous, unrelenting evil. It just never ends, until we leave.

When my birth-father feigned innocence and wanted to know what he had done wrong, my first thought was, "Where do I begin?" The feeling I had was just hopelessness. I had to bite my tongue to keep from asking him, "Do you want it alphabetically or chronologically?" If I took him at his word, and began listing fifty years of abuses, it would have taken months. The time, not to mention the emotional toll, would have been devastating.

As it was, I tested the waters with only one small example, and that resulted in an explosion of rage and more abuse, and certainly not even a shred of remorse. He didn't really want to hear what he had done wrong. *He just wanted me to say* ***anything,*** *so that he would have an excuse to attack me, just like old times.*

After seeing his response and discerning his intentions, why on earth would I continue trying to give him any more examples? Just so that he could keep me talking to him, and involve me in a six-month long argument? When you recognize this tactic, it is vital not to allow the abuser to take control of the discussion. My birth-father's reaction was my cue to end the conversation, because it was going nowhere and would not accomplish anything. It was not going to solve any problems, and it certainly was not going to be beneficial to *me* in any way to continue. If I had allowed myself to be dragged into it any further, I would have been playing right into his hands.

YOU'RE ALREADY PARANOID, SO I MIGHT AS WELL TELL YOU THAT IT *IS* YOU!

The problem with trying to explain to our abuser why we divorced her is that *it's not so much what she* ***did****, it's* ***who she is.*** Or rather, *what* she is. With an abuser, it is *not* any one incident. It is *not* just her behavior. It is *her.* It is the kind of person she is that we don't want to have anything more to do with. Abusers are evil, wicked, demonic people. Their behavior is merely an outward sign, a manifestation of the condition of their souls and the shriveled up, dead black hearts within them.

The reason we stay away is that we have finally sensed and internalized this. It's our abuser's whole persona that keeps us away, not any one incident or behavior. *It's everything about him.* It's his personality, his character, his unrighteousness, his ungodliness, his demonic spirit, his whole evil being. It's not just this thing or that thing or any of the things he does. It's *him!*

It would be more accurate to list his personality traits rather than his behaviors as the reason we disowned our abusive relative. Imagine telling our abuser *the truth~* that we refuse contact with him because ***he is*** nasty, cunning, spiteful, manipulative, belligerent, treacherous, critical, lying, untruthful, bullying, conniving, deceitful, sneaky, troublemaking, jealous, sabotaging, envious, bitter, sadistic, malicious, selfish, dishonest, narcissistic, hostile, dangerous, cruel, hateful, psychopathic, evil and abusive. That's who he is. Who in their right mind would want someone like that in their life? What normal, healthy person would want to deal with this, or to expose themselves and their children to it?

Our revulsion, repulsion, and avoidance are natural, normal, healthy reactions to exposure to evil. It is our God-given discernment setting off alarm bells in our heads and telling us to run for the hills. We left because we finally realized it was hopeless, and that changing these ingrained characteristics is impossible. Our abuser would have to change her very being, and that will never happen because she has no desire to. She left us no choice but to cut her off, in order to protect ourselves and our families.

The only way we can lead healthy, happy lives is to stay away from such evil people. We don't disown them because of one or two things they did. *We disown them because they are unfit as people to have in our lives.* My birth-father slammed the phone down before our conversation was finished, so I never got to tell him that. Satan took him a couple of years later without me ever getting the chance to enlighten him. Maybe now that he's burning in hell he finally got the answers he claimed to be searching for.

WHEREFORE COME OUT FROM AMONG THEM AND BE YE SEPARATE, SAITH THE LORD, AND TOUCH NOT THE UNCLEAN THING; AND I WILL RECEIVE YOU, AND WILL BE A FATHER UNTO YOU, AND YE SHALL BE MY SONS AND DAUGHTERS, SAITH THE LORD ALMIGHTY.....
2 Corinthians 6:17-18 KJV.

CHAPTER 11

"SHE CAN'T HELP THE WAY SHE ACTS," SO YOU'LL JUST HAVE TO ACCEPT IT, FORGIVE HER ANYWAY, AND NOT EXPECT HER TO CHANGE

How many times has this happened to you? You're upset over yet another incident of abuse, and you're venting, or crying, about it to another relative, who then tells you that *you have to understand* that's "just the way your abuser is", "she doesn't mean it," or "she can't help it," because of her own psychological problems.

I'M SPECIAL, AND YOU HAVE TO TREAT ME THAT WAY

Narcissists believe they are special and therefore worthy of special treatment. They know you have boundaries and rules for the way you expect people to treat you. But those only apply to *other* people. They fully expect you to make an exception for them. When confronted, many abusers will look you dead in the eye and state, quite simply and often with a shrug or a little smirk, that "that's just the way I am." The implication being that you should know me by now, and if you want to continue being in my royal presence, then you're just going to have to deal with it and accept whatever mistreatment I dish out.

When it became necessary for me to set limits on my contact with a very demanding and self-centered ex-friend, instead of apologizing for being so rude, pushy and nasty, and agreeing to control herself in the future, she chose to "take offense" and add fuel to the fire by becoming even *more* abusive. Later, she claimed she did this because *I* had "not handled her properly." She told me she "responded much better to a gentle hand guiding her in what's right." She added that this was "just the way she's wired," as if for some strange reason it was beyond her control to respond in a rational and polite way. Even more amazing was the fact that, although I had indeed finally set some limits on her selfishness and incessant demands, I nevertheless had still treated her gently and lovingly, while all the while *she* was treating *me* hatefully.

Unfortunately for my ex-friend, "that's just the way I'm wired" is not an acceptable excuse for abusing someone. I'm not her mother, and it's not *my* job to "guide her" or teach her what is "right" if she doesn't already know right from wrong by now. It is also not my job to make allowances for her "faulty wiring" by overlooking her hostile and offensive behavior. It's *her* job to "rewire" herself and behave properly. If she can't bring herself to act with love towards an old friend, then at least she can act in a civil and socially acceptable manner.

ARE THEY ALL CRAZY?

Perhaps even more frequently, some version of this ridiculous excuse is used by the Silent Partner (the abuser's chief enabler) or the Silent Majority (the whole toxic enabling family, church, or group) to defend an abuser. My mother had more excuses for my birth-father's abuse than *he* did. "That's just the way he is", "He can't help himself", "He can't handle his anger", "He doesn't know how to act right towards people", "He's always been that way", "He's very moody", "You know he just has a short fuse," and other lame excuses poured from her lips daily~ even though, paradoxically, *she* was the one who complained more about his behavior than anyone else.

The conclusions drawn by those offering these lame excuses are all pointing toward one and the same resolution to the problem~ *you! You* have to learn to accept that this is "just the way he is," *you* have to understand that he "has problems," *you* have to be more tolerant of his behavior because he "can't help it," and *you have to understand that none of this is his fault.* The entire responsibility for keeping the family running smoothly and not upsetting the apple cart is on *your* shoulders, because nobody else is going to do a thing. The abuser is simply not responsible for his own words or actions, which are supposedly completely out of his control. And his enablers are simply going to justify his abusiveness, not express any disapproval, never defend or protect you or the other victims, and not do anything to stop him. Therefore, *you* will just have to make allowances for his behavior, forgive him, and keep on forgiving him without ever expecting him to change, no matter what outrageous and destructive things he does, because otherwise *you* wouldn't be a "good Christian!"

Well, nice try. This is just more hogwash invented by abusers and their Silent Partners to allow them to get away with murder, so to speak. *Out of all the lame excuses abusers like to try, it doesn't get any lamer than "I can't control myself."* Here are some examples of the ridiculous excuses we've heard, which really are no excuse at all:

- "That's just the way she is."
- "She's always been like that."
- "She's like that with everybody."
- "When you love someone, you have to accept them as they are."
- "You have to take the bad with the good." (*What* good?)
- "He doesn't know how to talk to people."
- "It's because she was abused when she was a child."
- "He's not in his right mind."

- "He has a drinking problem."
- "She has trouble controlling her temper."
- "He has anger-management problems."
- "She's on drugs."
- "He gets very frustrated and takes it out on other people."
- "She's under stress."
- "He's having problems at work."
- "She's having problems with her boyfriend."
- "She's jealous of you."
- "He feels bad because you got a promotion and he didn't."
- "He's insecure and trying to make himself feel better by demeaning you."
- "She really admires you (translate: "envies") and wishes she could be like you."
- "She needs to bring you down to her level to feel better about herself."
- "When he thinks he's being attacked, his 'Reptile Brain' takes over."
- "He's afraid of losing you, so he's trying to push you away before you leave him."
- "He's afraid of getting too attached to you, so he's trying to push you away before you leave him."
- "He's afraid of intimacy, so he's trying to push you away."
- "He's afraid of commitment, so he's trying to push you away".
- "He loves you so much he doesn't know what to do, so he's trying to push you away."
- "He's afraid you'll see how inadequate he is, so he's trying to push you away."
- "It's subconscious. She doesn't know she's doing it.
- "It's false bravado. She's intimidated by you, so she's trying to show you that you'd better not mess with her."

- "She intimidated by you, so she's trying to show you that you're not so hot."
- "She admires your self-confidence, so she tries to undermine you."
- "She doesn't want you to realize what a pathetic loser she is, so she's trying to push you away before you see it."
- "She thinks you're pulling away from her, so she's trying to make you afraid of losing her."
- "She thinks you're pulling away from her, so she's avoiding you so you'll see how much you'll miss her if your relationship breaks up."
- "She can't handle confrontation, so she does passive-aggressive things instead of being direct."
- "She doesn't know how to express her feelings."
- "She doesn't think you'd understand if she told the truth, so she lies and covers up."
- "She has a lot of pride. That's why apologizing is so hard for her."
- "She just never admits she's wrong, but deep down inside she knows it."
- "Her parents always favored her sisters, so she has a lot of insecurities and anger."
- "Her parents always favored *her*, so she's spoiled and has an exaggerated sense of entitlement."
- "Nobody understands her."
- "She's a little eccentric."
- "She thinks everyone takes her the wrong way, so she's very defensive."
- "She thinks everyone loves her, so she's got a big head. She's just trying to see what she can get away with."
- "She can be a little difficult sometimes."
- "She gets overwhelmed."

- "She's a narcissist. She can't understand that the world doesn't revolve around her."
- "It's the way she was raised."
- "He thinks that whatever he wants is the most important thing."
- "He has trouble delaying gratification."
- "He has a problem with impulse control."
- "He doesn't mean the things he says."
- "He doesn't realize that words can hurt."
- "He doesn't mean any harm."
- "You just have to understand that he has some odd quirks."
- "He just reacts without thinking first."
- "She's confused."
- "She's depressed."
- "She's in a bad mood."
- "She's hormonal."
- "She has PMS."
- "She's menopausal."
- "She's going through a rough time right now."
- "She doesn't know any better."
- "They're having 'empty-nest syndrome' and they're just taking it out on you."
- "They don't want to admit you're all grown up. It's too painful for them."
- "They need reassurance that you still need them."
- "They were raised in a different time, when you respected your parents no matter what they did to you. So they don't understand why you have a problem with them doing all the things to you that their parents did to them. It's really just a culture clash."

YOU'LL BELIEVE ANYTHING I SAY IF I SAY IT WITH A STRAIGHT FACE

And the list could go on and on. It's funny that many of these preposterous excuses contradict each other and might even be exact opposites. Apparently just about every circumstance, good or bad, can be conveniently twisted into a lame excuse for being unable to control oneself and having no choice but to abuse other people. Abusers and their Silent Partners think that no matter what completely outlandish thing they say, as long as they say it in all seriousness and with a straight face, or repeat it often enough, we will be stupid enough to believe them.

Marcus, a sixty-two-year-old pedophile, was finally arrested and sent to prison after spending twenty-five years raping and molesting dozens of little boys, while his wife Lindsay, *who knew he was a pedophile because he had spent two years molesting her own child* ***and she caught him in the act***, covered for him, and even babysat other people's children and left them alone with him to be victimized. Lindsay also worked at an elementary school and refused to get a driver's license, very conveniently making it necessary for Marcus to drive her to and from work every day, and managing to expose every little kid in town to him as they tried to walk past his car while he waited for her.

When Marcus was finally arrested, Lindsay, who in my humble opinion should have been arrested as an accessory but for some reason wasn't, had this to say: "He has the mentality of a fourteen-year-old." This was followed by various versions of how he wasn't capable of understanding that what he was doing was wrong, he was "borderline retarded," he was very immature so he's "on the same level" as the children he raped and considered himself to be one of them (maybe it's just me, but, even so, I don't know many five-year-olds who have sex with one another), and so on.

She even went so far as to make the outrageous claim that the sex he had with his victims *was consensual,* and that these *little children had seduced her "helpless" husband!* Poor Marcus! All along *all those perverted little kids* had been the ones molesting *him* and taking advantage of *his* innocent gullibility, and now everybody else was blaming *him!* Apparently all of these children were just dying to have sex with him, and they knew he wouldn't say no because he was too dimwitted, so they seduced him. And then they got him in all kinds of trouble! Those mean kids are always picking on poor, dumb Marcus. It's all *their* fault he got twenty years in the state pen! According to Lindsay, although Marcus was in his sixties and many of his victims were as young as five or six, they were all on the same mental level, so they were all just....what? Playing doctor? Was she trying to say that Marcus' attacks were not really terrifying, painful, and traumatic to the children, because he was really just one of them~ a grey-haired, 6'3", 280-pound five-year-old lout?

As you can well imagine, there's a lot more to this story than I'm telling here. I'm not saying it doesn't happen, but personally I don't know too many fourteen-year-olds who rape other children and think it's all good. I don't know what kinds of kids this woman knows, but the fourteen-year-olds I know are indeed mature enough to be capable of knowing right from wrong. And they know that violence and forcible rape is very wrong. The kids I know would not want their age used as an excuse for sexually attacking a child, as if such behavior is "normal" for fourteen-year-olds. They would be mortified.

Suffice it to say that Lindsay's despicable and outrageous comments, as well as her refusal to be accountable for covering up for Marcus and practically hand-feeding him dozens of victims over the years, have caused her to be the talk of the town and to be shunned by just about every decent person who knows her.

My family, friends and neighbors had known this couple for many years. Marcus and Lindsay were quite the social butterflies, and all the townsfolk knew them. They lived in the same area they grew up in, and most folks had known them since they were children. All his life, Marcus carried on conversations like a normal person, was capable of understanding, problem solving, and rational thought, held a job like a normal adult, supported a house and a family for decades, drove a car, maintained his home, went out to dinner, and was able to complete transactions like selling and buying real estate and vehicles, filling out applications, purchasing insurance, paying bills, shopping, and applying for credit. He managed to get to doctor's appointments and maintain a social life. He served in the military, was married for thirty years, and had kids of his own (Don't ask).

If anything, he was cunning and conniving, and able to support his perversion with long-term advance planning. He volunteered as a little boys' sports coach. He wormed his way into positions of authority in the church that would allow him access to children. He "groomed" little boys to be future victims everywhere he went, going out of his way to be "friends" with them. He sweetly offered rides to children with no transportation and took the sons of single mothers to hockey games.

In other words, for decades, Marcus was a fully grown, fully functional, mentally competent adult of normal intelligence and ability, who displayed an age-appropriate maturity level. In fact, he was quite clever at scoping out potential victims and manipulating them into the necessary situations to be victimized, all while charming their unsuspecting parents. He was also adept at covering his tracks and making up alibis.

But as soon as the you-know-what hit the fan and his Silent Partner Lindsay went into damage-control mode, he magically morphed into a mentally challenged, big overgrown ape, with the mentality of a child, who had no idea that what he was doing was wrong, and who actually believed that his victims *wanted* to be raped by him. So essentially, *he was doing them a favor,* by giving them what they wanted. He thought they *liked* it! He thought it was okay. He just didn't know any better. Poor misguided, misjudged pervert.

Oh, pul-leeze. And abusers like this husband and wife team wonder why people get so enraged at them. The only thing that makes them look at all mentally challenged is that they actually think other people are stupid enough to believe this baloney. Other than that, this lowlife degenerate, and his equally lowlife wife, were smart enough to pull the wool over everyone else's eyes for a quarter of a century. How many fourteen-year-olds do you know who could pull *that* off?

The point of this disgusting story is to illustrate that there are apparently no limits as to how low an abuser and his enablers will sink to pretend that he is not responsible for the things he chooses to do. Their imaginations know no bounds when it comes to weaseling out of being accountable. They are absolutely shameless as they try to convince you that they just can't help themselves. They lie outrageously. No matter how ridiculous they sound, they will look you dead in the eye and continue to insist that they can't control their own words or actions. But, guess what? If *you* tried to do the same things to them that they do to you, you can bet that they would most certainly expect *you* to control *yourself!*

PROOF THAT "I CAN'T HELP MYSELF" IS A LIE

The whole concept of an adult who is powerless to control himself is just preposterous, and it insults our intelligence to expect us to fall for such garbage. Barring some catastrophic illness like a brain tumor, dementia or Alzheimer's, abusers can control themselves just as well as everybody else, if only they wanted to. And here's why:

1. Mentally ill people who have no control over themselves and are at the mercy of their impulses are not capable of the very deliberate and convoluted advance planning that goes into

most instances of abuse. They are not capable of the conniving and treachery required. They are not capable of the fabrications and lies needed to cover up what they're doing, or of making up complicated excuses. They are not capable of the sophisticated mind games and psychological battles-of-will that abusers play.

You are either out-of-control and unable to stop yourself from immediately acting on your impulses (in which case, you probably should be institutionalized to prevent you from being a danger to society), or you are perfectly capable of plotting and planning your next move over a period of time, and waiting for the best opportunity to carry it out. It's one or the other. You can't have it both ways! Think back and decide if your abuser *really* acts like she's "out-of-control," or if she's actually exquisitely *in* control.

2. The very nature of an out-of-control, impulsive act would mean that the chances of it being randomly repeated are probably one in a million. However, patterns of abuse are repeated again and again. An abuser does the same hurtful things and repeats the same unacceptable behavior over and over, forever, until he is stopped. Because he is capable of reasoning that it worked for him before, and since it worked for him before, it will probably work for him again.

3. The very same people who claim to be helpless to control the rude, nasty things that pop out of their mouths when they talk to *us* have no problem at all being polite and respectful to those whom they perceive as authority figures, such as their boss or their doctor. They behave completely normally with those whom they consider their equals, like the neighbors. They wouldn't dream of saying the things they say to *us* to a stranger on line at the deli.

> This is precisely why most people don't believe us when we start telling the truth about our abuser's behavior towards us. They've never seen the abuser in action, because he's clever enough to hide his true self around people he wants to impress or deceive. *This ability to display appropriate behavior when necessary or when advantageous to him proves that he does indeed understand what is and is not acceptable, and is perfectly capable of modifying his behavior.* Abusers manage to control themselves just fine when they have to. They just don't have to with us.

And *no,* "personality disorders" do not qualify as catastrophic illnesses. According to modern psychology, every one of us probably has some kind of personality disorder. But that's no excuse. None of us have the right to inflict our issues on anybody else, no matter how "special" we might arrogantly think we are. Instead of expecting everybody to make allowances for their "eccentricities", "bad moods," or "odd quirks," what abusers need to do is grow up and start taking responsibility for themselves and the things they say and do.

WHOSE JOB IS IT TO "FIX" AN ABUSER?

All kinds of treatments are available for those who *truly* want help with their "challenges." It's not *your* job to help your abusive father control his temper, nor to overlook his outbursts. It's not *your* job to help your manipulative sister with her "narcissistic personality disorder," or your control freak mother with her insecurities. It's not *your* responsibility to read two dozen self-help books trying to figure out *their* problems, when *they* could read the exact same books and *help themselves* if only they gave a hoot. It's not up to *you* to ask your therapy group or chat group to help you analyze why your parents behave so hatefully towards you. Those groups are not there to help *them* figure out *their* issues. They are there to help *you* with *your* issues~ the issues your family most likely is the cause of.

You are not your family's psychologist. It is not up to *you* to fix them. *God* can fix them, but the last thing they want is to submit themselves to his will and turn from their sin. So, because they are stubborn and "stiff-necked," the only choice left is for them to take responsibility for themselves, get into therapy or whatever, and get "fixed." You didn't cause their so-called problems, and you can't cure them. My favorite response to the "I can't control myself / he can't control himself" excuse for abuse is, "That is not my problem. I'm not running a mental institution for abusers."

I believe we waste altogether too much time and energy trying to psychoanalyze abusive psychopaths and figure out why they do the things they do. Therapy can be a very good thing for many people. But at times it can also be a bad thing, especially for abusers, narcissists and psychopaths, because it gives them a whole new repertoire of excuses for damaging other people. Modern psychology tends to make far too many excuses for inappropriate behavior by conveniently making the abuser into the victim of some psychological illness and then feeding into his narcissism by giving him attention for it. Of course he can't help himself. He has an "illness." Now he's *sick,* instead of just *evil.* Poor abuser~ turns out *he's* a victim too!

Of course, this puts the *real* victim in an impossible bind. How can we expect someone who can't control herself to be able to respect our boundaries and limits? Her behavior is out-of-control, and she can't help it. She wishes she could, but she can't. Oh, well. You're just out-of-luck, so there's really no point in setting limits in the first place. There's no point in rebuking her or confronting her or protesting your abuse, because there's nothing she can do about it. You'll just have to learn to live with it. That's just the way she is. And now that you understand, you'll *have to* forgive her, because you're a Christian.

THEY NEED TO LEARN SOME SELF-CONTROL, JUST LIKE EVERYBODY ELSE

One of the most common excuses we've heard for abusing children and Adult Children is that the parent was abused when she was a child. It's as if it's almost expected that she'll now abuse her own child. It's like a foregone conclusion. Of course your mother still screams at you, lies about you, and calls you names, because that's what *her* mother did to her! It's "the only thing she knows."

The biggest flaw in this line of reasoning is that plenty of adults who were abused by their birth-families do not go on to abuse their own children. I didn't. My husband didn't. My sister and numerous friends from abusive backgrounds didn't. We, and just about every person I've heard from so far in my ministry, are perfect examples of abuse survivors who do not abuse others, especially not our own children. Most of us would never want to put our children through what we have suffered, and are very careful not to repeat the things our parents did to us with our own kids. If anything, we go overboard in the other direction. I've always said that I have my parents to thank for teaching me how to raise children~ everything *they* did, *I* did exactly the opposite! *If coming from an abusive background turns you into an abuser, then how do you explain all of us?*

Studies have shown that psychopaths, with their emotional disconnect, are *less* affected by past experiences like trauma and child abuse than normal people are, ***not** more affected.* You cannot turn someone into a psychopath. No one is predestined to become an abuser. Being an abuser, or not being an abuser, is a choice we make. *Abusers choose to mistreat those who love them*, because it works for them and gets them what they want. The Lord gave all of us free will. We can choose to be loving and kind to others, or we can choose to be wicked and evil. We can choose to be righteous and godly, or we can choose to follow Satan. Abuse is not something we can't help. Abuse is a choice, and often a very deliberate, calculated choice.

Abusers and their Silent Partners are under the impression that once they manage to get it through our thick heads that the abuser really can't help himself because he has some mental condition, then we will just have to accept him the way he is. He "can't" change, so we can't expect him to. It's not his fault, so we can't blame him or hold him accountable. We just need to get over it, forgive him repeatedly, and let him continue on forever, abusing us and others without protest. Otherwise we wouldn't be good Christians. We can't be unforgiving. We'll just have to suffer in silence from now on, lest we cause a psychopath to feel bad about himself because he's helpless to make the changes we expect. God forbid an *abuser* should feel guilty or ashamed for a change!

GOD NEVER TELLS US TO BE "UNDERSTANDING" OF EVIL

So what exactly does the Bible have to say about all of this? Abusers and their enablers frequently try to justify their wickedness by claiming that God himself is on their side. They try to convince us that God wants us to be understanding about why our abuser acts the way he does. And, now that we know the reason for his behavior, to be forgiving also, because he can't help it. We should try to figure out what's wrong with him, and then overlook everything he does that damages us or the other people we love. We need to be sympathetic, accepting, patient and tolerant, and indulge his "little quirks."

But in fact, the Bible says nothing of the kind. No one who knows the Lord could think that he would ever tell us to make allowances for evil. That's completely illogical. Nowhere in God's Word are we told to be understanding of or patient with someone who deliberately and repeatedly hurts other people. Nowhere are we told to excuse or tolerate behavior that causes suffering for others, including ourselves.

We are *never* instructed to overlook abuse because the perpetrator has "problems of his own." That's like dismissing his actions by saying "Oh well, misery loves company." *He's* unhappy, so he's within his rights to make *us* unhappy, too. Then we won't be "better" than him, and that will make him feel better about himself, so it's okay. This is a ridiculous and nonsensical notion. Just because an abuser has problems doesn't mean he has to give everybody *else* problems. *His problems are irrelevant. They don't matter.* And they certainly don't give him license to abuse other people.

THERE ARE NO PSYCHOLOGISTS IN THE BIBLE

God never tells us to psychoanalyze anybody, good or bad, or to take into consideration their past, their anxieties, their addictions, their abusive childhoods, their stress levels, their anger-management problems, their insecurities, their personality disorders, or any other emotional or mental problems they might claim to have. Nowhere in the Bible are we told to try and figure out why wicked people act wickedly, because the answer to that question is already given to us:

DEAR CHILDREN, DO NOT LET ANYONE LEAD YOU ASTRAY. HE WHO DOES WHAT IS RIGHT IS RIGHTEOUS, JUST AS HE IS RIGHTEOUS. HE WHO DOES WHAT IS SINFUL IS OF THE DEVIL, BECAUSE THE DEVIL HAS BEEN SINNING FROM THE BEGINNING. THE REASON THE SON OF GOD APPEARED WAS TO DESTROY THE DEVIL'S WORK. NO ONE WHO IS BORN OF GOD WILL CONTINUE TO SIN, BECAUSE GOD'S SEED REMAINS IN HIM; HE CANNOT GO ON SINNING, BECAUSE HE HAS BEEN BORN OF GOD. THIS IS HOW WE KNOW WHO THE CHILDREN OF GOD ARE AND WHO THE CHILDREN OF THE DEVIL ARE: ANYONE WHO DOES NOT DO WHAT IS

RIGHT IS NOT A CHILD OF GOD; NOR IS ANYONE WHO DOES NOT LOVE HIS BROTHER....1 John 3:7-10 NIV.

The Lord has a very simple formula for dealing with those who damage us. We are told to rebuke them, forgive them *if* they repent, and have nothing further to do with them if they don't (Luke 17:3; Titus 3:10-11; Matthew 18:15-17; 2 Timothy 3:2-5). The Bible *never* tells us to forgive unrepentant evildoers who are unwilling to change. Biblically speaking, there is no such thing as a good excuse for abusing innocent people. Whatever reason an abuser has for his behavior doesn't make any difference at all. The only thing that matters is whether or not he chooses to repent when rebuked. It is his choice that dictates our next move~ either forgiveness, or having nothing further to do with him.

The Lord does not burden us with having to psychoanalyze our abusers, and we need to not take on this unnecessary burden. God is the one who judges men's hearts, not us, and we are not to step into this function that belongs to the Lord. Our Father in his infinite mercy also does not burden us with having to excuse and tolerate abuse forever, with no hope of it ever ending. He instructs us to confront and be ready to forgive if there is repentance (change), and he gives us an out if there is no change. We need to obey what the Bible *really* teaches, stop giving credence to the abuser's myriad of lame excuses, and take that out that the Lord is giving us. "Understanding" an abuser is not our burden, and God never meant it to be.

DO NOT BE DECEIVED: GOD CANNOT BE MOCKED. A MAN REAPS WHAT HE SOWS. THE ONE WHO SOWS TO PLEASE HIS SINFUL NATURE, FROM THAT NATURE WILL REAP DESTRUCTION; THE ONE WHO SOWS TO PLEASE THE SPIRIT, FROM THE SPIRIT WILL REAP ETERNAL LIFE.....
Galatians 6:7-8 NIV.

CHAPTER 12

THE OLD AGE EXCUSES: "SHE'S OLD, AND THAT'S HOW THEY GET" OR, "HE'S OLD, SO HE'S ENTITLED"

HE WHO TROUBLES HIS OWN HOUSE WILL INHERIT THE WIND....Proverbs 11:29 NKJV.

EVEN AS I HAVE SEEN, THEY THAT PLOW INIQUITY, AND SOW WICKEDNESS, REAP THE SAME. BY THE BLAST OF GOD THEY PERISH, AND BY THE BREATH OF HIS NOSTRILS ARE THEY CONSUMED. THE ROARING OF THE LION, AND THE VOICE OF THE FIERCE LION, AND THE TEETH OF THE YOUNG LIONS, ARE BROKEN. THE OLD LION PERISHETH FOR LACK OF PREY, AND THE STOUT LION'S WHELPS ARE SCATTERED ABROAD.....Job 4:8-11 KJV.

Those of us who have had to set limits on or divorce our abusive parents are often chastised by others who feel they have the right to judge us. Especially as our abusers age, if we continue to keep our distance, eventually someone will accuse us of being unkind or intolerant, and then attempt to "educate" us with some statement along the lines of, "She's old, and they get that way," or, "She's old, so she's entitled. You'd be that way too, if you were her age." I like to call this the "Old Age Excuse" for abuse, and it is amazingly popular with abusers and their Silent Partners. The Old Age Excuse is simply another version of the "She Can't Help the Way She Acts" and "She Can't Control Herself" excuse.

THE ENTITLEMENT MENTALITY OF THE NARCISSIST

Entitlement is a concept unique to narcissistic abusers and their Silent Partners. They believe that they are *entitled* to do whatever they want, because they are *"special"* in some way. Rules don't apply to them. They don't have to behave according to acceptable standards. They don't have to show kindness, consideration or good manners. They can lie, criticize, control, yell, scream, name-call, manipulate, steal, intrude or pry all they want to. Yes, it's true that *other* people are not allowed to get away with these things, but *they* are. You have to make an exception for them. They're not *like* everybody else. They're unique and wonderful and always right. You should be grateful that they even *talk* to you. Common people have limits and boundaries, but narcissists and psychopaths do not. *They are entitled* to do anything they want, and old age entitles them even more.

Well, here's a newsflash for them. *There is no such thing as being "entitled" to mistreat another person. Nothing* "entitles" you to walk all over a family member, or to cause pain for someone who loves you. *Nobody,* by virtue of their age or anything else, "deserves" to be allowed to hurt other people.

For years whenever I'd hear this asinine excuse, I'd get a silly picture in my mind of *me,* surrounded by my loving family, blowing out the candles on my 60th birthday cake, and then turning around with a wicked grin on my face and saying, "Oh, goody, goody! Now I can *finally* start abusing you all, and there's not a thing you can do about it! You have to let me get away with it from now on, because I'm officially *old!*" Seriously, what are the chances of our relatives accepting *our* advancing age as a valid excuse for *us* to abuse *them?* How come age doesn't mean anything when it's the *victim* who is getting older? And by the way, my 60th birthday came and went, and I'm *still* not getting cut any slack from my family and friends for being a cranky old lady!

A narcissist's typical mindset consists of "Me, me, me", "Me first", "Only Me", "Pay attention to Me", "It's all about Me", "My wishes are the only ones that count", "You don't matter unless you are giving Me what I want or I can use you in some way", "I have the right to do anything I like and behave however I want to," and "I'm entitled to whatever I want." And the answer the rest of us need to have to this outrageous arrogance is, "You wish!"

There is no difference between a young narcissist and an old one. They're all the same, and they all think they're "special." But that doesn't mean they really *are* special. Their concept of being a "special person" is not in the least bit rooted in reality. Being old does not make you special. We *all* get old. Being loving, caring and kind, being honorable and truthful, having integrity and righteousness~ these are the things that make you special. *Your* ***character*** *is what makes you a special person, not your age, your looks, or any other physical trait.*

Entitlement is a weird thing in some people's minds. It is common for abusers and their Silent Partners to try and make you feel guilty for setting limits on an "old lady" or an "old man," and I've been involved in several conversations to this effect over the years, including one concerning my own birth-father, which I'll tell you about later. Another of these discussions I once had concerned a perfectly healthy, manipulative and abusive mother in her late sixties. I found it incredible, and more than a little creepy, when her "well-meaning" Silent Partner gave me a meaningful look and said, "You know, she's getting on in years. She doesn't have much time left. You need to think about that!" As if we should all let her do anything she wanted to because she had one foot in the grave~ which she most certainly did not!

My response to this was, "No, *she* needs to think about that!" If her time is really so limited, is she going to choose to waste it by continuing to hurt her children and causing them to avoid her? Or is she going to change her ways and make the most of the time she has left? The choice to improve her relationships is the abuser's, and the best response to such a nonsensical statement is to throw it right back in her lap.

Nowhere in the Bible are we taught to make allowances for wickedness and evil behavior, and certainly not to make an exception just because the abuser is old. In fact, *fathers* (the *older* generation) are the ones who are admonished not to exasperate or provoke their children (the *younger* ones):

AND, YE FATHERS, PROVOKE NOT YOUR CHILDREN TO WRATH: BUT BRING THEM UP IN THE NURTURE AND ADMONITION OF THE LORD.....Ephesians 6:4 KJV.

FATHERS, PROVOKE NOT YOUR CHILDREN TO ANGER, LEST THEY BE DISCOURAGED......Colossians 3:21 KJV.

It doesn't say that it's okay for a father (or a mother) to start provoking his children after he reaches a certain age. It just says *"Don't do it."* Period. God makes no distinction based on age. Whether the parent is thirty or eighty doesn't make any difference. The Bible does not teach us that age "entitles" a parent to abuse her children. The Bible does not teach us that *anyone* is "entitled" to mistreat *anyone else* for *any* reason! Entitlement is another preposterous excuse that exists only in the minds of abusers and their Silent Partners. There is no such thing as being "entitled" to hurt other people.

SHE ONLY ABUSES YOU BECAUSE SHE'S OLD OH. SO IF SHE WAS YOUNG, SHE'D BE *NICE?*

Because of my role models, when I was a child I thought it was a given that you would get mean as you got old. But later on in life, I learned this was simply not true. In fact, what *is* true is that if you have always been a nice, kind, loving person, you will still be that way in your old age. And if you have always been nasty, intimidating, manipulative, rude, sneaky, belligerent, hateful, conniving, scheming, abusive, obnoxious, a liar or a bully or a user, you always will be. You might get a little worse as you age, becoming bitter and lonely as you realize that nobody is willing to put up with you any longer. But you're not going to do a 180 and take on a whole new persona that you never had before, just because you are now a senior citizen.

It wasn't until I was in my forties, when I got a job as a church secretary, that I learned the truth about "nasty" old people. The congregation had a great many senior citizens, and working with them was my first real eye-opener. Their cheerfulness and kindness, and the love in their hearts, was an inspiration. I knew people in their eighties who were visiting and helping shut-ins in their sixties. They were always ready to help someone else less fortunate, and treated other people with care, consideration, thoughtfulness, and concern. They had aged with grace, and taught me that I, too, could choose to age well. They were a joy to be around and I looked forward to my time with them every day. I did not meet one nasty old grouch the whole time I worked there. *If getting old automatically turns you into an abuser, then how do you explain all of them?*

My two American Bulldogs were therapy dogs, and my husband and I took them to nursing homes for many years. We logged over three hundred visits to various facilities. Although there were a few cranky, irritable seniors in these places, which is understandable due to their health conditions, the vast majority of them were as sweet as sugar. They were welcoming and appreciative that we were visiting them, instead of ungrateful and antagonistic like our relatives. They were polite and nice, never rude. They were adorable with the dogs. Even though they were living in a nursing home and dealing with a variety of illnesses and aches and pains, they were still pleasant and considerate of others. *If getting old is a valid excuse for mistreating others, then how do you explain all of them?*

On the other hand, my birth-father was rude, belligerent, manipulative, insulting, belittling, treacherous, underhanded, scheming and bullying for as long as I can remember. He was just as malicious, offensive, conniving, and hostile in his forties and fifties as he was in his eighties and nineties. He had been hateful his whole life, and he never changed, right up until the end. He always was, and always would be, an ugly, toxic lowlife. In fact, *pretty much every abuser I know has* ***always*** *been an abuser.* They didn't magically turn into abusers just because they grew older. It doesn't have to be that way. Abuse is still a choice, whether you're thirty or ninety.

Of course, if your relative has a specific medical condition such as dementia or Alzheimer's, it can cause her to be rude or irritable. We need to ask ourselves if this is out of character for her, which would indicate the onset of some illness. We also need to make a distinction between occasional inappropriateness or grouchiness, and abuse. Abuse is ongoing and greater in scope than a rare show of bad temper. Yes, we should be patient with her behavior if it results from an *actual* illness (not some "personality disorder" that we could all claim to have), and the best way to tell this is to compare her current behavior with her past behavior, as well as get a medical diagnosis from a doctor. If she has never acted this way before, then it would be reasonable to blame a medical condition. Not just "old age" in general, but a specific illness. However, if she has *always* been abusive and caused pain for others, then we can't blame it on old age and its infirmities.

Psychologists often say that the best way to predict future behavior is to look at one's past behavior. It is true that abusers usually do not mellow with age, and many get even worse as they get older. But they were still abusers when they were younger. They were always abusers. And if they didn't want to be alone in their old age, then they should have thought of that before they spent their entire lives alienating their families and driving everyone away. For an abuser, it is a Natural Consequence of his own bad decisions and offensive behavior that he should spend his old age alone. If the fact that he will age alone because of the way he treats people is not of any concern to him while he's having a field day tormenting his victims, then there is no reason for it to be of any concern to us, either.

After all, many of *us* qualify as senior citizens, too. And yet, instead of getting away with abusing others, *we* are still the ones being abused! *We* can't use *our* advancing age as an excuse to bully and abuse, or even to just be left in peace. How come nobody thinks that *we* should finally be treated well, with kindness, tolerance and respect, no matter how old *we* get? When is it *our* turn to have a loving family take care of us? Who makes allowances for *us* being "set in our ways," or tolerates *our* increasing inability to take on all the family holidays with no help?

I know women in their seventies who are still being abused by their ninety-year-old mothers. I got my first AARP invitation ten years earlier, but my birth-father still thought he was entitled to bully and threaten me even though I was pushing sixty, which is why I continued to refuse contact with him. We could be a hundred years old, and our families would still be abusing and exploiting us. Advancing age, aches and pains, moodiness, even serious illnesses don't cut any ice when it comes to giving the *victims* a break. As usual, our troubles don't earn us any understanding, consideration or thoughtfulness at all. Our problems are completely ignored, while more abuse is heaped on, and the Silent Partners keep on defending the abuser instead of standing up for her victims. *If getting older entitles one to special treatment, then why doesn't it apply to us?* Where is *our* special treatment?

I believe that if *we* can't use "getting older" as an excuse for miserable behavior, then neither can anybody else. There are just too many nice, kindly older folks around for age to be a valid excuse. It is offensive and insulting to senior citizens everywhere to assume that they're going to be abusive and hard to get along with just because of their age. No other demographic group would appreciate us painting them all with the same brush. It's obnoxious, not to mention politically incorrect, to lump a whole group of people together based on a physical trait, and demeaning not to view them as individuals capable of being rational and controlling their own behavior. That is an unfair prejudice and a form of age discrimination.

Most abusers do not mellow with age, and advancing age does not necessarily make an abuser any less treacherous or dangerous to be exposed to. The never-ending story of my ninety-something birth-father's abusive behavior includes him managing to get my unlisted phone number after ten years of no contact, and then taking less than three minutes to resume the threats, blackmail, screaming, name-calling, bullying and conniving he always inflicted on me, just because I wouldn't agree to his demands and give him information about my adult sons. Malicious, cunning, abusive old people were always malicious, cunning and abusive. They didn't suddenly turn into monsters when they got their first Social Security check.

So, before you accept another lame excuse for abuse, think back and ask yourself if your relative's behavior has only recently changed and become a problem, or if in reality he's been that way for pretty much as long as you can remember. If your abuser is a sibling, then you've known her all her life. Was she always a sweetheart in the past, or was she always a problem? If your abuser is a parent, and you have reached your mid-thirties, then chances are you'll have accurate and detailed memories of him when he was your age. What was he like back then? Do *you* now act the way *he* did at your age? How well did he treat you (and other people) ten years ago, twenty years ago, thirty years ago? What are his other long-term relationships and friendships like now, or doesn't he even have any? In the past, was he well-loved and a joy to be around? Or is the truth that nobody could *ever* stand him, even when he was much younger and "in his prime?"

An abuser's failure to plan ahead for his own old age does not mean that it's now *our* burden to jump in and fix his dilemma for him. There is no obligation, responsibility, or need for us to sacrifice our own health and happiness and expose ourselves and our families to more of our abuser's mistreatment just because he burned all his bridges, is now elderly, and didn't plan ahead for the time when he would be. I've always said that you can tell the kind of life a person has led by the crowd, or lack of same, at the funeral parlor when he dies. Sometimes the only tiny shred of justice a victim is going to see in her own lifetime is the chickens coming home to roost in her abuser's life.

There are *no* circumstances under which God tells us to tolerate abuse. There is no biblical precedent for allowing *anyone* to abuse another person, there is no scriptural teaching to overlook abuse because the abuser is elderly, and there is no justification for rewarding abuse. There is no reason to reward a lifetime of causing pain for others by being "family" for abusers in their old age. That would be interfering with God's Law of Sowing and Reaping (Galatians 6: 7-8). Having family and friends in your old age is the reward of a life well-lived, but abusers choose not to live their lives well. A loving family and friends to care for them is what seniors like the nice elderly church folks and nursing home residents deserve. Abusers are not "entitled" to that privilege.

THEN SAID HE UNTO THE DISCIPLES, IT IS IMPOSSIBLE BUT THAT OFFENCES WILL COME: BUT WOE UNTO HIM, THROUGH WHOM THEY COME. IT WERE BETTER FOR HIM THAT A MILLSTONE WERE HANGED ABOUT HIS NECK, AND HE CAST INTO THE SEA, THAN HE SHOULD OFFEND ONE OF THESE LITTLE ONES.....Luke 17:1-2 KJV.

CHAPTER 13

"YOU'RE NOT SUPPOSED TO JUDGE ME": THE DIFFERENCE BETWEEN JUDGING AND REBUKING

JUDGE: **To form an opinion about.**
REBUKE: **To express strong disapproval, to refuse to condone, to criticize severely, to reprimand.**

Have you ever told someone they've hurt you, and instead of apologizing, they tell you that you're not supposed to be judging them? It seems to be a popular defense for an offender to try and use a Christian's faith against her. Besides being under the misconception that you *must* forgive them, even if they are unrepentant and unremorseful, many abusers will tell you that you can't "judge" them when they have behaved offensively or wickedly. They will answer your rebuke by telling you that "the Bible tells us we are not to judge others." Or they will tell you that "only God" can judge them. They seem to think that this gives them free rein to carry on their unacceptable behavior just as before, without ever having to answer for it. Or *stop it* either, for that matter, until God himself judges them and sends them to hell!

What they are choosing to misunderstand is the difference between *judging* and *rebuking*. The distinction is that rebuking seeks to *correct* the offender rather than *condemn* her. Unfortunately, abusers usually take issue with being corrected, and prefer to turn it around and accuse the rebuker, or victim, of wrongdoing, rather than admit that *they* were wrong and change their own behavior.

Additionally, when we are talking about fellow "Christians," *it is not true* that the Bible tells us not to judge one another. If you do an internet search and study, you will find far more scriptures instructing us to judge those inside the church, who claim to be believers, than you will find instructing us to either judge or not judge those outside the church. There are supposed to be many checks and balances on ungodly behavior within church families. The Bible also instructs us very clearly to rebuke those who do evil, as well as those who hurt us.

Another way of looking at rebuking vs. judging is that rebuking involves *facts,* while judging often involves *assumptions.* Here is an example: When you disapprove of/protest/confront an abuser for behaving in ways that hurt other people (fact), and he responds by accusing you of not being a good Christian (assumption) because you are confronting him, not honoring him, or for whatever reason, *then you are **rebuking** him, but he is **judging** you.* Your *rebuke* is based on the *facts* of his behavior, which are not private or hidden in any way, but well known to you, him and everyone else, while his *judgment* is based on *assumptions* about your walk with the Lord, which he has no way of knowing anything about.

The best known scripture concerning not judging others is Matthew 7:1-5, in which Jesus tells us, *"JUDGE NOT, THAT YE BE NOT JUDGED. FOR WITH WHAT JUDGMENT YE JUDGE, YE SHALL BE JUDGED; AND WITH WHAT MEASURE YE METE, IT SHALL BE MEASURED TO YOU AGAIN. AND WHY BEHOLDEST THOU THE MOTE THAT IS IN THY BROTHER'S EYE, BUT CONSIDEREST NOT THE BEAM THAT IS IN THINE OWN EYE? OR HOW WILT THOU SAY TO THY BROTHER, LET ME PULL THE MOTE OUT OF THINE EYE; AND BEHOLD, A BEAM IS IN THINE OWN EYE? THOU HYPOCRITE, FIRST CAST THE BEAM OUT OF THINE OWN EYE, AND THEN SHALT THOU SEE CLEARLY TO CAST THE MOTE OUT OF THY BROTHER'S EYE"....Matthew 7:1-5 KJV.*

Perhaps you have judged someone by the way they look, their job, the clothes they wear, or the car they drive. Maybe you have gossiped about a woman who had a child out of wedlock, or parents who don't discipline their children. Maybe you have *formed an opinion about (judged)* a gay neighbor, a couple who got divorced, or a husband who had a new girlfriend before his divorce was final. These are examples of what this scripture refers to as judging~ forming an opinion about someone, who, whether you think they are right or wrong, has nothing to do with you or your loved ones and whose circumstances you might not know as well as you think you do, jumping to conclusions about things you do not necessarily know as fact, or making *assumptions* about the character of a person whom you are not in a position to judge, based on observations that could be faulty, biased, or none of your cotton-pickin' business.

Unfortunately, there are some people who have something to say about almost everyone. These folks think it's their place to pass judgment on everybody else, and to air their opinions to anyone who will listen. Their opinions are rarely based on known facts, but are often based on gossip, rumors, lies and innuendo. When you don't know someone well enough, you are simply not qualified to judge her. You have not walked in her shoes, you don't know what she's going through, there might be facts you are unaware of, and you are not in a position to decide whether or not her motives are pure. It's just not your place. Barring dangerous or criminal actions, if someone's looks, behavior or beliefs don't affect you personally and are not causing harm, and if you really don't *know* for sure what's going on, then Jesus is basically telling you to mind your own business, because you're not perfect either!

Sanctimonious abusers and narcissists who claim to be "Christian" often make it their life's work to pass judgment on other people's Christianity and walks with the Lord. This is very common in unrighteous church families. One time my family and I were in church, and it was about half an hour into the worship portion of the service. Some people were standing and praising God, and some were sitting and praying or praising. Suddenly one of the backup singers (not even the *lead* singer!), decided to promote herself to preacher status. She took it upon herself to interrupt in the middle of a hymn, stand and face the congregation, and begin chastising those who were sitting, demanding that everyone "stand on your feet!" "Come on," she shouted, "I know you have aches and pains from planting your gardens or chores or exercising! Stand up anyway! We are supposed to give God *sacrificial* worship! Get on your feet *now!*" Still, not everyone rose, so she called them to task. She shouted, "God asks so little of us in return for all he does! After all God has done for you, is it asking too much of you to praise him the way he deserves to be praised for a couple of hours a week?" This went on for several minutes, until she finally turned to face the altar and started concentrating on *her own* worship instead of everybody else's.

I was mortified by her behavior and her judging of other people's thankfulness to God, worship, praise, and walk with the Lord. Never before or since have I seen a backup singer get up, interrupt and stop the entire service dead, and start preaching as if she was the pastor. This person did not lead the kind of life that would qualify her to preach to anyone in church, and she had no godly authority over any of us, but that didn't stop her from trying to take unrighteous authority on her own.

Not everyone can stand up for an hour or more. Most of the people who had not been standing were senior citizens or disabled folks. Some were suffering from health problems that were not visible or obvious, such as cancer, breathing, heart, and back problems, and they had chosen to keep their health issues private and not share them with Miss Holier-Than-Thou. Others had obvious issues or had made them known, including people who were going to have, or had recently had, hip and knee replacements and foot surgery, and one or two pregnant women. Miss Holier-Than-Thou was aware of these, but she barreled on like a runaway garbage truck anyway, trying to shame them all for having to sit down to worship.

This dreadful scene brought to mind this story from the Bible:

AT THAT TIME JESUS WENT THROUGH THE GRAINFIELDS ON THE SABBATH. HIS DISCIPLES WERE HUNGRY AND BEGAN TO PICK SOME HEADS OF GRAIN AND EAT THEM. WHEN THE PHARISEES SAW THIS, THEY SAID TO HIM, "LOOK! YOUR DISCIPLES ARE DOING WHAT IS UNLAWFUL ON THE SABBATH." HE ANSWERED, "HAVEN'T YOU READ WHAT DAVID DID WHEN HE AND HIS COMPANIONS WERE HUNGRY? HE ENTERED THE HOUSE OF GOD, AND HE AND HIS COMPANIONS ATE THE CONSECRATED BREAD~ WHICH WAS NOT LAWFUL FOR THEM TO DO, BUT ONLY FOR THE PRIESTS. OR HAVEN'T YOU READ IN THE LAW THAT ON THE SABBATH THE PRIESTS IN THE TEMPLE DESECRATE THE DAY AND YET ARE INNOCENT? I TELL YOU THAT ONE GREATER THAN THE TEMPLE IS HERE. IF YOU HAD KNOWN WHAT THESE WORDS MEAN, 'I DESIRE MERCY, NOT SACRIFICE,' YOU WOULD NOT HAVE CONDEMNED THE INNOCENT. FOR THE SON OF MAN IS LORD OF THE SABBATH"...Matthew 12:1-8 NIV.

Hmmm. So Jesus himself said, *"I desire mercy, not sacrifice."* So much for Miss Holier-Than-Thou's idea that only "sacrificial" worship is acceptable to the Lord. I guess she skipped over *that* scripture when she was busy reading through the Bible looking for something to criticize other people on so she could make herself look superior. I've seen some rude, insensitive "Christians" in my day, but this sanctimonious Pharisee woman managed to hurt, offend, and embarrass plenty of her "sisters and brothers in Christ" at that service.

After feeling like they were being singled out, judged, and publicly called to task, some were hesitant to come back to church. Her actions made God's children feel unwelcome in his house. Do you think the Lord was happy with *her* behavior in church? Who do you think pleased God more that day? The worshippers who weren't feeling well, but came to church anyway and did the best they could to worship him to the best of their abilities, or Miss Holier-Than-Thou, who made them feel as if God would reject their heartfelt worship because it was not good enough~ in *her* opinion?

One of the most judgmental people I've ever known was my own ex-cousin, Delilah. When another of our cousins remarried after being divorced about five years, Delilah took an instant dislike to his new wife, a sweet, loyal and lovely woman who had a small child of her own, and who tried very hard to fit in with the family. Because the husband in this situation was a well-known narcissist, Delilah was positive he would not want his new wife's child around to compete with him for her attention. Eventually the child went to live with his father, and Delilah passed all around the family about how this woman had given up custody of him to please her new husband. "What kind of a mother *is* she?" ranted Delilah to anyone who would listen. "What kind of mother gives up her own child for a man? Just to please her new husband?"

She went on and on for years about this, never letting up on her opinion of what a terrible mother this lady was. But what Delilah didn't know (or maybe she *did* know and was just viciously lying about it) was that this poor woman did not give up her son willingly. She had fought a long, expensive, and draining custody battle, with the help and support of her new husband. But her own mother, a longtime alcoholic, went to court and testified for her ex-husband, causing the court to decide in his favor and her to lose custody of her child. She was devastated over losing her son, and so heartbroken over her mother's betrayal that she did not speak to her for many years. God is good to his own, and I'm happy to report that the wife and her mother eventually reconciled, and also that she has a wonderful relationship with her son and his family now that he is an adult. But she lost out on many years of his childhood and adolescence, when they should have been together.

Delilah's judgment, based on completely false *assumptions,* was one hundred percent wrong. It always seemed to be important to her to prove what a great mother *she* was, so I guess it made her feel superior to be able to gloat over what *she thought* was someone else's poor job of mothering, and to pass rumors around about the other person, so everybody would see how good *she* looked by comparison. Her cruel and malicious gossip accomplished nothing constructive, but only served to tarnish an innocent person's reputation and compound her pain and heartbreak after she had already suffered unimaginable sorrow.

THE JUDGMENT TRAIN NEVER GOES BOTH WAYS

Another judgmental busybody I knew was a pastor's wife. She made her disapproval crystal clear with numerous embarrassing and hurtful comments and gossipy whispers when the adult children and grandchildren of several of the church members had babies out of wedlock. And then it was *her* turn. Her unwed adult granddaughter had a child, *with a married man no less,* and suddenly Mrs. Sanctimonious Pastor's Wife had nothing to say. In fact, the child was brought to church and proudly paraded around on a regular basis, after the out-of-wedlock grandchildren and great-grandchildren of the other folks and their parents had been made to feel disgraced and unwelcome. *Their* out-of-wedlock grandchildren and great-grands were something to be ashamed of, but *hers* was something to be proud of, a fantastic blessing, so wonderful and cute and special.

Talk about hypocritical. Aren't *all* babies blessings? Or do you have to be the out-of-wedlock great-grandchild of the pastor and his wife before you can be considered a blessing? And why was *their* "disgraced" granddaughter encouraged to attend services and even picked up and chauffeured to church if necessary, when the other church members' children and grandchildren, who had been guilty of the very same "sin" (minus the adultery), had been made to feel humiliated and unwelcome?

Judgmental bigmouths often have a blatant double-standard. They can't wait to criticize and gossip about everybody else, but boy, when it's *their* turn to be in the exact same situation (or *worse*~ let's not forget *the adultery*), all of a sudden we don't hear a peep out of them. And unfortunately everybody else is usually too "polite" or spineless to remind them of how they condemned others for the very same "sin" and point out that what's good for the goose ought to be good for the gander! That kind of unvarnished truth-telling is what it takes to make them think twice before opening their big mouths and judging or gossiping about others, and it needs to be done more often.

REBUKING EVIL IS NOT THE SAME AS JUDGING

People who judge others in this way are not accomplishing anything good or helpful. Many times, they cause a great deal of damage. They are usually busybodies and gossips, holier-than-thou types who think they're perfect and everybody else should live up to their standards and play by their rules. They put themselves in God's place, and behave as if it's their job to decide whether others are sinning against *God.* They think it's their place to dictate how everybody else should live, and they often judge people who have done no harm. What they don't understand is that it is the Lord who makes the rules and sets the standards by which we are to live, *not them*, and *he* is the only one who has the right to judge each individual's success or failure in sinning or not sinning against *him.* He did not appoint worldly "enforcers" to judge for him.

On the other hand, in Luke 17:3, Jesus instructs us, *"TAKE HEED TO YOURSELVES. IF YOUR BROTHER SINS* ***AGAINST YOU,*** *REBUKE HIM; AND IF HE REPENTS, FORGIVE HIM"....Luke 17:3 NKJV.* Jesus does not tell us to keep silent about being offended, hurt or abused. He does not tell us to look the other way when we become aware of an innocent victim being abused. He tells us to *reprimand* and *express strong disapproval of (rebuke)* those who do something hurtful or offensive *to us.*

In Matthew 18, Jesus gives us a biblical model for rebuking:

"MOREOVER IF YOUR BROTHER SINS ***AGAINST YOU****, GO AND TELL HIM HIS FAULT BETWEEN YOU AND HIM ALONE. IF HE HEARS YOU, YOU HAVE GAINED YOUR BROTHER. BUT IF HE WILL NOT HEAR, TAKE WITH YOU ONE OR TWO MORE, THAT 'BY THE MOUTH OF TWO OR THREE WITNESSES, EVERY WORD MAY BE ESTABLISHED.' AND IF HE REFUSES TO HEAR THEM, TELL IT TO THE CHURCH. BUT IF HE REFUSES EVEN TO HEAR THE CHURCH, LET HIM BE TO YOU LIKE A HEATHEN AND A TAX COLLECTOR"....Matthew 18:15-17 NKJV.*

Heathens and tax collectors (also referred to as "publicans") were considered serious sinners and were to be shunned (Luke 18:11-13; Luke 5:30; Luke 7:34; Luke 15:1; Matthew 9:11; Matthew 11:19; Mark 2:16; Psalm 9:5, 15; Psalm 78:55; Psalm 80:8; Ezekiel 36:24; Ezekiel 39: 21-24).

In Titus, we are told, *REJECT A FACTIOUS MAN AFTER A FIRST AND SECOND WARNING, KNOWING THAT SUCH A MAN IS PERVERTED AND IS SINNING, BEING SELF-CONDEMNED... Titus 3:10-11 NASB.*

In Leviticus, we are instructed to confront one who sins against us directly rather than holding resentment in our heart:

YOU SHALL NOT HATE YOUR BROTHER IN YOUR HEART. YOU SHALL SURELY REBUKE YOUR NEIGHBOR, AND NOT BEAR SIN BECAUSE OF HIM...Leviticus 19:17 NKJV.

In Proverbs, we are told, *HE WHO REBUKES A MAN WILL IN THE END GAIN MORE FAVOR THAN HE WHO HAS A FLATTERING TONGUE ....Proverbs 28:23 NIV*. Fools, mockers, and the wicked do not listen to rebuke, but the wise and the righteous will learn from rebuke and love you for it (Proverbs 9:7-9; Proverbs 1:7; Proverbs 18:2). We may not know if someone is wise or a fool until we have rebuked him and his behavior gives him away:

FOOLS MOCK AT MAKING AMENDS FOR SIN, BUT GOODWILL IS FOUND AMONG THE UPRIGHT....Proverbs 14:9 NIV.

Fools just never learn~ *AS A DOG RETURNS TO ITS VOMIT, SO A FOOL REPEATS HIS FOLLY...Proverbs 26:11 NLT.* That is why we are instructed to rebuke a wrongdoer only once or twice, and after that, if he does not change, to have nothing further to do with him.

So there is a very big difference between *judging* others and *rebuking* evildoers, which we *are* biblically ordained and instructed very clearly to do. Sisters and Brothers, don't allow one who has sinned against you to confuse the issue. When the Lord has taught you what to do and how to handle a hurtful situation, do not get sidetracked by a foolish sinner. Telling you that you're not supposed to judge her is not an acceptable defense, when what is called for is an apology and repentance.

CHAPTER 14

THE MYSTERY EXCUSE FOR ABUSE: VARIOUS VERSIONS OF "YOU DON'T KNOW WHAT YOU'RE TALKING ABOUT," WITH NO FURTHER EXPLANATION GIVEN

HE WHO WINKS MALICIOUSLY CAUSES GRIEF, AND A CHATTERING FOOL COMES TO RUIN….Proverbs 10:10 NIV.

When we confront an abuser, the response will often be some form of "You're wrong," or, "You don't know what you're talking about," but then the abuser will refuse to elaborate any further. Even when asked what he means when he says we're "wrong," he will never be specific about exactly *how* we're wrong or *what* we're wrong about.

Some typical examples of the Mystery Excuse are:

- "You're wrong."
- "You're wrong about me."
- "You took it the wrong way."
- "You misunderstood what I said."
- "You misunderstood what I meant."
- "I didn't mean it that way."
- "I was only trying to help you, not hurt you." ("I did it for your own good.")
- "You don't understand."
- "You don't know what you're talking about."

- "You don't know anything about why I did what I did. I had my reasons!"
- "You don't know what was going on in my life."
- "You are misjudging me."
- "What you're saying isn't true."
- "What you're saying *about me* isn't true."
- "You've got it wrong."
- "Your facts are in error."
- "You heard me wrong."
- "You misinterpreted what I said."
- "You always think the worst of me."

A LESSON ON HOW TO NEVER GIVE A STRAIGHT ANSWER

THE WAY OF THE GUILTY IS DEVIOUS, BUT THE CONDUCT OF THE INNOCENT IS UPRIGHT....Proverbs 21:8 NIV.

E-mails and letters are always great study tools for learning about the defenses and excuses that abusers rely on. After the end of my relationship with a very narcissistic, selfish, and demanding ex-friend, I noticed some interesting patterns in her e-mailed answers to my rebuke of her hurtful behavior. Of course, the usual denial, pouting, anger, blaming others and refusing to be accountable or change anything were evident. But so was the "Mystery Excuse."

To make a long story very short, the beginning of the end of this relationship came when I was a few days away from a three-hundred-mile move, we were living in a tunnel of boxes, my son was graduating from college, one of my one-hundred-and-twenty-pound dogs was recuperating from knee surgery and couldn't walk, and various other family members and friends were dealing with *real* problems and tragedies, such as cancer and deaths in the family, which called for as much support and contact as I could manage under my own stressful circumstances.

Ignoring everything *I* had to deal with, my drama queen friend decided that this was the perfect time to demand attention for one of her typical life catastrophes~ her adult daughter, who lived five states away, breaking up with her boyfriend. Her daughter was perfectly happy and already dating someone else, but for some reason Miss Drama Queen decided that her daughter's love life entitled *her* to attention for herself. In fact, she believed she was so deserving of immediate attention that she became irate when I explained that a number of our loved ones were going through true tragedies and needed some of my time as well. My inability to drop everything going on in my own life so that she could vent caused a meltdown of narcissistic selfishness and rage.

When I could no longer give her all the attention she wanted, instead of being supportive of me as I had always been of her, she became demanding and abusive and caused a great deal of upset. Within a few days of my move, and the weekend of my son's graduation, she harassed me with nasty calls and e-mails several times a day, often without even giving me the chance to think over anything she had said previously or respond to it. Raving like a lunatic, she left long rants on my answering machine, which were overheard by other people who were mortified to have had the misfortune to be in the same room with my machine when she called. She accused me of lying about how busy I was and how often I read e-mails, and of being selfish and not putting people first (meaning only *her,* of course), among many other lies and false accusations.

Finally, I set strict limits on the contact I would have with her. She became resentful and spiteful, and the relationship deteriorated further over time, eventually ending a year and a half later. This saga generated the e-mail excerpts which I use as examples here, and also explains why they are dated over a period of a year and a half.

MYSTERY EXCUSE #1~ "YOU MISUNDERSTOOD ME"

LYING LIPS ARE AN ABOMINATION TO THE LORD, BUT THOSE WHO DEAL TRUTHFULLY ARE HIS DELIGHT.... Proverbs 12:22 NKJV.

The first version of this person's Mystery Excuse was to claim that I had "misunderstood" the nasty things she said and the false accusations she made. When I sent her back her own e-mails, in which she clearly said the things she was now claiming I "misunderstood," her response was to tell me that she "needed time to think about" what to say and would send me an explanation of her accusations in the form of a longer e-mail~ which, of course, never arrived.

But as I continued to hold her accountable for her abusive behavior, subsequent e-mails continued to include some version of me mysteriously "misunderstanding" her, with never anything more specific. No matter how many times I asked for clarification about what she meant and *what* exactly I had "misunderstood," she refused to answer me. She repeatedly ignored this request and never explained what she was talking about. Her excuse was that I had misunderstood what she said and did, but what and how I misunderstood was never explained. Whatever it was that I "misunderstood" remains a mystery to this day.

In the first exchange of e-mails, I have included the times she sent them to me, as well as the dates. This is a perfect lesson in the pressure an abuser will put on a victim for instant forgiveness, even though there has been no accountability and no promise of change. Unlike my ex-friend, I do not spend all day and night on the computer. At the time, my computer was in my basement, and she knew I only went downstairs to check my e-mails once a day. Yet she e-mailed me every hour or two, all the way up until almost ten o'clock at night. When she didn't get a response (because I hadn't even opened her e-mails yet, much less had time to think them over) by the first thing the next morning, her temper took over. She then decided that "God told her she had little to be forgiven for," and actually *demanded* to know whether I was going to forgive her or not.

However, it's interesting to note that *she* refused to respond to *me* quickly. She in fact *admitted* that she wanted "time to think about how to answer me" (making stuff up takes more time than just telling the truth), and said she would respond in detail "later," but refused to commit to when that would be. And yet, she didn't think that *I* deserved the exact same courtesy~ time to think it over before I replied to her. *She* demanded an instant response from *me,* although *I* apparently had no right to expect the same thing from *her.* So, for a bonus lesson on narcissistic pressure, as you read the following, take note of the times of each e-mail:

April 15, 7:54 PM~ (Her) "I'll respond to you in more detail later. Right now I'll just tell you that I didn't mean some things that you took the way you did. I will say more on that topic later."

April 16, 10:12 AM~ (Her) "I haven't written my long response yet. I want to do it when I have more time. I want to really think about it and not just answer you quickly. Unfortunately, I don't know when this will be. I'm sorry that we have had misunderstandings on *both* sides."

April 18, 4:18 PM~ (Her, after no apology, no explanation of what I had "misunderstood," no "long response" she supposedly was going to write, and still no clarification of what she meant) "I apologized days ago but have not heard from you yet. Am I correct in assuming you did not accept that apology? I don't understand what the problem is. If there is something specific that you want me to clarify, let me know."

4:46 PM~ (Me) I then re-clarified, for the second time, the false accusations she had made about me, which I wanted her to either explain or apologize for.

7:36 PM~ (Her) "I guess I just can't adequately explain what I meant, so my explanations aren't going to come out as I want or intend them to. I never *ever* meant to imply that you didn't put other people first!!!! (She didn't "imply" it, she *stated* it) I'm starting to think that you cannot and will not forgive me. This is very sad but mostly I'm saddened for you." (Illustrates pressure to forgive without proper apology, repentance, or even answering my questions.)

8:24 PM~ (Her, getting a little testy now, and without giving me a chance to reply to the last e-mail. Seriously, is this the way to try and make up with someone?) "Okay, that's *it.* If this is how you want to do it, fine, we will. Let's do this."

She then takes some of the points from one of my previous e-mails and "answers" them. Note, however, that her "answers" are really not answers at all, but yet another valuable lesson on an abuser's tactic of dodging a direct question:

My point: "You did not apologize for upsetting me just before my son's graduation."

Her response: "I did not apologize for upsetting you the night before your son's graduation, because I have no reason to apologize. I didn't deliberately set out to upset you just before his graduation!!!!"

My point: "You did not apologize for the things you said; you apologized for me 'misunderstanding' what you said."

Her response: "But if I never *meant* them that way in the first place......?"

My point: "I have asked you to clarify what you meant by 'Sorry but this time I'm very hurt by your one-sidedness', 'Everything has to be *your* way. All of our phone calls have to be your way and your timing', etc."

Her response: "I meant all the times *you call me and I miss your call*, and when *I* can call you back, then *you* are not available. So I have to 'know' via osmosis when *exactly* you are going to call or that's it and we won't be able to talk."

Absolutely amazing. I have no idea how this response was related to my original question of asking her to clarify how I was ever "one-sided" toward her, after I had literally spent decades listening to her laundry list of problems and complaints, and *she* was the one who couldn't have cared less when *I* was the one with the problems. It's downright bizarre that she blamed and resented *me* for not being there when *she* called, even though she readily admits that *she* wasn't there when *I* called. How dare I not just sit by the phone and wait for her to return my call! I have included this preposterous statement to illustrate a typical non-accountable offender's strategy of "crazy-making" irrational answers to direct, rational questions.

9:46 PM~ (Her) "Both of us are attacking each other, instead of attacking the person who is really responsible. *Satan* and his pals!"

Yep, it's everybody else's fault but hers. Even if we *could* blame this ridiculous fiasco on Satan, I wasn't "attacking" her. I was merely *holding her accountable* for what she had said about me. Interesting that she viewed this as an "attack."

April 19, 9:11 AM~ (Her, first thing the next morning) "This morning I was praying. I asked for forgiveness for the things I did against you, and God told me I have little to be forgiven for. Either you will choose to forgive me or you will not. Which is it going to be?"

This is yet another tactic used by abusers to avoid accountability~ going on the offensive, getting an "attitude," and making demands that they have no right to make. Many abusers operate under the old saying, "The best defense is a good offense." At least my abuser finally admitted that there *were* "things she did against me," although I don't think she realized she had admitted this.

Weeks and months would pass without my hearing from her, and then out of the blue I would get another wacky e-mail taking absolutely no responsibility for anything she did, but rife with yet more examples of the Mystery "You Misunderstood" defense:

February 4, the next year~ (Her) "I know that's what I did, but I was trying to do just the opposite! (What on earth does *that* mean?) This and *many* of the things you said about me were very, very misunderstood and taken wrong. I'm not going to try to defend myself anymore regarding any of this. That's God's job anyway. And even if it wasn't, I've come to the conclusion that you would just attack me further no matter what I say!"

So again I'm "attacking" her, simply because I'm still waiting for an apology for all the accusations she made against me that she was unable to justify. Note that I did not even initiate contact with her. *She* was the one who contacted *me* after almost ten months, still stewing about it!

May 3~ (Her) "I firmly believe that you and I *both* have misunderstood the other and taken what's been said out of context to a large extent."

Right. Now it's *my* fault, too.

February 12, the *next* year~ (Her) "However, most of the things you said are *not* true and you have misunderstood everything. Whether intentionally or not, I have no way of knowing. But your "facts" are very much in error."

Yet still no clue as to *which* of my "facts" are in error, even though I had asked her to clarify this numerous times.

It is amazing how repetitive these e-mails are, and how eye-opening it is to see in black and white just how many times an unaccountable offender will use the same old lame excuse. A year and a half had passed, and I had long since given up on the relationship and had not initiated any contact with her. Yet, *she* continued to contact *me* (narcissists don't give up their supply so easily), and in every single e-mail, she still claimed that I had "misunderstood" her direct, written statements. *She* wasn't wrong, *I* was wrong! Or at the very least, we were *both* wrong. *I* "misunderstood," but she was never going to explain *what* it was that I "misunderstood." In her last e-mail, she added insult to injury by implying that I might even be *intentionally* "misunderstanding." This is a tactic meant to bait me into indignation, so that I would respond to her and start up the discussion all over again. But it didn't work. By this time, as far as I was concerned, it was more than over. I wasn't going to get dragged in again, only to go around endlessly in circles for another year or two.

Unfortunately, there can be no repentance (change) if an offender never acknowledges that she did anything wrong, or that she has any understanding at all of what it was she did wrong. Claiming that the victim "misunderstood" a clear statement made by the offender does not show any remorse at all. The offender cannot ask for forgiveness and promise never to do it again if she never takes responsibility for what she did in the first place.

When lies or false accusations are challenged, an offender who genuinely wants to resolve the disagreement and repair the relationship can have only two possible responses. Either:

1. *She must prove that she did not lie and her accusation was not false*, by explaining exactly what she meant when she made the accusation.

Or,

2. *She must apologize for lying about you.*

There is no other way to weasel out of being accountable for making a false accusation and defaming someone else's character.

How to respond to this particular Mystery Excuse? Insist on clarification. Don't get sidetracked. *Make your abuser explain herself.* If she lies about you, call her on it. If she makes a false accusation or an untrue statement, *don't allow her to change the subject.* Make her explain what she meant, or else admit that what she said was not true after all and apologize. Insist that she take responsibility for her words. In other words, hold her accountable.

MYSTERY EXCUSE #2~ "YOU HAVE NO IDEA WHAT I'VE BEEN GOING THROUGH"

WITH NARROWED EYES, THEY PLOT EVIL; WITHOUT A WORD, THEY PLAN THEIR MISCHIEF....Proverbs 16:30 NLT.

The second version of the Mystery Excuse illustrated in my ex-friend's e-mails consisted of broad hints that I "had no idea what had been going on in her life," so I had no right to "judge" her. In her mind, holding her accountable for her own behavior meant that I was "judging" her. Apparently whatever had been "going on in her life" was supposed to give her license to behaving abusively. Therefore, *I* was in the wrong for even confronting her. I should not have even protested her mistreatment, because she had a *reason* for doing all the nasty things she had done to me. Whatever it was that was going on in *her* life made it all okay.

The silliness of this premise is obvious enough on its own. The catch, however, is that she never said *what* exactly it was that was supposedly "going on in her life." All she would do was to vaguely and mysteriously refer to "all the things going on in her life" that I was not aware of. Somehow, *I was supposed to feel responsible, and guilty, for not knowing things she had never told me.* And I was supposed to *care*, so much so that I would let her get away with abusing me.

This is typical of a narcissistic abuser who actually believes that you should be so interested and concerned about *her* life that you will forget all about the problems she's causing in *your* life, stop right in the middle of requiring accountability from her, shift gears completely and ask her what *is* going on in her life~ and then turn your full attention to *her* needs instead of *yours.* It's an attempt to change the subject, create a diversion, get you off the track, and dodge responsibility for her behavior. It's also fishing to see if you're still interested in her histrionics, and if her life is still of utmost importance to you. She's trying to pique your curiosity and get a response.

Mystery Excuse #2 is also a form of "punishment." Because I had rebuked her and set limits on her and the contact I would have with her, my ex-friend was letting me know that I had been demoted. I was no longer a confidante. I was out of the loop, thank the good Lord! In the following excerpts, notice how she mentioned that she "never even told me about her (abusive and estranged) father's passing." Then, when I sent her back her own e-mail, in which she had announced his passing to me, she responded coldly with, "I stand corrected. I did not think I included you in that e-mail." Oh, really? Why not? I was one of her oldest and closest friends. Why would she "leave me out" of this big news in her life? What message was she trying to send? *That because I had set limits on her, I was no longer considered a good enough friend to be told that her father had died?* So I was either being set up to be blamed later on for not knowing something I had never been told, or I was being "punished." Except that not having to endure every detail of a drama queen's life anymore isn't exactly punishment.

Here are some examples of the Mysterious "You Don't Know What's Been Going On So You Have No Right To Expect Me To Be Accountable" excuse taken from my narcissistic ex-friend's e-mails:

April 15~ "I have far from told you *all* my hurts and *all* the things going on in my life and the people I know."

April 17~ "This is *only one* of the things going on in my life the past few months. I could fill volumes, just like you!!!! Different, but still the same."

January 31, the next year~ "Besides *you have no idea* of the things going on in my life. So I'd be very careful about judging me, lest you be judged."

February 4~ "As humans, we are *all* selfish and I'm no exception. I have not been telling you anything that has been going on in my life since last summer. If you'll recall I didn't even tell you that my father died. I had been having very *major* problems and hard things to deal with. Several *very* serious things were going on."

My reply~ "Actually, you did tell me your father died." I then sent her own e-mail back to her.

Her reply~ "I stand corrected. I did not think I had included you in that e-mail."

More of my response to her~ "I take issue with your assumption that all humans are selfish. I do not consider myself to be a selfish person, nor do I consider my friends and loved ones to be selfish. In fact, I have made it a point of eliminating people like that from my life. I know far too many kind, generous, loving, caring, giving, self-sacrificing, completely *un*selfish and even *heroic* humans to agree with that statement. So speak for yourself. I'm glad you at least admit that *you're* selfish, but don't try to make it sound like everybody *else* is, too."

February 12, the *next* year~ "As a matter of fact, you have had no way of knowing of any or all of the things going on in my life for some time now."

Again, I am struck by the repetitive nature of these statements, even though they were made weeks, months, and even a year apart. It sounds like a broken record. This shows that the Mystery Excuse is a pattern with this person, something she falls back on as a matter of habit whenever she needs to explain herself, instead of just being honest and accountable. Knowing that it's an "automatic" response causes it to lose its credibility. It's impossible to actually believe a defense that's repeatedly pulled out of storage, dusted off, and trotted out whenever a convenient excuse to avoid responsibility is needed.

The narcissistic nature of these relentless repetitions is glaring. It's all about *my* life, *my* life, *my* life, and *my* life, ad nauseum, because the narcissist's life really *is* the only thing that matters. Because I never responded to this ploy or showed any interest in whatever it was that was "going on in her life," she became fixated on it, repeating it endlessly, determined to get a response from me and insisting on using it to garner some attention. *After all, she had no idea what was going on in **my** life, either, during that time, but **that** didn't matter to her at all.*

It jumps out at me that she used the exact phrase "things going on in my life" six times over the course of a year and a half, in just about every e-mail I received from her during that time, and then expected me to excuse her behavior toward me because of these mysterious "things." Each time she pointed out to me, with an almost self-satisfied smugness, that I "had no idea" what these inexplicable yet monumental things were. And she wasn't telling me what they were, either. She wanted to *make me ask.*

After reading all of these "broad hints," most of us would ask ourselves, "What on earth is the big secret? What is she hiding? Why doesn't she just spit it out? If something is really going on in her life, then why doesn't she just come right out and say it?" Again, for all the reasons we discussed above~ fishing to see if the victim still cares, throwing her off the track, and smugly showing her that she's persona non grata, no longer important enough to be told all the gory details.

And, obviously, *because there* **is** *nothing* so earth-shattering *really* going on in her life. *She couldn't go into details because there were no details to go into.* When I failed to take the bait, elaborating any further would have necessitated obvious exaggeration and proven that she really was just what other people in her life suspected all along~ a drama queen who makes catastrophes out of normal life events to get attention for herself. Remember, this particular disagreement originally started when my time was very limited by *my own* life crisis, and my ex-friend became enraged because I paid more attention to and spent more time on *my own problems and relatives who were dying of cancer* than I did consoling *her* when her daughter dumped her boyfriend and started dating someone else.

How to react to this second version of the Mystery Excuse? When your abuser tries to use whatever is supposedly "going on in her life" as an excuse for mistreating you, it is best not to give it any credence at all. If it was *so* important, she'd come out with it already, instead of pretending that it's some deep, dark secret. *She is trying to change the dynamic of your exchange back to* ***her*** *being the center of attention, instead of* ***you.*** She is trying to get you to ask her about it. She wants her narcissistic supply, to know that you *care.* This will turn the whole discussion back to her and her life, and feed into her narcissism by giving her the attention and sympathy she craves.

Simply *don't take the bait* when she hints around about all the "things" you don't know.If a friend or relative was truly stressed out over a major life event that might have caused her to behave out of character, you'd know about it, because she would have told you. She would have no problem being honest with you about what was happening. If she consistently uses this as an excuse but doesn't share the details, then you can be sure it's because *there is nothing to share.* If you ask what *is* going on, you'll just be allowing her to change the subject from *your* issues back to *her* issues and rewarding her baloney with narcissistic supply.

The fact is that *whatever* is "going on in her life" is completely irrelevant, anyway. It has nothing to do with the issue at hand. It does not give her license to lie about you, be nasty or rude, make demands, control you, criticize you, bully you, or treat you badly in any way. The best strategy here is to *ignore* all the hinting around, and tell your abuser plainly that no matter *what* is happening in her life, it still doesn't give her the right to act badly towards you. Inform her that you still expect her to grow up, get a grip, control herself, take responsibility, and be accountable for her behavior. Then get back to discussing *your* issues, without letting her sidetrack you.

These are just two versions of the very versatile Mystery Excuse. All Mystery Excuses need to be taken with a grain of salt and a healthy dose of skepticism, because for the most part, they're fabrications that are *just not true.* It's *not true* that you "misunderstood," it's *not true* that you "don't know what you're talking about," and it's *not true* that some strange, top-secret, unknown events caused your abuser to lose control of herself and lie about you, harass you, falsely accuse you, or otherwise mistreat you.

HOW TO SEE IT COMING

A FALSE WITNESS WILL NOT GO UNPUNISHED, AND HE WHO SPEAKS LIES SHALL PERISH….Proverbs 19:9 NKJV.

How can we recognize the Mystery Excuse when we confront an offender? It's really very simple. When we confront her or try to set limits on her, and her responses to our rebuke don't add up and don't make sense, *there it is!* When the conversation becomes irrational, responses become vague and nonsensical, and straight answers don't follow straight questions, some version of the Mystery Excuse is being used on us.

Many of us have spent our lives taking at face value the infinite variety of preposterous statements and vague, evasive answers that abusers come up with to justify their behavior. When faced with an unexpected and nonsensical Mystery Excuse, we often become flustered and slightly confused, drop the subject, and let the offense slide. This is exactly what our abuser wants, and exactly what she was trying to manipulate us into doing when she tossed out the Mystery Excuse.

It takes some re-conditioning on our parts to learn to stand firm in the truth and hold an abuser accountable for what she says and does, while refusing to get sidetracked by various versions of the Mystery Excuse and the other inane gibberish in her repertoire. Trying to convince your victim that she can't understand plain English, or has some mental problem which causes her to take every innocent little thing the wrong way, is hardly an appropriate way to show remorse and make amends. We need to stop accepting vague explanations and mysterious excuses for abuse, and be firm in our expectation of true repentance~ an apology and a permanent change in behavior.

THERE ARE SIX THINGS THE LORD HATES, SEVEN THAT ARE DETESTABLE TO HIM: HAUGHTY EYES, A LYING TONGUE, HANDS THAT SHED INNOCENT BLOOD, A HEART THAT DEVISES WICKED SCHEMES, FEET THAT ARE QUICK TO RUSH INTO EVIL, A FALSE WITNESS WHO POURS OUT LIES AND A MAN WHO STIRS UP DISSENSION AMONG BROTHERS.....Proverbs 6:16-19 NIV.

CHAPTER 15

THE "CHRISTIAN" ABUSER: TWISTING GOD'S WORD TO JUSTIFY ABUSE

BUT THERE WERE FALSE PROPHETS ALSO AMONG THE PEOPLE, EVEN AS THERE SHALL BE FALSE TEACHERS AMONG YOU, WHO PRIVILY SHALL BRING IN DAMNABLE HERESIES, EVEN DENYING THE LORD THAT BROUGHT THEM, AND BRING UPON THEMSELVES SWIFT DESTRUCTION. AND MANY SHALL FOLLOW THEIR PERNICIOUS WAYS; BY REASON OF WHOM THE WAY OF TRUTH SHALL BE EVIL SPOKEN OF. AND THROUGH COVETOUSNESS SHALL THEY WITH FEIGNED WORDS MAKE MERCHANDISE OF YOU: WHOSE JUDGMENT NOW OF A LONG TIME LINGERETH NOT, AND THEIR DAMNATION SLUMBERETH NOT...2 Peter 2:1-3 KJV.

FOR YOU HAVE BEEN CALLED TO LIVE IN FREEDOM~ NOT FREEDOM TO SATISFY YOUR SINFUL NATURE, BUT FREEDOM TO SERVE ONE ANOTHER IN LOVE. FOR THE WHOLE LAW CAN BE SUMMED UP IN THIS ONE COMMAND: "LOVE YOUR NEIGHBOR AS YOURSELF"...Galatians 5:13-14 NLT.

I hear from victims of "Christian" and church family abusers on a regular basis, and of course that's to be expected. But it never ceases to amaze me when I hear from the "Christian" abusers themselves.

Their conversations, e-mails, and letters are a great learning tool, and a window into the sinful minds of those who pervert the Word of God for their own selfish and abusive ends. It is a very great sin to use our precious Lord as a cover for wickedness and evil, and such so-called Christians give all the rest of us a bad name. But the Lord turns that which was meant for evil to be used for the good of those who love him (Genesis 50:20; Romans 8:28). One conversation I had with just such an abuser, which took place over a period of a few weeks, is a perfect example. In this chapter, I will use that discussion as a study tool to illustrate several examples of how such so-called "Christians" often twist the Bible to justify damaging other people.

AN OXYMORON: "THE CHRISTIAN ABUSER"

To many of us, the words "Christian" and "abuser" don't seem to belong together in the same sentence. They are, or should be, a contradiction in terms. And yet how many of us have heard of a minister's children who were raised with cruelty and abuse? How many of us know of an upstanding, church-going man or woman of God, who turns out to be a criminal or a child molester? Who can forget the huge scandal in the Roman Catholic church, when so many of their so-called "men of God" priests were exposed as pedophiles~ child molesters who were using their position in the church as a source of obtaining new victims~ and the higher-ups who covered up for them and even moved them to new parishes where they could continue to rape even more children? Calling oneself "Christian" does not make one exempt from abusive behavior. And calling oneself "Christian" does not make one a *real* Christian, either!

One scripture which addresses this point is 1 John 3:

NO ONE WHO LIVES IN HIM KEEPS ON SINNING. NO ONE WHO CONTINUES TO SIN HAS EITHER SEEN HIM OR

KNOWN HIM. DEAR CHILDREN, DO NOT LET ANYONE LEAD YOU ASTRAY. HE WHO DOES WHAT IS RIGHT IS RIGHTEOUS. HE WHO DOES WHAT IS SINFUL IS OF THE DEVIL, BECAUSE THE DEVIL HAS BEEN SINNING FROM THE BEGINNING. THE REASON THE SON OF GOD APPEARED WAS TO DESTROY THE DEVIL'S WORK. NO ONE WHO IS BORN OF GOD WILL CONTINUE TO SIN, BECAUSE GOD'S SEED REMAINS IN HIM; HE CANNOT GO ON SINNING, BECAUSE HE HAS BEEN BORN OF GOD. THIS IS HOW WE KNOW WHO THE CHILDREN OF GOD ARE AND WHO THE CHILDREN OF THE DEVIL ARE: ANYONE WHO DOES NOT DO WHAT IS RIGHT IS NOT A CHILD OF GOD; NOR IS ANYONE WHO DOES NOT LOVE HIS BROTHER….1 John 3:6-10 NIV.

For some reason, the one thing I never anticipated when I started a ministry for abuse victims was that I would be hearing from the abusers themselves. You wouldn't think they'd have the nerve. Sometimes I receive e-mails from them. But more frequently, abusers who cross my path as I go about my life and find out what I do, or who already know about Luke 17:3 Ministries, will look for the opportunity to "discuss" an issue such as forgiveness or repentance with me. Many times this is simply a thinly disguised challenge to what we are teaching. Often they will be quite candid about how they have abused a loved one, and then follow that admission with a long list of excuses and rationalizations.

Once in a blue moon, I'll be approached by an offender who is truly contrite and looking for guidance in repairing the relationship she had damaged. But most of the time, the abusers who wish to "discuss" their situations with me are simply looking for validation of their unacceptable behavior. They often use typical abuser tactics in their attempts to force me to admit that their wicked behavior was really innocent, unintentional, misunderstood, or even justified.

They will defiantly trot out the usual manipulation, deception, belligerence, pouting, pretending to be insulted, and whatever else they have in their narcissistic arsenal. Sometimes it's as if they've read every book ever written about their dysfunctional defenses, and now they're just sticking to the script and doing everything you'd expect them to do.

Occasionally, abusers will try to trick me into contradicting myself, or contradicting the Bible~ or better yet, will try to prove that the *Bible* contradicts *itself!* The amusing thing about this is that in trying to trap me~ or even worse, the Lord~ in a contradiction, they usually wind up contradicting themselves instead. And most of the time, they don't even realize it.

A LITTLE KNOWLEDGE IS A DANGEROUS THING

The most fascinating abuser of all to have these discussions with is the one who claims to be a Christian herself. Some of these wicked people are influenced by the Spirit of False Religion, and some by the Jezebel Spirit or Ahab Spirit. Some may have been "born again" decades ago, but never grew in the Lord or developed into a mature Christian, remaining instead in bondage to the sins of the flesh such as selfishness, pride, bitterness, envy, jealousy and unlovingness. Some are the result of a combination of all three of these issues.

Then there are others who were believers at one time, but have fallen away. They just won't admit it to you, or sometimes even to themselves. There is indeed such a thing as an abuser who is *technically* a "Christian" in terms of believing in Christ as the Son of God, but who is still not a Spirit-filled, sanctified, *real* Christian. Remember, even *Satan* believes in Christ (Luke 4:1-13). Those who have the most vested in denying this and convincing you that a "Christian" couldn't possibly be abusive are usually none other than the abusive Christians themselves.

One thing we know for sure that we will never have to worry about is meeting up with our "Christian" abusers in heaven. They are not going to be there. The Bible says that if they deliberately continue to sin after having been saved by Jesus' precious blood, then they have doomed themselves. There is nothing they can ever do to make up for it. Such "Christian" sinners are an abomination to the Lord and are condemned to destruction:

FOR IF WE SIN WILLFULLY AFTER WE HAVE RECEIVED THE KNOWLEDGE OF THE TRUTH, THERE NO LONGER REMAINS A SACRIFICE FOR SINS, BUT A CERTAIN FEARFUL EXPECTATION OF JUDGMENT, AND FIERY INDIGNATION WHICH WILL DEVOUR THE ADVERSARIES. ANYONE WHO HAS REJECTED MOSES' LAW DIES WITHOUT MERCY ON THE TESTIMONY OF TWO OR THREE WITNESSES. OF HOW MUCH WORSE PUNISHMENT, DO YOU SUPPOSE, WILL HE BE THOUGHT WORTHY WHO HAS TRAMPLED THE SON OF GOD UNDERFOOT, COUNTED THE BLOOD OF THE COVENANT BY WHICH HE WAS SANCTIFIED A COMMON THING, AND INSULTED THE SPIRIT OF GRACE? FOR WE KNOW HIM WHO SAID, "VENGEANCE IS MINE, I WILL REPAY," SAYS THE LORD. AND AGAIN, "THE LORD WILL JUDGE HIS PEOPLE." IT IS A FEARFUL THING TO FALL INTO THE HANDS OF THE LIVING GOD....Hebrews 10:26-31 NKJV.

WILL THE REAL CHRISTIAN PLEASE STAND UP?

What is intriguing about having an exchange on evil behavior with a "Christian" (or ex-Christian) abuser is that she actually has a working knowledge of the Bible, which she will often use to twist or misinterpret scripture to suit her own purposes. She will pick and choose the scriptures she thinks she can use to justify her wickedness, and conveniently omit the scriptures that would condemn her behavior and show her for what she is. She can use her "insider" knowledge about how a Christian is supposed to behave to give the *appearance* of being a godly, righteous person to the uninitiated. But she cannot fool those who know enough to look at her *fruit.*

It serves an abuser's purposes to pretend to be a believing Christian. She thinks she'll be able to convince people that she *must* be a good person, innocent of whatever abuse you might accuse her of, because she "believes in God." To which I would have to say, so what if she "believes in God?" *Satan and his demons believe in God, too~* and that doesn't make *them* good! (James 2:18-19).

Satan is the father of deception, deceit and lies. He is the father of trickery and treachery. He has many disguises and many faces. He is well able to disguise one of his children as a "religious" person in order to fool others. But the Lord has that covered. In the Gospel, Jesus himself teaches us how we can tell the difference:

BEWARE OF FALSE PROPHETS, WHICH COME TO YOU IN SHEEP'S CLOTHING, BUT INWARDLY THEY ARE RAVENING WOLVES. YE SHALL KNOW THEM BY THEIR FRUITS. DO MEN GATHER GRAPES OF THORNS, OR FIGS OF THISTLES? EVEN SO EVERY GOOD TREE BRINGETH FORTH GOOD FRUIT; BUT A CORRUPT TREE BRINGETH FORTH EVIL FRUIT. A GOOD TREE CANNOT BRING FORTH EVIL FRUIT, NEITHER CAN A CORRUPT TREE BRING FORTH GOOD FRUIT. EVERY TREE THAT BRINGETH NOT FORTH GOOD FRUIT IS HEWN DOWN, AND CAST INTO THE FIRE. WHEREFORE BY THEIR FRUITS YE SHALL KNOW THEM. NOT EVERYONE THAT SAITH UNTO ME, LORD, LORD, SHALL ENTER INTO THE KINGDOM OF HEAVEN; BUT HE THAT DOETH THE WILL OF MY FATHER WHICH IS IN HEAVEN. MANY WILL SAY TO ME IN THAT DAY,

LORD, LORD, HAVE WE NOT PROPHESIED IN THY NAME? AND IN THY NAME HAVE CAST OUT DEVILS? AND IN THY NAME DONE MANY WONDERFUL WORKS? AND THEN WILL I PROFESS UNTO THEM, I NEVER KNEW YOU: DEPART FROM ME, YE THAT WORK INIQUITY....Matthew 7:15-23 KJV.

God never intended his holy Word to be used as a cover for sin. This is an abomination to him. Deliverance ministers know that one of Satan's favorite tricks is to use scripture against God and the deliverance team. The devil loves to argue God's Word. Many deliverance ministers advise against quoting the Bible during a deliverance unless you are reading directly from it or are very sure you are completely accurate, because the devil is just itching for the opportunity to trap you and be able to say "Aha!" if you falter.

During a deliverance, demons will use this tactic to distract the deliverance team from their purpose, which is to bind and cast out the demons. Demons are very clever, and if they can get the team off-track, they will be able to remain in control longer.

Children of the devil use the same ploy when it comes to being held accountable for their actions. If they can somehow manage to get you off the track when you rebuke them, then they will never have to answer for their wrongdoing. If they can confuse the situation enough, they might even be able to get you to just give up, without ever having to commit to repentance or a change in behavior. And what more satisfying way for a child of Satan to confuse a child of God than to use God's own holy Word against her?

Besides trying to use the Bible to justify their wickedness, some who call themselves "Christians" will engage in other pseudo-religious behaviors. They might attend church on a regular basis, tithe every week, speak in tongues, be "slain in the spirit," raise their hands to "worship" God, tell you they will "pray for you," shout "Hallelujah!", and use all the right words and phrases. How could anyone possibly believe that such a "godly" person is actually evil and malicious, and that all of this is just an act?

Such people are modern-day Pharisees, deceptive and untruthful, full of the "appearance" of holiness without the substance:

BUT DO NOT DO WHAT THEY DO, FOR THEY DO NOT PRACTICE WHAT THEY PREACH....EVERYTHING THEY DO IS DONE FOR MEN TO SEE....Matthew 23:3,5 NIV.

Jesus reserved his harshest rebukes for the Scribes and Pharisees and his very strong reprimands are recorded in the Seven Woes of the Pharisees in Matthew 23. He refers to the phony Pharisees as hypocrites, sons of hell, snakes, and a brood of vipers, among other choice words. He chastises them for tithing and yet lacking the "more important matters" of justice, mercy and faithfulness (Matthew 23:23).

Some so-called "Christians" are anything *but* humble servants. They are filled with pride, even about their faith, and try very hard to impress others with their righteousness~ claiming that they are "growing every day in their walk with the Lord," that the Lord is doing or has done "a great work in them," that they are "falling more in love with Jesus every day," that the Lord has healed them, blessed them, and given them all the wonderful gifts that he reserves for his children. An abuser will tell you all of these things, because she is trying very hard to convince you that *she* is counted in that number. She is one of God's children, *just like you!*

For a sincere Christian, such incredible blessings from God fill us with humble gratitude. But for an "unrighteous Christian," such statements are a very calculated attempt to seem holier-than-thou, a clever smokescreen to hide their true nature, and spoken of with great pride instead of humility and appreciation. Such people know the right words to say, but they are empty words and their purpose is to impress and deceive. Who would dare to challenge the sinful words or actions of one who obviously walks so closely with the Lord and is so filled with the Holy Spirit? But although they know enough to talk the talk, they are not really walking the walk. They are not dwelling with God, and they are not Spirit-filled. Again, we cannot judge a book by its cover. Remember what the Lord Jesus teaches us~ to know them by their fruit.

True Christians are not selfish narcissists, who behave as if other people exist only for their use and exploitation. True Christians do not bully, manipulate and abuse others. True Christians love others, and true Christians *serve*. The Bible teaches us that people of faith are expected to do good works:

DEAR BROTHERS AND SISTERS, WHAT'S THE USE OF SAYING YOU HAVE FAITH IF YOU DON'T PROVE IT BY YOUR ACTIONS? THAT KIND OF FAITH CAN'T SAVE ANYONE.... SO YOU SEE, IT ISN'T GOOD ENOUGH JUST TO HAVE FAITH. FAITH THAT DOESN'T SHOW ITSELF BY GOOD DEEDS IS NO FAITH AT ALL~ IT IS DEAD AND USELESS. NOW SOMEONE MAY ARGUE, "SOME PEOPLE HAVE FAITH; OTHERS HAVE GOOD DEEDS." I SAY, "I CAN'T SEE YOUR FAITH IF YOU DON'T HAVE GOOD DEEDS, BUT I WILL SHOW YOU MY FAITH THROUGH MY GOOD DEEDS." DO YOU STILL THINK IT'S ENOUGH JUST TO BELIEVE THAT THERE IS ONE GOD? WELL, EVEN THE DEMONS BELIEVE THIS, AND THEY TREMBLE IN TERROR! FOOL! WHEN WILL YOU EVER LEARN THAT FAITH THAT DOES NOT RESULT IN GOOD DEEDS IS USELESS?....SO YOU SEE, WE ARE MADE RIGHT WITH GOD BY WHAT WE DO, NOT BY FAITH ALONE....JUST AS THE BODY IS DEAD WITHOUT A SPIRIT, SO ALSO FAITH IS DEAD WITHOUT GOOD DEEDS.....James 2:14, 17-20, 24, 26 NLT.

ONE CLUE FOR SPOTTING A "CHRISTIAN" NARCISSIST

Here's a helpful clue for spotting a phony "Christian" narcissist: Is she always "worrying" about other people, or asking you to pray for them? At first this clue seems contradictory, but when you think about the narcissist's "concern," there will be a phony and self-serving feel to it. Narcissists exist and get away with their inappropriate behavior by presenting a false persona, a facade of being normal and nice, so that other people doubt their own perceptions or don't believe what you say about the narcissist's true nature. Narcissists also do not accept boundaries between themselves and other people, and look at others as mere extensions of themselves. They use other people and their good times (weddings, etc.) and bad times (illnesses, etc.) for their own drama or benefit. If someone else has a happy occasion, the narcissist will manage to make it about herself, and if someone else has a misfortune, the narcissist will use it to pretend to be concerned so that she can impress bystanders.

Non-religious narcissists will pretend to fret or worry aloud about someone else to make you think they care. "Religious," holier-than-thou narcissists will ask for prayer for another person to make you think they care. Either way, *they don't care.* But they can get attention from you, *thanks to someone else's problems.*

A big hint is who and what they are asking for prayer for. Do they seem to be dragging the bottom of the barrel to come up with something and someone to "pray" about, while ignoring *real* problems faced by people you both know? If they ignore a major misfortune, like a housefire or a car wreck, or the serious illness, like cancer or heart trouble, of someone close to them or well-known to you (because it might cause you to turn your attention to that person and away from them), but ask you to pray for their cousin's son to pass a test in school or their neighbor's sister who is being sued by her landlord for back rent, then you know they're dramatizing to get you to say what a nice, lovely, caring and concerned person they are. They are *using* the other person to get narcissistic supply (attention, approval, admiration) for themselves from you! Beware of someone who always pigeonholes you to tell you she's "worried about" or "needs prayer for" people she barely knows and their minor setbacks that every other normal human being deals with just fine, but doesn't express any concern for people you know or those who are dealing with *real* disasters.

THE NUT DOESN'T FALL FAR FROM THE TREE: CHILDREN OF THE DEVIL DO THE DEVIL'S WORK

My birth-father was just about the farthest thing you could get from a Christian. But when I was little, every now and then, I'd learn something valuable from him. He always loved goading people into an argument. It was like a hobby to him, or maybe more like a calling. He got a power high from getting someone all riled up. He often reminded us that he was "on the debate team in high school," and he loved the "intellectual sport" of debate. But for such a big "intellectual," he had no hesitation in making himself look like a complete fool. He would make the most absurd, outrageous and idiotic statements just to get someone to respond to him. He would contradict himself, or argue forcefully about something, and then, as soon as you agreed with him, change his opinion and argue just as forcefully for exactly the opposite viewpoint.

When challenged on this, he would smile slyly and say, "I was just playing devil's advocate!" In other words, he didn't really believe any of the nonsense he spouted. He was just baiting the other person and trying to get a rise out of them. He was also trying to be the center of attention. Winning the "debate," or "argument," as everyone else called it, wasn't the point. Controlling his "opponent," tricking him into falling for his little "deception," and keeping him enmeshed, was.

It is no coincidence that one who is trying to "use" being a Christian to justify his wrongdoing often makes preposterous or nonsensical statements, tries to confuse you, especially on issues of faith, or even totally contradicts himself. Satan is the father of chaos and confusion. All lies, deception, deceit and trickery originate with him. Such people are choosing the devil's way over the Lord's way. They are, in every sense of the word, the "devil's advocate," and they are doing his dirty work for him.

From the time he was thrown out of heaven, Satan has not learned his lesson about challenging God. The Book of Job tells just one story of the lengths Satan will go to in order to "win" by making a child of God doubt his faith or question the Lord and his Word. The temptation of Jesus as recorded in Matthew 4:1-11 is another example of the devil challenging God. But Jesus did not take the bait. He did not have to prove himself to the devil. And we, also, don't have to prove anything to those who try to use the Word of God, or our faith, against us.

A "CHRISTIAN" ABUSER IN ACTION

I was once a participant in an ongoing discussion with a totally unrepentant "born-again" abuser, which took place over the course of several weeks. It concerned her absolutely abominable behavior toward her oldest, and pretty much only, friend, a good-hearted woman whom I also happened to know very well. I had a long-standing familiarity with both women, and an intimate knowledge of their characters and personalities as well as what had transpired between them. This afforded me a rare chance to observe the deterioration of a relationship in which one person's love, caring and generosity was repaid with ongoing and continual selfishness, envy, ungratefulness, neglect and pride. I was a firsthand witness to this decades-old friendship ending for no other reason than the offender's stubborn refusal, despite being given many chances by the victim, to act like a *real* Christian (or at least like a mature adult), be accountable and accept responsibility for her own behavior, apologize sincerely and humbly, change her wicked ways, and do whatever she could to make amends.

This woman used many of the tactics so typical of abusers when someone rebukes or challenges them. At a certain point the tone of our discussions changed and deteriorated. I realized that, although she pretended to want my help in mending fences with her ex-friend, she really never gave any thought to anything I said. The Lord showed me that what she *really* wanted to do was to put *me* in the position of defending *myself,* so that I would keep on talking to her, keep on giving her attention, and keep up this ongoing "discussion." She was using *me* to get the narcissistic supply she was no longer getting from our mutual friend, who was no longer speaking to her.

This "born-again" abuser often claimed she "forgot" or "didn't mean" what she had plainly said or e-mailed to me, contradicted herself outright a number of times, twisted my words or what the Bible says, whined about being "misunderstood," and at times became angry, nasty and abusive toward *me.* Abusers usually drop all pretense of niceness and let their true colors show when you fail to go along with their program.

A couple of times, after she denied saying something that she had said, I sent her own e-mail back to her to prove my point, only to have her backtrack and claim that I had "misunderstood," even though her own words were right in front of her in black and white. Then she would pretend to become insulted. In very sly, devious, "innocent" ways, she tried to test me and my knowledge of scripture, and to challenge *my* walk with the Lord. All this because I rebuked her, instead of agreeing with her and supporting her abuse. I didn't take her side, so that gave her license to start abusing *me*, too. I can only imagine what she must have put her ex-friend through. As far as I'm concerned, if she didn't want my honest opinion, then she should not have started the discussion in the first place.

Like many abusers, this woman didn't even mind it if the things she said made her sound like she had mental problems and I wound up thinking she was just nuts, as long as she could still delude herself into believing that she had "won" the argument. These strategies are referred to as "crazy-making" because they are used to make you think that *you* are the crazy one. But they usually have exactly the opposite effect as you start to think your abuser would have to be mentally ill to come up with the wacky, outlandish, completely ridiculous things she says, and to say them in all seriousness. It is at this point that many victims and bystanders decide that, like me, they're not running a mental institution for abusers, and it's time cut bait and to run for the hills.

Although she was attempting to get me to "see things her way," absolve herself of any wrongdoing, and have me validate and agree with her, what this abuser actually did was to make herself look far worse. Once the phony mask of righteousness dropped off, no preconceived notion that I may have held about her was anything close to as bad as she really was. While trying to justify her point of view, she gave away many clues as to her true nature, inadvertently revealing an unloving heart controlled by envy, pride, resentment, bitterness, competitiveness, jealousy and hostility. And all masquerading in the disguise of a "good Christian woman."

During our exchanges, it was ironic that this woman habitually and repeatedly stated, "I will own what is mine, *but*.....", the implication being that *the problem was also someone else's fault* besides hers. However, she *never actually did* "own what was hers." Repentance is not a negotiation, and neither are apologies. Incredibly, from our discussions, I was actually able to compile a list of *thirty-six excuses* given by this abuser to justify her repeated, continuing and persistently inexcusable behavior toward her friend, one more lame than the next. She may have had her faults, but a lack of creativity wasn't one of them!

In this chapter, we will discuss four of these excuses in particular, since they serve as excellent illustrations of a Christian offender who tries to use her knowledge of God's Word to get away with ungodly behavior. In this woman's case, her two main tactics consisted of either misquoting or misinterpreting scripture to her own advantage, or trying to make herself appear too "godly" and too "righteous" to have really done what she did with any ill will or malicious intent. Her defense basically amounted to all of the selfish, uncaring, unloving things that she had done being merely "misunderstood" by her ex-friend and me, because she was *much* too good of a Christian to have ever really done those things deliberately.

THEIR FRUIT WILL GIVE THEM AWAY EVERY TIME

This abuser was a person who knew the "Born-Again Christian" drill well. She was able to display many of the outward signs of being a "good" Christian, and she used her knowledge to get away with as much as possible, all while trying to convince others that they must have misjudged her because she is obviously so holy.

But she could not fool anyone who knew enough to look at her fruit. Her life, her house, and her finances were all in chaos. She wasted most of the day and night on the computer, instead of cleaning or doing anything constructive. She did not work, and had not held a job for many years. She had troubled relationships with almost every family member, and very few friendships. She never followed through on plan after plan to change her life, get a job, move to a new house, start a ministry, or any of the other grandiose ideas she carried on about.

She was often upset or angry with everyone from her vet, to her hairdresser, to her church, to her children, and has accused almost every person who has had the misfortune of crossing her path of not doing right by her in some way. She was unreasonable, narcissistic, and almost always worked up over something or other.

She was selfish and self-centered. She was spoiled, attention-seeking, and irrationally demanding of other people's time and energy, without giving any thought to what anyone else might be going through. She had no concept of boundaries, or that she might be intruding on another person with her demands for attention. She was filled with pride. She was dishonest and untruthful. She never got anything accomplished, and was envious of those who did. She was a drama queen who treated every little thing in her life as if it was a huge catastrophe~ and then ignored, *or even contributed to*, the *real* catastrophes in the lives of her friends. She had no appreciation. She had an unloving heart. She used people when she needed them, but if they needed her, she was nowhere to be found. She took, but she did not give, and she did not serve.

If you are thinking that none of the above makes her sound like much of a "good" Christian, I would have to say you are right. But what this person failed to realize is that someone with discernment can see all of these things and will know her by her fruit. She thought that the phony façade she presented worked with everyone. Using her "Christianity" as a cover-up for her sinful nature may not work all of the time or with every person, but it does work enough times and with enough people that it was worth it for her to continue doing. And so, whenever she was rebuked or challenged, trotting out her "Christianity" was her automatic response. Yet, to one with understanding, her fruit gave her away and her true nature was painfully obvious.

Here are four of this so-called "Christian" abuser's best excuses/contradictions out of the thirty-six that she gave me, and what the Lord showed me about why they just don't hold any water:

1. "THE LORD HAS HEALED ME, PRAISE THE LORD!"~ FOLLOWED BY "I ACT THE WAY I DO BECAUSE OF MY PAST."

This abuser made many statements to the effect that the Lord had healed her, the Lord had done or was doing a great work in her, and that her walk with Jesus was deepening every day. The point of these statements was to mislead the listener into believing that she was a mature Christian who walked with the Lord, and therefore could not possibly be capable of abusing others. Again, her defense was that everybody else just "misunderstands" her.

But then she went on to blame her "abusive childhood," forty years in the past, for her current "actions and reactions" toward her friend. This is a huge contradiction. One of this woman's biggest problems was that she just didn't know enough to quit while she was ahead. Part of the response the Lord gave me to this inconsistency was:

"People who have been healed by the Lord no longer act or react according to their histories. If the Lord has healed you, then the past no longer has any control over your life. That is what healing is. I know this from my own healing from my own abusive past. The lives of mature Christians are controlled by the Holy Spirit. When God heals you, he makes you a new person and puts a new spirit in you (Ezekiel 36:26-27). The past is ancient history and you are no longer influenced by it.

The Lord's healing is perfect and complete. It is not imperfect or incomplete. He dries all our tears and fills us with his grace. The Lord knows the plans he has for you (Jeremiah 29:11). If you are a person who loves him, he will turn that which was meant for evil in your life to good (Romans 8:28). In my own case, his will was for my testimony and experiences to be used to help others. Once he has healed you, he certainly doesn't intend for you to use your past to *hurt* others. We need to learn from the past, but if we still let it influence how we treat others in the present, or influence anything else in our lives, then we are not healed and we are not Spirit-filled."

Another interesting observation is that this woman had been "saved" some thirty-five years previously, and yet she was *just now* claiming to be "deepening her walk with the Lord", "being healed," and "having a great work done in her." This indicates someone who, although she has been a Christian for decades, had never become a *mature* Christian. And, as her continuing abusive behavior demonstrated, had never had her "second salvation," which is going through the process of sanctification. Although she knew the right words to say, she did not really "dwell with God." She was not being truthful. She was deceiving herself, and trying to deceive others as well. But her fruit gave her away.

When rebuked, this abuser had nothing to say in terms of repentance. But she did have a huge inventory of excuses, which she somehow felt justified her repeatedly hurting another person. One of the excuses she was now offering was her own abusive past. So another point which I needed to make in my discussions with her was that, concerning one's "past" (or any other excuse for that matter), the fact is that the Bible does not tell us to "analyze" or "understand" the reasons why someone might be acting unacceptably. Scripturally, that is a non-issue. We tend to spend far too much time talking to therapists, reading books on why people behave badly, and in general trying to give abusers the benefit of the doubt and convince ourselves that they "can't help it" and they "don't really mean it."

But nowhere in the Bible are we told to "be understanding of" an abuser's past, her abusive childhood, alcohol or drug addiction, oversensitivity, anger issues, stress, trauma, personality disorders, or any other reason she might think she has for hurtful words or behavior. No one has the right to inflict their issues on anyone else. We make it far more complicated than it is, but in God's Word it really couldn't be any simpler. The only way in which the Bible instructs us, very clearly, to deal with an offender, is to rebuke her, forgive if there is repentance, and have nothing further to do with her if there is not (Luke 17:3). Nothing more, and nothing less.

2. "THE DEVIL MADE ME DO IT!"

At one point in my ongoing discussions with this person, I mentioned that the Lord had revealed to me a demonic influence in what she was doing to her friend. I urged her to honestly and prayerfully search her heart so that she might recognize these things for herself and be delivered of them. What I saw were the Spirits of Envy, Pride, Jealousy, Bitterness and Resentment. However, the Lord told me not to reveal them to her, because she would not hear it coming from me. She needed to see it for herself, confess it, and repent of it.

But she did not prayerfully search her heart and wait on the Lord's word. Instead, she guessed on her own that the "Spirit of Strife" was at work in her situation. She then went on to say that she believed this was "probably on both sides" (like I said before, she doesn't know enough to quit while she's ahead), when in reality, her friend had done nothing wrong at all, had actually been very patient for many months with her uncalled-for histrionics, and had been loving and forgiving toward her, only to be repaid again and again with nastiness, selfishness, lies, deceptions and unreasonable demands. This abuser's pride would not let her admit that the wrongdoing was really only on her side. There was no wrongdoing at all on the other side. She was one hundred percent at fault, but she needed to feel that her ex-friend had contributed to the problem and shared in the guilt.

Upon hearing this, I realized that I would need to be a little more specific. I then clarified my point. I told her that she needed to discern how these spirits had influenced *her, not* her friend, or their "situation."

After giving some more thought to my words, this abuser managed to come up with yet another angle. This time, the idea was to absolve herself completely with the old "the devil made me do it," or in her case, "the devil made *us* do it" defense.

One persistent theme in our ongoing discussions was that this person's most frequent, and almost reflexive, response to someone letting her that know she had been hurtful was to accuse the other person of "attacking her" or "blaming her." Apparently, since I was not agreeing with what she was doing to her friend, in her mind, both I and her friend had been "attacking" and "blaming" her. When I mentioned the demonic influence in her behavior, she jumped on it almost gleefully, quickly twisting what I had said to completely avoid taking any responsibility. She was very excited that we could finally agree on something! And in yet another attempt to make an ally out of someone who wasn't buying what she was selling, she tried enlisting me to "stand together with her against the devil," who, according to her, was now *the only one* really causing "all of this."

She began by telling me that she totally agreed that "there is a demonic force at work here. No doubt about it!" This was her attempt to sucker me into thinking that she agreed with me and we were all seeing the same things. She then went on to inform me that it was the "Spirit of Strife." Still "educating" me, she told me this is a demonic spirit sent out straight from hell for the express purpose to steal, kill and destroy. She asked if I could see that it had done just that.

And then she went on to say that here we three friends were "blaming each other" (Whoa! *She* certainly has nothing to "blame" anybody for! *No one else but her did anything wrong!*) and "anything and everything else," instead of placing the blame right where it belongs! She repeated that she would "own what was hers," but that it was time we "attack the correct person!" Really on a roll here, she continued that she wanted to stand up *now* against Satan, and bind and rebuke him for what he did and was still trying to do in this situation. Her excitement was palpable as she declared, "We've let him go far enough!!! It's time to stand together against him!!! Are you with me on this?"

My goodness, I felt like one of the Three Musketeers. Here was a real drama queen at work, trying to sweep everybody else up in her performance. But in reality, this was just another diversionary tactic. The truth got completely distorted and twisted. Like all narcissists, she did not differentiate between herself and others. She assumed we were all thinking alike, "blaming each other and anything and everything else," when we most certainly were not.

Notice that she wanted me to be "with her on this"~ *on the same side as she was.* On *her* side instead of on the side of her victim~ a verbal sleight of hand and a very subtle maneuver for a declaration of loyalty from me. One of Satan's tricks is to try to get you to agree that some form of his evil is acceptable. So in situations like this, there really is no compromise and no aligning yourself with the wicked person. Wrong is wrong, plain and simple. The smokescreens and diversions that an abuser will throw at you are meant to confuse you and to help her avoid being accountable. Here is the response the Lord gave me to her defense of "the devil made me do it!":

"First of all, I don't agree that "blaming each other" is what is happening here. Every conflict cannot be referred to in terms of "blame." That automatically makes the situation adversarial instead of cooperative, and accomplishes nothing toward resolution. I am not "blaming" you, and I am certainly not "blaming anything and everything else." Holding you accountable for what you do is not the same as "blaming" you. Also, I have not wronged you and neither has our friend, so you don't have anything to "blame" me for, or to blame her for, either. If your first or most common response when someone lets you know that you have hurt them is to feel as if you are being "blamed" or "attacked," then you need to think about why you are so defensive.

I am also not "blaming" Satan and never meant to imply that I was. I do not agree that he has any power or control over my actions, because I am a child of God. Satan does not control me because I do not give Satan control. I give control only to the Lord. I said there was a demonic *influence, not* demonic *control.* You still have free will. Satan can only tempt, but he cannot make you follow that temptation. Satan is not controlling this situation. It is an easy out for people to try and blame Satan in order to absolve themselves of the responsibility for what they've done wrong. But the devil doesn't *make* anybody do anything. *Everyone has free will,* and makes their own choice about whether to listen to him or not. Humans are ultimately accountable for their own decisions and behavior, not Satan. *You* made the choice to act the way you did, over and over again, for all these months. No growth is ever possible if you are going to blame anyone or anything else for your own wrongdoing."

3. "I HAVE REPENTED *TO GOD* FOR HURTING *HER*, AND MY CONSCIENCE IS NOW CLEAR."

This is another ploy used by this abuser to avoid having to make amends directly to the person she hurt. She was basically saying that she only has to answer to God for harming someone, and that no one else has the right to "judge" her or to expect her to make amends for what she did or change her behavior. She is letting us know that, in her mind, she does not have to show repentance to her victim because she has repented to God, and that's the end of it! Her conscience is now clear! So let's change the subject and move on!

She told me that she had indeed repented to God "for any and all of her part" in this situation, and that she now had "a very clear conscience." But in the Bible, the apostle Paul writes, *"MY CONSCIENCE IS CLEAR, BUT THAT DOES NOT MAKE ME INNOCENT. IT IS THE LORD WHO JUDGES ME".....1 Corinthians 4:4 NIV.*

Here we have a clear example of a so-called "Christian" who is simply too prideful to face her victim, apologize sincerely, accept responsibility, admit she was wrong, and change her ways. She thinks she can now put it all behind her and hold her head up high without ever doing the right thing by her victim. Any humility this person had shown in the past was false humility, calculated again to make her seem more righteous than she was. It wasn't until she was caught in this conflict over her wrongdoing that her pride-filled heart became obvious.

In the Bible, when you damage another person, you are expected to make restitution *to that person. "Repenting to God" does not get you off the hook.* You are told to go face the person you hurt and make it right by making him whole. And *then* you still have to repent to God for your sin (Exodus 22:3-15; Leviticus 6:5-7; Numbers 5:5-8; Proverbs 6:2-5; Proverbs 6:31). The Bible does not tell us that "repenting to God" is sufficient, or that doing so absolves us of the obligation to make amends directly to the person whom we have injured.

Additionally, when this abuser implied that because she had "repented to God," no one else had the right to judge her, she was conveniently forgetting that the children of God (one of whom she claimed to be) are held to an even *higher* standard than the children of the world, and certainly than the children of the devil. The Bible *does* repeatedly instruct the children of God to judge one another.

In Galatians chapter 5, Christians are instructed to expel an immoral brother from among them. Paul specifically tells us not to judge those *outside* the church, but we *are* told to judge those *inside* the church:

I WROTE YOU IN MY LETTER NOT TO ASSOCIATE WITH IMMORAL PEOPLE; I DID NOT AT ALL MEAN WITH THE IMMORAL PEOPLE OF THIS WORLD, OR WITH THE

COVETOUS AND SWINDLERS, OR WITH IDOLATERS, FOR THEN YOU WOULD HAVE TO GO OUT OF THE WORLD. BUT ACTUALLY, I WROTE TO YOU NOT TO ASSOCIATE WITH ANY SO-CALLED BROTHER IF HE IS AN IMMORAL PERSON, OR COVETOUS, OR AN IDOLATER, OR A REVILER, OR A DRUNKARD, OR A SWINDLER~ NOT EVEN TO EAT WITH SUCH A ONE. FOR WHAT HAVE I TO DO WITH JUDGING OUTSIDERS? DO YOU NOT JUDGE THOSE WHO ARE WITHIN THE CHURCH? BUT THOSE WHO ARE OUTSIDE, GOD JUDGES. REMOVE THE WICKED MAN FROM AMONG YOURSELVES.....1 Corinthians 5:9-13 NASB.

In Deuteronomy, the children of God are told six times to purge wicked people from among themselves (Deuteronomy 17:7; 19:19; 21:21; 22:21 & 24; and 24:7). These are just a few of the scriptures instructing us to hold fellow "children of God" accountable for their behavior.

Notice also the vague reference to "her part in all of this" without any mention of exactly *what* that was. There was never anything specific in any of our discussions that she would admit to and agree to be accountable for. Also, *by referring to "her" part in it, she was implying that the other person also had a part in it,* another attempt to divert attention away from *her* wrongdoing and place at least part of the "blame" (as she would call it) on the innocent victim. She tried this ploy several times. But whenever I asked her specifically what the victim had done wrong, she would either ignore me and not answer, babble something that made no sense or was completely untrue, or change the subject. The reality was that *the victim had done absolutely nothing* to contribute to the situation between them, or to deserve the treatment she got. The arrogant abuser was trying to keep her own dignity intact and save face by refusing to acknowledge that no one else did anything wrong!

Part of my response to her "clear conscience" was:

"It is great when someone repents to God, and I am very happy that you have done that. But repentance means a change in behavior and turning from wrongful ways, not just remorse. Besides God, the person you have injured has the right to a meaningful apology, a guarantee that it will never happen again, and whatever else you can possibly do to make amends. Once trust has been broken, and someone has learned to expect unacceptable or destructive behavior from another person, she would need reassurances and a promise of change before she would again be able to feel comfortable with the person who had hurt her.

Apologies are a great first step, but they are only a first step. You have a history of apologizing whenever you make anybody angry at you, just to get back into their good graces. But then you never change anything. You have even done this with me, several times. I also remember you apologizing last year after the way you were acting toward our friend. Although she wasn't comfortable with it and the grudging way in which it had been given, she accepted your apology anyway, and thought you had both put it behind you and that you then would be a loving and considerate friend. In fact, a number of things which you now say to make it seem as if you have changed, such as the Lord is now "doing a great work" in you, you have said many times before. But then more of the same always happens in your behavior with both me and our friend. So there have been several apologies over the years, but no actual change in your heart toward me or our friend. How can she know that anything will be different after *this* apology? Why should she believe you now?

Although there are times when you appear to be seeing clearly, gaining wisdom, or growing in the Lord, later on it turns out that you are not and nothing has actually changed. Your fruit is the clue. Not until you discern the spirits that are influencing you in your life, as well as in your feelings toward our friend, confess them, and are delivered of them will this happen.

When you refer in general terms to "your part in all of this," or that you "will own what is yours," without ever mentioning what exactly that is, there is nothing to indicate that you have actually been given any knowledge or understanding of these things from the Lord. It could just as easily be Satan trying to trick or deceive you, or me, or our friend.

Someone who has treated another person poorly needs to be very specific about exactly what behaviors they now recognize are unacceptable and are committed to permanently changing. Generalities, "making an effort", "growing," or "trying" to change isn't good enough. These are just ways to avoid making a definite and permanent commitment. In order for trust to be restored, there needs to be a promise that certain explicit things will simply never happen again. This is the kind of response our friend would need from you before she could feel that the Lord's hand is truly on a restoration of your friendship, and that it is really he who is speaking to your heart and *his* word that you are following.

Also, time needs to pass with the "repented" person proving that she meant what she said. Not that she's still "trying" weeks, months, or years later. There is much growth that still needs to happen and that is more important than anything else. If the Lord uses the end of your friendship to do this work in you, then it will be done according to his perfect will. Until your understanding is complete, you are fully accountable and commit to a permanent change, and a new heart and spirit is put in you, God will not bless a reconciliation."

4. "I HAVE RECEIVED THE BAPTISM OF THE HOLY SPIRIT AS EVIDENCED BY SPEAKING IN TONGUES; THEREFORE, I AM A GODLY AND RIGHTEOUS PERSON."

This person did not go into any details about how long ago she received this gift, whether she still spoke in tongues, or whether she prays in tongues or truly speaks in tongues. I have never heard her speak in tongues, and would have no way of knowing if she had a genuine gift, or if she was manifesting a counterfeit gift or speaking through the Spirit of False Tongues. She boasted of this gift, and used it to imply that she was being "misjudged" by both me and our friend, because if she was "holy" enough to have such a gift, then she could not have done what we all knew perfectly well she *had* done. However, the Bible is clear that speaking in tongues does not necessarily equate to being a truly godly, righteous Christian.

In 1 Corinthians, chapters 12-14, the apostle Paul goes into a very detailed account of the Gifts of the Holy Spirit, and discusses speaking in tongues at length. He tells us very clearly that not everyone will receive every gift, but that *all* of the gifts are important in the body of the church. Some will be given the gift of tongues, some will be given the gift of prophecy, some will be given miraculous powers, some will be given wisdom, and so forth. The Holy Spirit gives these gifts to each person, just as he determines (1 Corinthians 12: 4-31).

Paul doesn't pull any punches when he tells us that it doesn't matter what gifts we have been given~ if we do not have *love* in our hearts, then we are nothing. In 1 Corinthians 13, he says, "*THOUGH I SPEAK WITH THE TONGUES OF MEN AND OF ANGELS, BUT HAVE NOT LOVE, I HAVE BECOME SOUNDING BRASS OR A CLANGING CYMBAL. AND THOUGH I HAVE THE GIFT OF PROPHECY, AND UNDERSTAND ALL MYSTERIES AND ALL KNOWLEDGE, AND THOUGH I HAVE ALL FAITH, SO THAT I COULD REMOVE MOUNTAINS, BUT HAVE NOT LOVE, I AM NOTHING. AND THOUGH I BESTOW ALL MY GOODS TO FEED THE POOR, AND THOUGH I GIVE MY BODY TO BE BURNED, BUT HAVE NOT LOVE, IT PROFITS ME NOTHING."… 1 Corinthians 13:1-3 NKJV.*

Paul then goes on to discuss the gift of tongues, and its desirability and value compared to the other gifts, especially the gift of prophecy:

PURSUE LOVE, AND DESIRE SPIRITUAL GIFTS, BUT ESPECIALLY THAT YOU MAY PROPHESY. FOR HE WHO SPEAKS IN A TONGUE DOES NOT SPEAK TO MEN BUT TO GOD, FOR NO ONE UNDERSTANDS HIM; HOWEVER, IN THE SPIRIT HE SPEAKS MYSTERIES. BUT HE WHO PROPHESIES SPEAKS EDIFICATION AND EXHORTATION AND COMFORT TO MEN. HE WHO SPEAKS IN A TONGUE EDIFIES HIMSELF, BUT HE WHO PROPHESIES EDIFIES THE CHURCH. I WISH YOU ALL SPOKE WITH TONGUES, BUT EVEN MORE THAT YOU PROPHESIED; FOR HE WHO PROPHESIES IS GREATER THAN HE WHO SPEAKS WITH TONGUES, UNLESS INDEED HE INTERPRETS, SO THAT THE CHURCH MAY RECEIVE EDIFICATION.....1 Corinthians 14:1-5 NKJV.

THEREFORE LET HIM WHO SPEAKS IN A TONGUE PRAY THAT HE MAY INTERPRET. FOR IF I PRAY IN A TONGUE, MY SPIRIT PRAYS BUT MY UNDERSTANDING IS UNFRUITFUL.... OTHERWISE, IF YOU BLESS WITH THE SPIRIT, HOW WILL HE WHO OCCUPIES THE PLACE OF THE UNINFORMED SAY "AMEN" AT YOUR GIVING OF THANKS, SINCE HE DOES NOT UNDERSTAND WHAT YOU SAY?....1 Corinthians 14:13-14, 16 NKJV.

I THANK MY GOD I SPEAK WITH TONGUES MORE THAN YOU ALL; YET IN THE CHURCH I WOULD RATHER SPEAK FIVE WORDS WITH MY UNDERSTANDING, THAT I MAY TEACH OTHERS ALSO, THAN TEN THOUSAND WORDS IN A TONGUE. BRETHREN, DO NOT BE CHILDREN IN UNDERSTANDING; HOWEVER, IN MALICE BE BABES, BUT IN UNDERSTANDING BE MATURE.....1 Corinthians 14:18-20 NKJV.

THEREFORE TONGUES ARE FOR A SIGN, NOT TO THOSE WHO BELIEVE BUT TO UNBELIEVERS; BUT PROPHESYING IS NOT FOR UNBELIEVERS BUT FOR THOSE WHO BELIEVE. THEREFORE IF THE WHOLE CHURCH COMES TOGETHER IN ONE PLACE, AND ALL SPEAK WITH TONGUES, AND THERE COME IN THOSE WHO ARE UNINFORMED OR UNBELIEVERS, WILL THEY NOT SAY THAT YOU ARE OUT OF YOUR MIND? BUT IF ALL PROPHESY, AND AN UNBELIEVER OR AN UNINFORMED PERSON COMES IN, HE IS CONVINCED BY ALL, HE IS CONVICTED BY ALL. AND THUS THE SECRETS OF HIS HEART ARE REVEALED; AND SO, FALLING DOWN ON HIS FACE, HE WILL WORSHIP GOD AND REPORT THAT GOD IS TRULY AMONG YOU….1 Corinthians 14: 22-25 NKJV.

And so we are taught that not all Christians receive every gift, but that *all* of the gifts are important to the body of Christ. We see that, despite what this particular abuser apparently thinks, the Bible does not place such a high priority on tongues that it should be considered the true test of a believer. In fact, the gift of prophecy is assigned a much greater importance.

I'm not quite sure why she chose to "boast" about tongues in particular, and no other gifts, as some sort of proof that she should be considered a godly person (probably because she had no other gifts to boast of). But in any case, God's Word is still very clear on the most important point of all~ *the gift of tongues, or any of the other gifts, are meaningless and worthless if the person does not have love.* This individual was sadly lacking in that department; therefore, according to the infallible and holy Word of God, whatever gifts she claimed to have didn't mean a thing.

The Bible gives very clear examples of the fruit of a true Christian who lives by the Spirit, as opposed to the behaviors of one who might claim to be Christian, but who really lives by the flesh or by her sinful nature. This is how we can tell the difference:

SO I SAY, LIVE BY THE SPIRIT, AND YOU WILL NOT GRATIFY THE DESIRES OF THE SINFUL NATURE. FOR THE SINFUL NATURE DESIRES WHAT IS CONTRARY TO THE SPIRIT, AND THE SPIRIT WHAT IS CONTRARY TO THE SINFUL NATURE. THEY ARE IN CONFLICT WITH EACH OTHER, SO THAT YOU DO NOT DO WHAT YOU WANT. BUT IF YOU ARE LED BY THE SPIRIT, YOU ARE NOT UNDER THE LAW.

THE ACTS OF THE SINFUL NATURE ARE OBVIOUS: SEXUAL IMMORALITY, IMPURITY AND DEBAUCHERY; IDOLATRY AND WITCHCRAFT; HATRED, DISCORD, JEALOUSY, FITS OF RAGE, SELFISH AMBITION, DISSENSIONS, FACTIONS, AND ENVY; DRUNKENNESS, ORGIES AND THE LIKE. I WARN YOU, AS I DID BEFORE, THAT THOSE WHO LIVE LIKE THIS WILL NOT INHERIT THE KINGDOM OF GOD.

BUT THE FRUIT OF THE SPIRIT IS LOVE, JOY, PEACE, PATIENCE, KINDNESS, GOODNESS, FAITHFULNESS, GENTLENESS AND SELF-CONTROL. AGAINST SUCH THINGS THERE IS NO LAW. THOSE WHO BELONG TO CHRIST JESUS HAVE CRUCIFIED THE SINFUL NATURE WITH ITS PASSIONS AND DESIRES. SINCE WE LIVE BY THE SPIRIT, LET US KEEP IN STEP WITH THE SPIRIT. LET US NOT BECOME CONCEITED, PROVOKING AND ENVYING EACH OTHER.

BROTHERS, IF SOMEONE IS CAUGHT IN A SIN, YOU WHO ARE SPIRITUAL SHOULD RESTORE HIM GENTLY. BUT WATCH YOURSELF, OR YOU MAY ALSO BE TEMPTED. CARRY EACH OTHER'S BURDENS, AND IN THIS WAY YOU WILL FULFILL THE LAW OF CHRIST. IF ANYONE THINKS HE IS SOMETHING WHEN HE IS NOTHING, HE DECEIVES HIMSELF. EACH ONE SHOULD TEST HIS OWN ACTIONS. THEN HE CAN TAKE PRIDE IN HIMSELF, WITHOUT COMPARING HIMSELF TO SOMEBODY ELSE, FOR EACH ONE SHOULD CARRY HIS OWN LOAD. ANYONE WHO RECEIVES INSTRUCTION IN

THE WORD MUST SHARE ALL GOOD THINGS WITH HIS INSTRUCTOR. DO NOT BE DECEIVED: GOD CANNOT BE MOCKED. A MAN REAPS WHAT HE SOWS. THE ONE WHO SOWS TO PLEASE HIS SINFUL NATURE, FROM THAT NATURE WILL REAP DESTRUCTION; THE ONE WHO SOWS TO PLEASE THE SPIRIT, FROM THE SPIRIT WILL REAP ETERNAL LIFE....
Galatians 5:16-26 - 6:1-8 NIV.

Thank you, Father God, for your Holy Word. Help us never to stand by silently while others defile your Word by perverting it to justify their wickedness. Bless us, Holy Spirit, with your priceless gifts of discernment, understanding and wisdom. Lord Jesus, give us the courage to speak out against all evil, even if we have to rebuke a "fellow Christian," and to stand fast and bind Satan in all his clever disguises, in your glorious Name we pray. For greater is he that is in us than he that is in the world (1 John 4:4). Amen!

CHAPTER 16

DESPERATE MEASURES: WHEN THEY SENSE THEY'RE LOSING THEIR GRIP ON YOU, FIVE SURPRISING WAYS OF KEEPING YOU ATTACHED

DON'T WASTE YOUR BREATH ON FOOLS, FOR THEY WILL DESPISE THE WISEST ADVICE.....Proverbs 23:9 NLT.

FATHERS, PROVOKE NOT YOUR CHILDREN TO ANGER, LEST THEY BE DISCOURAGED...Colossians 3:21 KJV.

Once upon a time, I used to have a pleasant fantasy. In it, I would tell my birth-mother that her behavior was upsetting to me. She would apologize, assure me that she would never dream of continuing to hurt me because she cared for me a great deal, and promise to stop her offensive behavior immediately. Then, true to her word, she would never do it again, enabling our relationship to be happily restored. Boy, was I living in la-la land.

When *that* never worked, I had a slightly more complicated delusion. In this version, after I complained about her mistreatment, Mommy Darling would continue hurting me anyway. Since it stressed me out to be in her presence, I would stop constantly placing myself in that position, and begin avoiding her instead. I would start to emotionally detach and to feel distant from her. I might even decide to take a break from the relationship for a few weeks or months, of which I might or might not choose to inform her, to get my thoughts together about what to do next. Mom, sensing my withdrawal, would realize what she was doing and become concerned about losing the relationship. Afraid that she might *really* be driving me away, she would come to her senses, immediately stop her hurtful behavior, and make every effort to be as pleasant to be with as possible. Her turnabout would enable me to enjoy spending time with her, and our relationship would be happily restored. Yeah, right. What in the world was I thinking?

Now, if we were talking about *normal* people, who truly do love and care for those who love them, this might really happen. In fact, the very reason why we try to talk things out with a loved one who is hurting us is that we are hoping against hope for such a happy ending. But those of us who have had the misfortune to try and reason with a control freak or an abuser quickly learn there is almost *no chance* that this will actually ever happen in *our* situations.

No matter how calmly and politely we request a change, things will go south fast. Any attempt we make to have a loving and rational discussion will quickly degenerate into a nasty, crazy-making argument. We will be left scratching our heads and wondering what on earth went wrong, and why a simple plea for a little consideration had to be blown up into such a big deal.

On the surface, abusers seem to have absolutely no sensitivity to others at all. *But in reality, they are acutely sensitive to their victim becoming stronger, beginning to heal, or pulling away from their toxicity.* Control freaks sense instantly when they begin to lose their grip on their victim, which will mean losing their ability to control him. They are desperate to prevent that from happening, and will pull out all the stops to keep him enmeshed with them.

Many of us have tried to limit our time with our abusive relatives, rather than to cut off all contact. Many of us have decided to take a "vacation" of several weeks or months from our relatives, to see if we can clear our heads and reconcile the relationship down the road from a fresh perspective. This can increase our self-esteem, independence and growth. *And that is the **last** thing an abuser wants.*

Abusers will not allow you any distance, any room to breathe, or any time to think. They will not respect your request for even a short break from their toxicity. They will allow us no more than a few days before intruding on our "sabbatical" with another call or e-mail. Totally lacking in self-control or any consideration for what *we* might want, they just can't wait to continue the discussion, add something else to what they've already said, or throw more fuel on the fire. When *they* decide we've taken enough time, then time's up! They will demand that we hear them out. They will pressure, hound, and harass us to speak to them again before we are ready. If, instead of insisting on the time we requested and just cutting them off, we give them an audience, then before you know it we will find ourselves right back in the same old argument.

Some of their tactics are quite obvious, but some are much more subtle. In this chapter, we will discuss five very clever strategies designed to manipulate you into staying connected and under your controller's thumb. These strategies are very deceptive and not at all what they seem to be. At first glance, they appear to be aimed at driving you further away and daring you to really end the relationship. It is almost as if your abuser is saying, "You can't tell me what to do! I'll show you! If you don't like it, then get out!"

But in reality, he never expects you to actually do that! Appearing to repulse you even further is really a clever disguise for tightening the noose and reeling you in. Keep in mind as you read on that, *contrary to appearances, these ploys are not meant to push you away. Their real purpose is to **keep you connected** to your abuser by forcing you to continue to respond to him.* His goal is to keep you talking to him, even if the "talk" is an argument. If he wins, you will still be having the same argument, and therefore still be attached to him, a year from now, and maybe even ten years from now.

STRATEGY #1
INCREASING THE ABUSE

Normal people, upon learning that they are causing pain for another human being, do their best to change upsetting behaviors immediately. Most of us would never deliberately hurt another person, especially someone we loved and who loved us. So we are naturally dumbfounded when our abusive relative does just the opposite. When a control freak senses that you are pulling away or gaining strength, *instead of stopping her offensive behavior, she continues it, or even escalates it.*

After being rebuked, not only will many abusers not stop their hurtful behavior, they will do it even more! They're not going to let you tell them what to do! It's as if they are daring you, challenging you, and saying "Oh, yeah? And what are you gonna do about it?" But remember, although it seems as if they are *trying* to drive you away, they are not. They are trying to do just the opposite~ to keep you arguing with them, and therefore still connected to them and still in a relationship with them.

This is when we can clearly see that our relative is operating in an adversarial spirit instead of a cooperative spirit. When you begin to set limits, your abuser will balk at you taking control. She feels as if you are challenging her for domination and power. You are growing and becoming stronger, which threatens her. You are no longer intimidated by her histrionics. What she is doing no longer works. So instead of stopping, she ups the ante.

When this happens, you are going to have difficulty comprehending it. You will be flabbergasted, confused, upset, and maybe even angry, because you approached your relative in the spirit of goodwill to resolve a problem between you, and she reacted by getting even worse. After telling her that her behavior is hurtful, to have her continue, or do it even more, removes all doubt as to whether she was intentionally trying to hurt you or not. Now you will know that *all along, it was deliberate.* You have revealed your feelings, and she now knows what gets your goat. So escalating the abuse instead of stopping it makes it a very personal and intentional slap in the face.

You will not want to believe that a person you love and have always treated well is doing this to you. You will be devastated and appalled. You will be compelled to express your righteous indignation, and to tell her how terrible she has made you feel. Doing this keeps you communicating with her and enmeshed with her. Bingo! She wins!

STRATEGY #2
ESCALATING THE ARGUMENT

Escalating the argument is another way of protesting that you are growing strong enough to set limits or to distance yourself. This happens when a narcissist overreacts to your complaint, no matter how polite and carefully worded it was. You probably spent time rehearsing how to approach your relative or church family member in as respectful a way as possible. You were sure if you could keep things calm and explain your feelings, that he would listen to reason. You had high hopes of resolving the issue to everyone's satisfaction, but you can see now that you needn't have bothered.

What should be so simple to resolve, if everyone involved truly cared for each other, will turn into a huge battle. No matter how nicely you try to start out, things will go downhill real fast. There is no reason at all for a big fight, but an abuser will start one out of any perfectly nice attempt to clear the air. Your abusive relative will make a mountain out of a molehill and blow a slight disagreement all up out of proportion.

Once again, *normal people* do not react this way. How simple it would be for your relative to just say, "Oh, sorry. It won't happen again." End of discussion, problem solved, and everybody's happy. Now wasn't that easy? But, noooooo...... It's gotta turn into World War III!

Why? Again, it's the adversarial spirit versus the cooperative spirit. Abusers regard such discussions as golden opportunities to vent and have temper tantrums. Your abuser isn't looking for a compromise, a mutual solution, or a relationship in which everyone can be happy. *He is looking for power, domination and control.* This isn't a partnership. He wants to be *the boss!* How dare you? Who do you think you are to speak like this to him? You are just a bug he can squash under his feet.

Now, he can't come right out and tell you that he won't stand for anything less than total submission to his will. If he was *that* honest, you would probably run for the hills, and then he wouldn't have you to kick around anymore. But he *can* get more and more outrageous and demanding, secure in the knowledge that you will feel obliged to respond. He can get all worked up and enraged, knowing you will probably feel you must stick around to try to calm him down and reason with him, because it was never your intention to upset him. As long as you try to explain yourself, justify your position, or even scream and yell back, he has won~ because you're still attached to him.

When you realize that your attempt to have a nice, calm, rational, respectful discussion is being turned into a nasty, full-blown argument, take control back and *end it.* Just stop talking, hang up the phone, or turn your back and walk away.

STRATEGY #3
PUTTING YOU ON THE DEFENSIVE

Putting you on the defensive takes many forms, from voicing a complaint about you to complete character assassination. Your abuser might claim that you are wrong for taking offense at offensive behavior. She might question your motivations for refusing to continue to be her doormat. She might say that you deserved whatever was done to you, or that you brought it on yourself. She might tell you that you are emotionally or mentally defective ("You're too sensitive", "You take everything the wrong way", "You misunderstood what I said", "You always make mountains out of molehills") My birth-mother conveniently forgot all the battles *she herself* had had with my birth-father, as well as the lifelong parade of fed-up ex-friends and relatives, when she stated, with a perfectly straight face, that *I* was "the only one who had a problem him."

Your relative might make an outrageous accusation or tell a blatant lie. The more outrageous or blatant, the better, because that guarantees you will feel compelled to respond. And how many of us *wouldn't* feel compelled to respond and defend ourselves when someone is lying about us or accusing us of something we never did? Our abusers often know us better than we know ourselves. They know exactly how to push our buttons. They know that we care about what other people think of us. They know that we're so careful to be kind, nice, good and righteous. They know we try our best to be loving and good-hearted. So they aim right for the personality traits that they know we value the most. *They are counting on us being horrified that anyone might actually think we were not nice.*

Once you have fallen into the trap of defending yourself, you are in for a very long night. A skillful abuser will have you justifying every word you have ever said since the year of the flood. You will find yourself trying to explain the rationale behind every perfectly reasonable thought and every perfectly correct feeling you have ever had.

Just remember, *your abuser doesn't really believe what she is accusing you of, anyway.* She knows it's not true, so you don't have to convince her. She is not really trying to resolve anything with you. She is simply trying to keep you connected and responding to her. And while she's at it, she's having a little fun by getting a rise out of you and seeing that she can still make you get all upset and flustered. When you allow this, you have given her far too much power over you.

Sisters and Brothers, you do not have to prove yourself to anyone but the Lord. You are never going to satisfy or please critical relatives or bullies anyway, no matter how much you try, so you might as well save yourself a lot of time and trouble and just give up. More than once I have had to inform my hypercritical birth-parents that their opinion of me didn't matter anymore. It was always going to be negative, anyway. They seemed to have a great deal of difficulty comprehending this. It's tough for a control freak to realize that one of the most effective weapons he once used to control you no longer works, and that whatever he thinks, you no longer care about.

When faced with a silly and nonsensical allegation, don't give your abuser the satisfaction of getting all worked up and defensive. The best answer is to simply shrug and say, "That's ridiculous, and I'm not even going to justify it with a response."

STRATEGY #4
PROLONGING THE DISCUSSION AD NAUSEUM

I was a witness to an interesting conversation between my friend Rachel and her birth-father, with whom she has had a strained relationship all her life, and especially since her parents' divorce. Dear old dad is an arrogant, obnoxious, intimidating, belligerent man who had spent years bullying Rachel and her mother. For some reason, when Rachel turned thirty, he suddenly decided it was time to improve his relationship with his daughter, because she was now "old enough to make her own decisions." (The implication being that his ex-wife, rather than his own behavior, had turned Rachel against him.)

So he summoned Rachel to a pow-wow at a local diner, and she asked me to accompany her for moral support. Although I remained silent for most of the meeting, I did have some insights which I was able to pass on to her later. The most obvious problem to me was that every time Rachel very clearly expressed her thoughts or feelings to her father, he "gaslighted" her by pretending that he had no idea what she was talking about.

For instance, when she told him he had been "mean and cruel" to her mother, he asked her, "*When* was I mean or cruel?" Then, whenever she recalled a specific incident of abuse, he would never acknowledge her perfectly accurate memory, take responsibility for what he had done, or show any remorse. Instead, he would put her on the defensive again by asking, with feigned innocence, "*When* did I do that?"

Notice he did not outright deny what she was saying. That might have caused her to become angry and end the conversation. He only *questioned* what she was saying. This tactic was not only designed to cause her to doubt her perceptions and memories, but also to force *her* to keep answering *him*. Then, when she answered, instead of admitting anything, he would ask yet another question, and another, and another~ thus prolonging the conversation indefinitely.

Whoever is the one asking the questions has taken control of the conversation and the direction in which it is headed. Rachel's father knew that if he could keep it going long enough, eventually he might be able to lighten things up a little, share a few "good" memories or an inside joke, and basically soften Rachel up. The point of this strategy was to seduce the "weak-willed" victim into continuing to accept the status quo, and maintain a relationship with the abuser without requiring anything at all of him.

Questioning you interrupts your train of thought. It literally gets you off the track of what you wanted to discuss. It puts you in the position of answering your relative, while getting none of your own questions answered, and none of your points addressed. It makes you stop and think, forces you to remember details and to repeat dates, circumstances, etc., to the abuser, *even though he already knows perfectly well what you are talking about.* It is a diversion, and a very effective one.

Rachel was uncomfortable with the direction the conversation had taken, which included many abusive or overbearing tactics and numerous veiled criticisms of her mother. She could see that they weren't getting anywhere, but every time she tried to disengage and end the discussion, her father kept peppering her with questions and overwhelming her with chatter. It's amazing how long a skilled control freak can drag a discussion out, while still managing to duck all accountability. After three hours, we made a break for it~ and he followed us all the way out to the parking lot and kept blathering on for another half-hour until she finally closed the car door in his face.

Thinking about it later, Rachel realized that none of the issues she wanted to address were ever resolved. Most hadn't even been discussed. Her father had totally monopolized the whole conversation with his agenda. Rachel's goal for this meeting was to give her father a chance to show her that he had changed, and hopefully to repair the relationship. But her father's ulterior motive was to seduce or coerce a relationship with Rachel without being accountable in any way for the things he had done to her and her mother, and without committing to any changes.

If fences had truly been mended and a happy reconciliation had taken place, then both parties involved would now feel joy and peace about their relationship. But Rachel came away from this discussion feeling stressed, unsettled and uncomfortable, because she realized that nothing had changed and she still could not have a relationship with this man. She was exhausted, drained, and felt like she had spent three hours being browbeaten.

What upset her the most was knowing that, down the road, her conniving father would use this whole episode against her, and would claim that he "couldn't understand" why she still didn't want to see him, after they had spent such a "nice" afternoon together, cleared the air, and parted on such "friendly" terms. He would never look to himself, but would either declare that her mother had turned her against him again, or that Rachel must have some kind of mental problem to still be "carrying a grudge." And she was right. A few weeks later, that's exactly what he did.

When I was in the real estate business, lawyers would often call me to negotiate deals at 11:00 PM or midnight, claiming that they were "tied up in court all day." Eventually, I realized that this was a strategy they used to catch me when I was not at my best. If I was tired or sleepy, I would not be thinking clearly, and they might get me to slip up and make a mistake or make a concession that I would not normally agree to. When I realized what was going on, I began turning my phone off at nine o'clock every night. There was nothing so urgent that it couldn't wait until morning, when I was refreshed and clear-headed.

An abuser who keeps hounding you long after you have tired of the discussion is using this same strategy. *He is trying to wear you down.* He is trying to exhaust and confuse you until you are no longer thinking straight, so that you will either give up on holding him accountable, or be convinced to concede some of his points and "see things his way."

Sometimes, you might think that the argument is over, that everything is settled, or even that the relationship has ended. And then the next thing you know, your abuser is back on the phone, starting the whole thing up again. This is because he does not feel he "won" the first time around, so now it's time for round two. But just because the donkey brays doesn't mean you have to answer him!

When the conversation is just going around in circles and nothing is ever getting settled, it's time to say, "We're not getting anywhere with this," and *end it.* Enough is enough. You can always revisit it later if you see any indication that further discussion might actually accomplish something useful.

STRATEGY #5
DISOWNING YOU

Of all the tactics utilized to keep you enmeshed with her, being disowned by your abuser is my personal favorite. It is inherently fascinating just because it's so contradictory. It's like the oxymoron of abusive artillery.

Disowning is a threat or an implied threat that is not often actually carried out~ although it might be, which in most cases would be a blessing. It ranges from pouting, to hanging up on you, to refusing to speak to you, to shunning you from the family, to cutting you out of the will. It's telling you that if you don't toe the line, you're out. It is blatant emotional blackmail.

Disowning is often threatened or alluded to, but rarely carried out simply because the abuser does not *really* want the relationship to end. After all, if she loses you, she also loses the ability to control you, which is what she lives for. If you're out of her life, then who is she going to have to use and abuse? Let's face it. All this time your relationship was unbalanced at best, one-way at worst, with *you* doing most, if not all, of the giving and *her* doing most, if not all, of the taking. What idiot would want to give *that* up? Your abuser doesn't really want to set you free. You might actually *like* that! She only wants to keep you in line; hence the threat to cut you off.

Occasionally, an abuser really does carry out her threat and stops speaking to you. When she senses that you are growing stronger and distancing yourself from her anyway, this is often the last-ditch effort of a control freak to remain in control, by dumping you before you can dump her. Of course, *actually changing her behavior in order to make a pleasant relationship possible is out of the question* in an abuser's mind. Treating you with love and respect is simply not an option. Somebody dumping somebody is the only alternative as far as she is concerned.

It's a matter of pride. No way is she going to let you take control and make this decision. *She* wants to end the relationship before *you* do, just to prove that she's still calling the shots (but be prepared for her to lie to the rest of the family about what really happened between you). She is going to control the path of your relationship right down to the bitter end, and sometimes even from the grave! Little does she know that when she cuts you off, it will be the biggest favor she's ever done for you.

One thing I learned is not to take it personally when narcissists, abusers and psychopaths disown you. *Many times, the reason they disown you is not that **you** did something wrong. It's that **they** did something wrong.* And now they're either embarrassed at getting caught, too ashamed to face you, afraid of your anger, or trying to discredit you by making *you* look bad before you can expose *them*. They don't want to have to answer for what they did, so they turn it all around and pretend *you* hurt *them*, and then they make themselves scarce and get out of range before you can hold them accountable~ and usually before you can even realize the full extent of what they did to you. If they are refusing to speak to you, then how can you ever confront them or ask for an apology?

When my birth-mother and her supporters (birth-sis, one aunt and two cousins) disowned me, what started the final disagreement was Mommy Darling demanding that I choose between her and my son. She knew she had crossed the line when she did that, so instead of backing off and apologizing, she went even crazier and stopped speaking to me, to make it look like *I* was the selfish, unreasonable lunatic instead of *her*. By the time they took my abusive birth-parents' side and joined them in disowning me, Mommy Darling's Silent Partners/Flying Monkeys had *already* done me wrong, by listening to and spreading lies about me, gossiping about me, meddling, egging on my abusers, and taking their side, when none of what was going on between me and my parents was any of their business. Instead of doing anything constructive, they added fuel to the fire. So the next logical step was to shun me and rob me of the opportunity to confront them for their betrayal when I eventually found out about it. They had to justify stabbing me in the back somehow, so they pretended I deserved it and *they* were *angry* at me, when the truth was that my issues with my birth-parents had absolutely nothing to do with them. One of Daddy Darling's favorite sayings always was "the best defense is a good offense." *In other words, the best way to defend your actions when you do wrong is to attack the person you hurt.* This way, you put the victim on the defensive and turn everybody's attention to *her*, and *you* never have to explain yourself or be accountable for *your* behavior.

When your abuser disowns you, or threatens to disown you, the last thing she expects is for you to shrug, say "Okay, if that's what you really want," and let her go. She has watched one too many soap operas. What you are supposed to do is start crying and begging her not to leave. You are supposed to hang on to her ankles, screaming "No, no~ please stay! I'll do anything you want!" as she drags you to the door. Then, when you have properly humbled and humiliated yourself, she can forgive you and agree to stay, but only after making *you* apologize to *her* and promise to change *your* ways!

Thankfully, this tactic usually backfires on abusers. Many victims are relieved and only too happy to let their abusers go, and can then move on with a clear conscience, knowing it was the abuser's decision to end the relationship even though the victim was willing to try and make it better.

In my own situation, when my mother disowned me, I made the decision to leave well enough alone and simply do nothing further. *BUT IF THE UNBELIEVER LEAVES, LET HIM DO SO. A BELIEVING MAN OR WOMAN IS NOT BOUND IN SUCH CIRCUMSTANCES; GOD HAS CALLED US TO LIVE IN PEACE....1 Corinthians 7:15 NIV.* I felt very strongly that the Lord had removed me from an extremely toxic situation of which he no longer wanted me to be a part. So I did not call her or make any attempts to get back together. I figured that *she* had been the one to end our relationship, and if she had a change of heart, then *she* needed to be the one to restore it. I was heartbroken at first, but eventually I became at peace with it. And after a while I felt relief, joy, and profound gratitude. I understood that my Father was protecting me, and that he loved me so much that he had taken this burden from me. Thank you, Abba Father!

ENOUGH, ALREADY!

Let's be honest. When everyone is acting in love, asking for a favor such as a positive change that will improve your relationship, and coming to an agreement, should take all of five or ten minutes, at most. When it starts to drag out longer than that, it is only because someone is being stubborn. When it goes on for hours, days, or weeks, then somebody is refusing to cooperate and is intentionally obstructing a resolution. That person is deliberately preventing the confrontation from ending. Abusers and bullies are not interested having constructive conversations that result in nice solutions. They are only interested in *winning*.

Because we are so predictable, our abusers know that we are going to react the same way every time. This is how we wind up repeating the same patterns and getting dragged into the same arguments over and over again. In order to free ourselves, we need to start being *unpredictable.* Our relative manipulates confrontations to keep us engaged and force us to respond to her. The only way for us to counteract this is to do just the opposite of what she is trying to get us to do, which means to *disengage and stop responding.*

After all, you wouldn't spend time arguing with the patients in a mental asylum, would you? It is just as futile to continue arguing with an unreasonable hostile abuser, who says nonsensical preposterous things, and acts in crazy irrational ways. We need to let go of the need to set the record straight, defend ourselves and get things resolved, and embrace the need to just have a little peace and quiet!

As long as we continue to respond to a control freak's nonsense, she wins. *When we stop responding and leave,* ***we*** *win!* The idea is to *detach,* leaving her no one to argue with. If we simply disappear when the same old arguments start, then she will be left all alone with no one to listen to her, and plenty of time to think over her behavior and change her attitude.

No matter how hard you try, you are never going to convince an unwilling person to start treating you with love and respect. We need to train ourselves to recognize the point at which further discussion ceases to be productive. *A general rule of thumb is that this point has been reached when you find yourself repeating or rephrasing your request for the third time.*

That is when we need to *stop*, pick one of the following statements, say it, and *walk out:*

- "We're just going around in circles. I've had enough."
- "We already discussed this and I'm not going to keep rehashing it."

- "I'm going to take that as a "no." I'll just have to go ahead and take other measures to protect myself."
- "I'm not going to waste any more time on this. These are my terms. Take it or leave it."
- "I've made up my mind and I'm not going to discuss it anymore."
- "We're not getting anywhere with this. I'm leaving."
- "I'm not going to repeat myself again. If we're going to see each other anymore, then this is the way it has to be."
- "This discussion is going nowhere, so I'm ending it. I'm hanging up now. Don't call me again until you agree with what I'm asking of you."
- "I told you what I need from you, and it's non-negotiable. You're either going to do what I ask, or not. When you let me know your decision, then I'll let you know my decision about continuing this relationship."
- "I can't explain it any better than I already have. If you refuse to get my point, then there's no point in continuing to discuss it."
- "I can see we're not going to agree on this. Let me know when you're ready to do what I'm asking of you."
- "I've made myself perfectly clear. I have nothing more to say."

So, what's the bottom line here? Basically, control freaks want power and narcissists want attention. The combination of a narcissistic control freak results in an abuser who's harder to get rid of than chewing gum in your hair. By staying connected and continuing to argue with her, you are feeding into *both* her addiction to power *and* her demands for attention. *You are giving her everything she wants, at your own expense.*

Such abusers have nothing positive to offer, like kindness or love, which would persuade you stick around and pay attention to them.

So they manipulate you into sticking around and paying attention to them by picking a fight. They force you to repeat your pleas over and over again. They upset you, put you on the defensive, and maneuver you into asking why they are doing this to you, so that they can involve you in an endless, pointless discussion. They have exasperated you so many times before, and you always stuck around and tried to resolve it. And that's exactly the reaction they're counting on this time, as well.

So this time, we need to spring a little surprise of our own. We need to break the old pattern, be tough, and let them know firmly that enough is enough! We need to say, "Okay, I tried. I'm outta here. Bye!" *And then refuse to discuss it anymore, disengage, leave, hang up that phone, walk out that door, end it!* If, sometime down the road, our abusive relative decides to honor our request for a change in behavior, then she can always let us know. Showing your abuser that you mean business is the only way to get through to her.

AND IF THE HOUSE BE WORTHY, LET YOUR PEACE COME UPON IT: BUT IF IT NOT BE WORTHY, LET YOUR PEACE RETURN TO YOU. AND WHOSOEVER SHALL NOT RECEIVE YOU, NOR HEAR YOUR WORDS, WHEN YE DEPART OUT OF THAT HOUSE OR CITY, SHAKE OFF THE DUST OF YOUR FEET. VERILY I SAY UNTO YOU, IT SHALL BE MORE TOLERABLE FOR THE LAND OF SODOM AND GOMORRHA IN THE DAY OF JUDGMENT THAN FOR THAT CITY. BEHOLD, I SEND YOU FORTH AS SHEEP IN THE MIDST OF WOLVES: BE YE THEREFORE WISE AS SERPENTS AND HARMLESS AS DOVES.....Matthew 10:13-16 KJV.

CHAPTER 17

"LET'S GO TO COUNSELING TOGETHER AND WORK ON *OUR* PROBLEM"

When I started setting and enforcing limits on birth-father and his behavior, Mommy Darling called me up and announced that her husband was "willing" to go into joint therapy with me. Now to a novice, inexperienced in dealing with really dangerous narcissists or psychopaths, this might sound just peachy. Finally, we're getting somewhere. At first glance, an abuser offering to go to counseling with you appears to be a hopeful sign. It sounds like he's willing to change, to make some concessions, and try to work out the problems in your relationship. But before you agree, stop and think twice.

If your abuser decided to go into therapy *by himself,* then we might assume that at least he's admitting that *his* behavior needs to change and is owning his part in the problems between you. But when your abuser thinks *you* need therapy too, then doesn't it follow that he believes *your* behavior *also* needs to change, and *you* also bear some responsibility for the problems in your relationship?

Abusers sometimes suggest joint counseling, like my birth-parents did, "to work on *our* problem." But I took issue with the idea that it was *our* problem. *I* didn't have a problem. My abuser did. I was actually quite offended by the insinuation that I needed any kind of therapy, and the implication that I was contributing to the problems caused solely by my birth-father's abuse. There was nothing wrong with me. In fact, I was finally becoming healthy enough to start standing up for myself, have appropriate boundaries, and expect to be treated with respect.

I was not about to let my parents blame me, even partially, for my birth-father's inability to get along with me or anyone else. There was nothing wrong in my relationship with Daddy Darling that a change in *his* behavior wouldn't fix. Then we could all be pleasant and enjoy each other's company. It was that simple. But he was unwilling to do this. And I, having a full-time job, children to raise, and a heavy load of volunteer commitments, was unwilling to waste any more of my valuable time playing games with him.

I had already literally spent years going around in circles with my birth-parents over their abuse, and getting absolutely nowhere. The joint counseling "offer" came at a time when I was enforcing my boundaries much more firmly than I had ever done in the past, because I had finally begun to realize that my parents' unacceptable behavior was negatively affecting my children. My parents' stubborn refusal to respect those boundaries had made it necessary for me to curtail the time my family and I spent with them. The more they acted out, the more I cut back on our time together, to give them less opportunity to inflict their drama and abuse on me and my family. They knew I was getting stronger, and they were losing their grip on me. It had gotten to the point where I hardly ever spoke to birth-father and pretty much never saw him. Hence, the joint counseling idea, a typical narcissistic black-hole Hoovering attempt to suck me back in and get me trapped in the same room with him, having to talk to him and listen to more of his abuse. Daddy Darling always loved a captive audience.

And an important part of that audience would have been the therapist himself. Someone who was getting paid to listen respectfully to Daddy Darling and take him seriously while he dominated the whole conversation with his mind games and perversions of the truth. Someone who was supposed to be "neutral"~ meaning able to be swayed to *his* side by the wiles of the psychopath (remember, psychopaths always underestimate everyone else's intelligence and insight). Someone whose job it was to actually pay attention to the narcissist. Someone who, in birth-father's opinion, would have no choice but to allow him to control and take over with his drama~ while I would sit there, trapped like a rat, session after session, never getting any of my points addressed, my blood pressure skyrocketing as my abuser did his best to undermine my credibility and make me look like a crazy person. What better source of narcissistic supply could there be than weekly meetings with two people stuck in the same room with him for an hour, forced to listen to every pearl of wisdom and outrageous fabrication that drooled out of his mouth? And you can bet it would have been quite a show!

Study after study on narcissists and psychopaths shows that therapy does not work for them. They do not change, and they are never "cured." They manipulate and toy with therapists, play mind games, lie and twist everything. You cannot possibly make any progress in therapy if all you are going to do is lie, deny, try to make the therapist feel sorry for you, and blame everyone else for your problems and the problems *you* cause~ and that is exactly what narcissists and psychopaths do. They also use therapy to learn psychological jargon and the latest fad "personality disorders," so they can use them as excuses for why they behave the way they do. Then they can claim they're "sick" and can't help it, and try to get sympathy for themselves.

Your abusive parent is not going to change. *If she really wanted to change so badly, then she would go to counseling without you. The reason she's willing to go to counseling* ***with*** *you is not to change* ***her,*** *but to change* ***you.*** Back to the way you were before you decided to grow a backbone and start standing up to her. Everything was fine before *you* up and went crazy and changed it all. She also wants to get the therapist on her side~ and get him thinking, and trying to convince you as well, that *you* are at least part of the problem. If the therapist shows even a hint of neutrality, she will take it as confirmation that "a professional" thinks *you* have a problem, and you will never hear the end of it.

Also, keep in mind that your abuser is *not* going to keep your counseling sessions confidential. She will repeat and twist anything you say, to make herself look good to others and make *you* look like the nut-job. At the very least she will let the rest of the family know that you are in therapy with her. Since it's *her* therapy, too, she will claim that she has the right to tell anyone she wants to about it. She will also do everything she can to imply, if not state outright, that *you* are having "issues" that you need help with, and make it seem like she is heroically donating her time to help you. It's a huge mistake to make yourself vulnerable to an abuser unless you want your personal business~ *or rather, her version of your personal business~* blabbed to anyone who will listen and give her narcissistic supply. If you go into counseling with her in good faith, and speak about your feelings openly and honestly, *rest assured that every word you say will eventually be used against you.* With narcissists and psychopaths, I have always found it much safer to play it close to the vest and never let them know what I'm really thinking.

Relationship therapists often insist on *separate* counseling first, before they will see a couple together, so that each one can work on his or her own issues before they try to work out their joint issues. However, in my case, my "issue" was not that I was sick, neurotic, or had mental or emotional problems, despite the fact that my parents would have loved to make me believe that, and were in fact trying to make it seem that way. My "issue" was that I was finally growing, becoming healthy and getting stronger, by the grace of God. This was a *good* thing, not something I needed therapy to undo.

My answer to my birth-mother's "generous" offer was "No, thanks." I informed her that I did not need counseling, because there was nothing wrong with me. It did not matter what any counselor might say, anyway. I had already made up my mind that I was unwilling to continue having a relationship with birth-father if *he* did not change. The one who had something wrong with him was *him.*

However, I did offer a compromise, which I thought was quite reasonable, and certainly more than I owed to either of them. I agreed to cooperate with therapy for *him*, on *my* terms. I told birth-mother that her husband could pick the therapist of his choice, and I would be willing to have a telephone consultation with whomever he picked and bring them up to speed on what the problems were from my perspective. They could then go to work on him with my best wishes. And after six months of therapy for *him,* I would be willing to once again speak on the phone with the therapist to discuss what, if any, progress he felt they were making. First of all, I wanted to see if birth-father was serious enough about changing *himself* to make a commitment to long-term therapy. And second of all, this was all the time and effort I was willing to devote to making *him* normal. He wasn't worth any more than that, and it was a losing proposition anyway. I also agreed to continue consulting by telephone every six months until such time as I was satisfactorily convinced that Daddy Darling was genuinely changing, and only then would I consider a face-to-face joint meeting with the therapist present. I made it clear that I was in no rush and would not be pressured. I would only take it *very* slowly.

Not to worry~ we never got that far. I never heard another word about therapy. My control freak parents were not about to "obey" me and allow *me* to take control by setting *my own* terms and conditions for *my own* cooperation. And of course, my abusive father was neither interested in going, nor willing to go, if it meant that *he* would be the one doing the work and making the changes. He had no desire to change. He never intended to go in good faith, so he was not interested in going alone. He would only go to *joint* therapy, because he wanted *me* to change, and go back to the way I was, once again accepting his abuse. His other motivation for only going *with* me was that this was yet another attempt to control me, by forcing me to sit in a room and talk to him, or rather, listen to *him* talk. So much for being sincerely willing to look at himself and be accountable for his own unacceptable behavior. This whole charade had just been another one of my birth-parents' manipulations.

Just because you are refusing to be abused anymore does not mean there is something wrong with you. You do not need to be "fixed." I have a huge problem with giving an abuser any ammunition by which to claim, and to tell other people, that his *victim* is the one with the mental problems. So, if your abuser or her Silent Partner ever suggests it, be very cautious about an offer for *joint* therapy. It's extremely doubtful that it's coming from a sincere desire to change and restore your relationship, and all the other relationships she has damaged as well. Someone who is accountable and willing to admit that *they* are causing *their own* relationship problems would be eager to change. They would get themselves into counseling ASAP, and would not make *your* attendance a condition of *them* going into therapy so that they could improve the way *they* relate to people and make *their own* lives better. The one who has a problem is your abuser, and if she is serious about accepting the responsibility for the results of her own actions, then she should be willing to go into therapy alone and work on herself. You will know she's really trying if and when you begin to see some positive changes.

There is no psychology in the Bible. Therapy for abusers is not their victim's burden. The biblical view of abusive people is not that they are suffering from some sickness or mental disorder requiring patience and sympathy. The Bible tells us that people who abuse others are *evil*, not sick. They *choose* to cause pain for others. Our only obligation is to rebuke them in the hope that they will see the light, and to forgive them *only* if they repent (change). *We have absolutely no obligation to "help" them change; in fact we are warned against having continued contact with them.* If they do not change their ways, then we are instructed to have nothing more to do with them (Luke 17:3; Matthew 18:15-17; Titus 3:10-11, etc.)

WARN A DIVISIVE PERSON ONCE, AND THEN WARN HIM A SECOND TIME. AFTER THAT, HAVE NOTHING TO DO WITH HIM. YOU MAY BE SURE THAT SUCH A MAN IS WARPED AND SINFUL; HE IS SELF-CONDEMNED.....Titus 3:10-11 NIV.

CHAPTER 18

"MY DAYS ARE NUMBERED" (AND YOU'RE SPEEDING IT UP BY CONFRONTING ME) OR, "I'M SICK, SO YOU CAN'T HOLD ME ACCOUNTABLE"

IS ANY ONE OF YOU SICK? HE SHOULD CALL THE ELDERS OF THE CHURCH TO PRAY OVER HIM AND ANOINT HIM WITH OIL IN THE NAME OF THE LORD. AND THE PRAYER OFFERED IN FAITH WILL MAKE THE SICK PERSON WELL; THE LORD WILL RAISE HIM UP. IF HE HAS SINNED, HE WILL BE FORGIVEN. THEREFORE CONFESS YOUR SINS TO EACH OTHER AND PRAY FOR EACH OTHER SO THAT YOU MAY BE HEALED....James 5:14-16 NIV.

WHEN A WICKED MAN DIES, HIS HOPE PERISHES; ALL HE EXPECTED FROM HIS POWER COMES TO NOTHING.... Proverbs 11:7 NIV.

Sooner or later, every narcissist and sociopath tries a pity ploy of one kind or another. The pity ploy is designed to make you feel sorry for your abuser and guilty for confronting her, so you will relent from expecting her to be accountable for her own behavior.

After my birth-mother died, I had to sue my birth-father for the return of the money he had stolen out of the trust account my mother left for me, and for the diamond jewelry she had willed to me, which he claimed he couldn't find~ actually expecting us to believe that he sold his house with my mother's diamonds in it. During the proceedings, the judge asked him by what date he could have the jewelry appraised. Daddy Darling hemmed and hawed, trying to avoid making a commitment. First he said he didn't know, because he had doctors' appointments coming up. The judge repeated the question, and he continued to stall, saying he had to take a trip to the V.A. Hospital to pick up his prescriptions. The pity ploy wasn't working too well on the savvy judge, who repeated his question one last time. Assuming the judge must be too dense to get his point, Daddy Darling sighed heavily and tried making it a little clearer with, "You know, I'm not a well man…." To which the judge, now out of patience, banged his gavel down and said, "Two weeks!"

Fast forward to ten years later. Seven of those years, Daddy Darling had spent stalking me and my family, until we finally moved away. As I mentioned previously in Chapter 10, a few weeks before we left, he accosted my husband in the street in front of our house and requested a meeting (to be kept secret from me), which he didn't get. Instead, I proceeded to write him a long letter detailing decades of his abuse and instructing him not to contact me or my family again until and unless he met my conditions, which included the appropriate apologies, repentance and restitution. We never heard back from him, and shortly thereafter we moved, leaving no forwarding address.

Control freaks hate it when they lose control. They typically panic when you get away from them, and become obsessed with finding you again. It took him almost three years to locate us, but eventually birth-father managed to get my unlisted phone number and call me.

CORRECTION IS GRIEVOUS UNTO HIM THAT FORSAKETH THE WAY: AND HE THAT HATETH REPROOF SHALL DIE….
Proverbs 15:10 KJV.

Once he had me on the phone, there was no hint of an apology, no attempt to make things right, and no promise of change. *In fact, he completely ignored every single condition I had set forth in my letter.* Instead, after a decade-long estrangement and a minute or two of pretending that he was thrilled to hear my voice and wanted to be back in the family, he became enraged when he realized that I still intended to hold him accountable. When I refused to give him my adult children's phone numbers and other private information without their permission, he had his usual meltdown~ screaming at me, threatening, and calling me names. He tried to blackmail me, yelling that he would not put my children back in his will if I did not give him information about them. Yes, he had disowned them~ punishing his "grandsons" along with their mother. Nobody cared about being in his will and no one ever asked him for a dime, but he still thought he could use his money to control us. Of course, as soon as any of us did anything he didn't like, my children would be right back out of his will. Eventually, when he failed to coerce my cooperation, he slammed the phone down in my ear.

After this, his new wife and I spoke briefly. I told her what had happened, that it was obvious he hadn't changed a bit, and that my family and I were not interested in going back to the way things were with him. She agreed that he hadn't changed. And then she added, "You know, he only has a few years left." To which I gave my stock reply, "Yeah, well, maybe he'd better think about that."

THE EVIL DEEDS OF A WICKED MAN ENSNARE HIM; THE CORDS OF HIS SIN HOLD HIM FAST. HE WILL DIE FOR LACK OF DISCIPLINE, LED ASTRAY BY HIS OWN GREAT FOLLY....
Proverbs 5:22-23 NIV.

A week later, I wrote him another note spelling out my conditions for ever speaking to him again~ an apology for the way he had acted on the phone as well as the things he had done in the past, and proof that he had changed his ways, including a guarantee that there would be no further voice-raising, name-calling, threats, blackmail, hang-ups, or disrespect of any kind. He responded two weeks after that with yet another blackmail attempt, this time voided checks to be replaced only if we called him by a specific date. None of us ever replied to him.

After that, my family and I got an occasional holiday card, which we ignored, just like *he* persisted in ignoring my terms. The last time, he included a message, written in heavy black marker and big capital letters to convey the sense of urgency characteristic of an estranged abuser's attempt to suck you back into the relationship. "My days are numbered!" it said, "I want to see or hear from you and your family." But still no apology, no offer to make amends, and no promise of change. It was all about what *he* wanted, with no mention at all of anything I had said *I* wanted. As usual, *my* conditions and desires were completely ignored, and *his* were all that mattered. He wanted contact, but he didn't want it badly enough to apologize and agree to treat us all nicely. Once again, he got no response from me, and he never would. Because as long as he continued to ignore what *I* wanted, which he did for the rest of his life, then he wasn't going to get what *he* wanted, either.

JUST AS MAN IS DESTINED TO DIE ONCE, AND AFTER THAT TO FACE JUDGMENT....Hebrews 9:27 NIV.

What is interesting in this whole crazy-making chronicle is the psychopath's consistent use of the pity ploy, even though it's not working. Three times in this decade-and-a-half-long saga, either he or his wife alluded to him having some mysterious ailment for which he should be given a free pass, or hinted and expected that I should give him whatever he wanted without requiring anything in return from him, because, after all, he's got one foot in the grave. To hear him tell it, by this point he had been on borrowed time for the last fifteen years. And yet, he was still well enough for all of his usual conniving, plotting, manipulating, screaming, scheming, name-calling and bullying. You'd think that instead of antagonizing his victims even *more*, someone who *really* thought his days were numbered would spend whatever time he had left mending fences and making amends for all the wrongs he did in his life, so that he could die in peace and be right with God.

When you finally start to stand up to your abuser, confront, set boundaries, or limit your exposure to her, don't be surprised to hear that all of a sudden she's a sick woman, when all along she seemed as healthy as a horse, and certainly hale and hearty enough to heap abuse on you and cause all kinds of family upheaval. Your abuser might announce this herself, or she might have a Silent Partner/Flying Monkey do it for her. Playing sick gives the impression that your abuser couldn't possibly be doing what you say she is, because she's much too frail to be abusing you. And telling other people that you're aggravating her so much you're making her sick has the added benefit of making *you* look heartless. Gullible or meddling friends and relatives will just eat this nonsense up.

You can expect to hear various hints, histrionics and drama along the lines of:

- "I'm not well."
- "I'm a sick man *(and you're making me sicker)*."
- "Your mother is old and not in the best of health. She shouldn't have to deal with these family problems *(that **she** causes)*."
- "I don't have a lot of time left *(so you'd better enjoy me while you can!)*."
- "All this arguing is making me sick."
- "My doctor says I can't have any more stress."

- "Your father is getting older. You might never see him again. Aren't you going to feel bad if something happens to him and you were on the outs?"
- "I have to go for tests next week." *(said mysteriously and with an ominous tone and expression.)*
- "I'm so depressed over the things you said to me that my doctor had to increase my medication."
- "You're the one who changed. You used to be so easy to get along with *(because you used to tolerate her abuse)*. I don't even know you anymore! Why are you trying to drive me crazy?"
- "Why do you keep upsetting me like this? You're going to give me a stroke!"
- "This constant arguing is killing me. I can't take it anymore."
- "You're giving me a headache."
- "You're giving me an ulcer."
- "You're giving me heart trouble."
- "You're killing me!"
- "I'm up all night crying because of the terrible things you said."
- "You know I have high blood pressure. Why are you making it worse?"
- "You know I have health problems. Can't we just let bygones be bygones? Talking about this is not good for me"
- "I can't keep fighting like this. I just want to live in peace."
- "All I want to do is die in peace."

A variation on this theme is the abuser who actually *does* apologize, or at least concedes some of your points, because she's "too sick to argue with you anymore." She'll make it clear that you're *forcing* her to agree with whatever you say, because you are making her "sick" or worsening her condition by expecting her to behave herself.

She'll pretty much tell you that she doesn't really mean it, but is just apologizing to get you to drop it, since you're upsetting her so much. An abuser might even say, "I'm too sick to argue with you, so alright, I'm sorry!" or, "Okay, I apologize. I can't take any more of this," or, best of all, "I just want peace in the family." Don't believe it and don't pay any attention to a phony, self-serving apology.

These statements are what I like to call "Nonsense Statements." They don't actually mean anything of any importance or relevance, and are simply another diversion. They do not constitute any accountability or any admission of wrongdoing. They're the same as saying, "I didn't do anything wrong. But I'll tell you what you want to hear, because that's the only way to get you to stop upsetting me by holding me accountable for what I do. I'll tell you and everyone else that you're making me sick. I don't care if a lifetime of enduring my abuse is making *you* sick. And I don't mean a word I'm saying. I'll just pretend to smooth things over because now it's affecting *me*."

AS I HAVE OBSERVED, THOSE WHO PLOW EVIL AND THOSE WHO SOW TROUBLE REAP IT. AT THE BREATH OF GOD THEY ARE DESTROYED....Job 4:8-9 NIV.

Before you accept any guilt in this situation, realize that the assertions your abuser is making about his health and who's responsible for it are all twisted backwards. *By confronting your abuser, you are* ***not*** *making him sick. He's making* ***himself*** *sick (and he's making everybody else sick, too) because of his unacceptable behavior.* If he's so concerned about his health, then he needs to stop doing whatever he's doing that's making it necessary for you to confront him.

All the discord *starts* with your abuser and his behavior. *He* is the one who is causing all the upset in the family, *not you.* If he wasn't misbehaving, then you would have nothing to confront him about, his so-called health wouldn't suffer, and he would be able to live in the peace he claims he longs for. It is the height of arrogance to suggest that he should be permitted to continue abusing other people as much as he wants, and no one even has the right to protest, or *they* are being the "troublemakers." All he has to do is just *stop.* And then there will be nothing to fight about. You are not responsible for an abuser's health and not to blame for his medical issues, if in fact any actually exist.

Sometimes, an abuser might have a legitimate health problem, although she will probably exaggerate it greatly to engender as much sympathy as possible. In which case, *we would need to ask ourselves why* ***she*** *persists in causing the arguments that are supposedly negatively impacting her own health.* Really sick people have more important things on their minds and other things to worry about than bullying or controlling us.

However, in many cases, our abuser's so-called "illness" is entirely fabricated. It's usually vaguely alluded to and mysteriously hinted at, with no details given. Notice that my birth-father said his "days were numbered," *but he didn't say why.* There were no specifics, no mention at all of heart problems, cancer, or any other illnesses. Technically, *all* our days are numbered, aren't they? Eventually, we're *all* going to die. Is that supposed to give *all of us* the right to do as much damage to other people as we can while we're still alive?

At the time he sent this message, Daddy Darling still drove his car, ran errands, took care of business, socialized, showed up at family events such as funerals, and kept in touch with people who he didn't know were talking to me. For all I knew, he still played golf and took his boat out to go fishing. He had been "sick" with who-knows-what-because-he-never-said for over fifteen years by then, and yet he was still going strong. It was entirely possible for him to be prowling the earth ten years down the road. He might even have outlived me! In fact, he lived another seven healthy years with no serious illnesses (a total of *twenty-two years* of supposedly being on his last legs!), and died at the ripe old age of ninety-three after a few days in the county home, where his relatives put him when he got too hard to handle.

I rarely suggest giving narcissists any more attention. It's far better to completely ignore their drama. But if you really want to get to the bottom of your abuser's claims, then start asking questions. Like, *exactly what illnesses are we talking about here*, specific types of tests, dates of tests, test results, treatments and medications given, procedures she's had, the next steps in treatment, referrals made, and doctor's names and phone numbers~ and settle for nothing less than every minute little detail. *Do not accept any vague or evasive answers.* Keep questioning until you get sensible information and direct answers.

Your abuser's responses will give you a clue as to whether her "disease" is exaggerated, or even an outright lie. Hey, maybe there really *is* a genuine illness that *you* might need to talk to her doctor about. *Which of course, you would not do without* ***telling her*** *you're going to call the doctor and insisting she sign the patient privacy permission form for you to speak with him~ and then observing her reaction.* If she's telling the truth, then she won't have anything to hide, and she should have no problem with you talking directly to her doctor. If she goes ballistic or protests you having a little chat with her doctor, then you can pretty much figure she's hiding something. Don't let her turn it around now and tell you that her medical problem is none of your business. Remember, *she made it your business*, because *she's* the one who *told* you about it in the first place, and then tried to use it as an excuse for not being able to resolve the problems between you. So it's hardly a secret anymore.

ALL GO UNTO ONE PLACE; ALL ARE OF DUST, AND ALL TURN TO DUST AGAIN....Ecclesiastes 3:20 KJV.

Probably the most important thing to keep in mind is, if our relative is really so sick, then how come she is still perfectly capable of causing so much family chaos? Why does she always seem to be at the center of whatever turmoil is going on? Where on earth is she getting the strength? If she doesn't feel well, then shouldn't she be minding her own health and resting, instead of conniving, bullying, manipulating and controlling? You'd think she wouldn't feel up to all that. A *really* sick person wouldn't have the energy for it. She'd have other things to concentrate on and worry about, like her impending doom. Abusers are always healthy enough to *start* a fight, but when you stand up to them, all of a sudden they're not healthy enough to *finish* it. If your abuser really has health issues like high blood pressure, heart problems or ulcers, then shouldn't she be concerned enough about her own health to avoid starting problems that are supposedly going to aggravate her illnesses? Why should *you* worry about raising her blood pressure when *she* doesn't? How serious could it be, if she doesn't care about it herself, and is still willing and able to cause all of these problems?

To break free of the guilt mode, it helps to throw the responsibility for her own health, stress and depression right back into our abuser's lap. We need to replace our relative's pity ploy with a mantra of our own:

- When she says, "My doctor says I can't have more any stress," we say, "*I* am not giving you stress. *You're giving yourself stress,* and you're giving it to everybody else, too."
- When she says, "You're making me sick," we say, "*I* am not making you sick. *You're making yourself sick.* And you're making *me* sick, too."
- When she says, "I have a bad heart," we say, "If you're so worried about your heart, then you should stop causing all this trouble."

- When she says, "You're making my depression worse," we say, "Then why don't you try being nice and getting along with people? I'm sure that would make you happier."
- When she says, "I don't have much time left," we say, "Well then, you'd better get to work making amends for all the bad things you've done, before your time runs out!"
- When she says, "All this arguing is killing me," we say, "Then stop arguing. Just apologize and agree to respect my boundaries. It's *your* choice."
- When she says, "I just want to live in peace," we say, "That's up to *you*. You're the one causing all the problems. Just knock it off, start being nice, and then we can *all* live in peace."
- When her Silent Partner/Flying Monkey says, "Your mother is old and sick and shouldn't be dealing with all of these problems," we say, "My mother shouldn't be *creating* all of these problems for *the rest of us* to have to deal with."
- When she says, "You're driving me crazy!", we say, "It's too late for that. You were *born* crazy." Oops, was that naughty of me? Sorry, I couldn't resist!

Sisters and Brothers, don't allow your abuser to twist and confuse the situation, and don't accept any guilt that he or his Silent Partners might try to lay at your doorstep. It is our relative's abuse that causes all the problems, arguments, disagreements and fights, not our reaction to his abuse. The buck stops with the abuser himself. As soon as he decides to start behaving himself and treating us nicely, then all the problems will disappear. The price for this would be giving up his control and abuse, and then he could spend the time he has left on earth doing what he says he wants so badly~ enjoying his family and living in peace. But he doesn't want it that badly, now does he?

IF YOUR HAND CAUSES YOU TO SIN, CUT IT OFF. IT IS BETTER FOR YOU TO ENTER LIFE MAIMED THAN WITH TWO HANDS TO GO INTO HELL, WHERE THE FIRE NEVER GOES OUT. AND IF YOUR FOOT CAUSES YOU TO SIN, CUT IT OFF. IT IS BETTER FOR YOU TO ENTER LIFE CRIPPLED THAN TO HAVE TWO FEET AND BE THROWN INTO HELL. AND IF YOUR EYE CAUSES YOU TO SIN, PLUCK IT OUT. IT IS BETTER FOR YOU TO ENTER THE KINGDOM OF GOD WITH ONE EYE THAN TO HAVE TWO EYES AND BE THROWN INTO HELL.... Mark 9:43-47 NIV.

IT IS BETTER TO GO TO A HOUSE OF MOURNING THAN TO GO TO A HOUSE OF FEASTING, FOR DEATH IS THE DESTINY OF EVERY MAN; THE LIVING SHOULD TAKE THIS TO HEART....Ecclesiastes 7:2 NIV.

FOR THE WAGES OF SIN IS DEATH; BUT THE GIFT OF GOD IS ETERNAL LIFE THROUGH JESUS CHRIST OUR LORD..... Romans 6:23 KJV.

CHAPTER 19

"I'M ONLY HUMAN!" ....AND NOBODY'S PERFECT ....AND HUMAN BEINGS ARE ALL SELFISH ....AND I MAKE MISTAKES JUST LIKE EVERYBODY ELSE

WHEREFORE BY THEIR FRUITS YE SHALL KNOW THEM...
Matthew 7:20 KJV.

EVEN A CHILD IS KNOWN BY HIS DOINGS, WHETHER HIS WORK BE PURE, AND WHETHER IT BE RIGHT...Proverbs 20:11 KJV.

I'M ONLY HUMAN....

This lame excuse for abuse is the condensed version of "Hey, what do you expect from me? After all, I'm only human." It will often be accompanied by some type of theatrics for emphasis~ feigned frustration, phony impatience, crocodile tears, or a casual shrug. All intended to convey how silly and unreasonable *you* are being for expecting accountability and proper behavior from a mere human being.

Right off the bat, I take issue with the "I'm Only Human" claim. Psychopaths are not human~ at least not like *we* think of humans.

They lack the basics of what makes someone a human being~ a conscience, for starters. Not to mention any feelings or emotions that aren't negative and destructive. They manage to feel anger, selfishness, hatred, resentment, envy and jealousy (although a lot of that is just an act, too), but they do not feel empathy, kindness, sympathy, mercy, compassion, pity, remorse or love. They view those who are "stupid" and "weak" enough to have such emotions with contempt and scorn, including the people who love them. In their minds, your stupidity and weakness is what makes you *deserve* what they do to you.

Humans have morals and abide by a code of ethics acceptable in human society. Psychopaths are completely *amoral.* They do not consider themselves to be a part of human society, and see no reason to abide by its rules. A psychopath will use, abuse, and even destroy anyone they perceive as vulnerable, without batting an eye, as long as it suits them. Their relentless cruelty to innocent human beings, both children and adults, as well as helpless animals, is how they get their kicks. They do it just for amusement. Your life is merely a game to them, and if something is important to you, that's reason enough to spoil it or destroy it, just to show you who's more powerful. That's what they consider "winning" the game. They enjoy watching the suffering of others. In fact, they *love* it. They are soulless predators disguised as humans, the better to walk amongst us undetected. Ruthless, remorseless, malevolent, primitive, reptilian evil~ encased in a human shell. *Just because it **looks** like a human being, doesn't make it one, any more than a figure in the wax museum is a real human.*

...AND NOBODY'S PERFECT

This is a Nonsense Statement. Whether or not there are any perfect people in the world is completely irrelevant to the fact that an evil person is abusing you and you are confronting her for it. Yes, nobody's perfect and everybody has their flaws, but not everybody's "flaws" include bullying, manipulating, conning, lying or abuse. Harmless little quirks are not in the same category as behavior that damages other people. You don't have to be *perfect,* you just have to be *nice.* Your so-called "imperfections" do not give you the right to hurt anybody else.

The "Nobody's Perfect" premise is an example of black-and-white thinking. If you can't claim to be perfect, which your psychopath or narcissist already knows your humility won't allow you to do, then your only other choice is to be an abuser. There's no happy medium. So unless you claim perfection, then you are just as bad as your abuser is~ you just don't want to admit it. This is an absurd statement, with no logic behind it. Let's not get side-tracked here. Regardless of the "imperfections" of other people, the fact remains that *this one person* is causing pain and harm for people who don't deserve such treatment, and most of the *other* "flawed human beings" are not.

....AND HUMAN BEINGS ARE ALL SELFISH

No, they're not. In fact, without even thinking about it, I can rattle off at least two dozen people I know personally who don't have a selfish bone in their bodies. If I take a few minutes, I can come up with plenty more. I know dozens of people who have literally spent their lives serving the Lord, doing good deeds and sacrificing to help others, while not expecting or receiving any payback, and who have never benefited themselves at someone else's expense.

I've heard abusers use this argument to justify their abuse many times, and my response is "Speak for yourself." Not only are most people *not* inherently selfish, but some of the *least* selfish people in the world are survivors of child abuse, most of whom have been raised to put other people before themselves at all times and no matter what.

Many abused children have been "parentified," expected to run the household, raise younger siblings, take on adult responsibilities, and take care of their parents and solve their problems. My birth-mother frequently complimented me on how "unselfish" I was and told me that my birth-sister was not like me~ she was "more selfish" and "not as generous." I was chosen to fill the caretaker role, and birth-sis was not. So our mother reinforced "unselfishness" in me, but did not expect it of her other daughter.

This childhood brainwashing molds our adult personalities into compliant, selfless, patient, long-suffering and uncomplaining caretakers whose own needs never get met, and sets us up as prey for predators and targets for abusers for the rest of our lives. I spent my entire childhood caring for my neglectful and abusive parents, their other child, and their house. No self-preservation or self-defense was allowed, much less outright selfishness. They continued to take full advantage of my generosity and self-sacrificing personality long into my adulthood. Finally, I had to *learn* to put my own needs first, and to internalize the concept that it wasn't "bad" of me to do that. I had to force myself to be a little "selfish" sometimes, just as a matter of survival, and it was very uncomfortable for me. One of the biggest problems that abuse victims have is their extreme reluctance to set boundaries, *because they don't want to be "selfish."* Of all the good, kind, caring, giving, generous *unselfish* people in the world, abuse survivors top the list, even to their own detriment.

It is ironic that selfishness is literally ***the*** *defining trait of narcissists, psychopaths and abusers, and yet they dare to project this same trait onto everybody else, in an attempt to make it sound like normal human behavior.*

The "Selfish" premise states that selfishness is universal among human beings. Your abuser can't be one of the unselfish humans, because there *are* no unselfish humans. That is a ridiculous statement to make, and a complete lie.

....AND I MAKE MISTAKES JUST LIKE EVERYBODY ELSE

Yeah, but everybody else's "mistakes" don't cause harm to other people on a regular basis, and the abuser's "mistakes" do.

Let's start off by defining a "mistake." A mistake is something you do *accidentally, unintentionally* or *inadvertently.* There is no such thing as "accidentally" abusing someone, so abuse cannot be defined as an all-too-human "mistake." Your abuser's "mistakes" are repeated over and over again, because he knows he can get away with it with someone who loves him. He uses your love for him against you. Abuse is an ongoing pattern of behavior, often planned out in advance, and carried out with callous disregard for the feelings and welfare of the victim. It isn't just a little "whoopsie." People who make genuine mistakes apologize and make sure it doesn't happen again. They don't keep repeating the same "mistake" over and over again.

Have you ever watched a talk show and seen a husband who cheated on his wife (with her sister or best friend, just to make it interesting) turn the "blame" around and pretend to lose patience with his wife's continued lack of trust in him? Time and again, I have watched cheaters, both male and female, state something to the effect of, "Yes, *I've made some mistakes.* But that was in the past, and I'm sick of you not trusting me now. You need to get over it." None of them ever explain how you can possibly have an affair "by mistake." What, you didn't know you were having sex? You thought you were imagining it? You "accidentally" slept with someone other than your spouse? How? You forgot what your wife looked like and mistook her best friend for her? Just an innocent little mistake, right? Just for once, I would love to hear somebody explain exactly how it is possible to "accidentally" have sex~ with anyone!

You cannot gossip and lie about someone "by mistake." There is no such thing as "accidentally" gossiping or "unintentionally" telling a lie. You can only make a conscious decision to do it, because you *want* to and you don't care about the pain you will be causing. You cannot lie *to* someone "by mistake." You can only lie on purpose, because you are a liar.

Exactly how is it possible to "accidentally" snoop through somebody else's closets? Were you sleep-walking? How is it possible to "mistakenly" pry into someone else's business, or "accidentally" ask nosy questions and try to get information about your child from one of her friends?

Criticizing or belittling another person is not a "mistake." How is it a "mistake" when you raise your voice at another adult? Or call them a name? Are you trying to say that you made a mistake and called them the *wrong* name, when you meant to call them a *different* name?

You cannot "accidentally" steal from or con a relative. You cannot cheat your child or your friend "by mistake." You make a *decision* to steal, cheat or con someone.

There is no such thing as "accidentally" disowning your adult child, so you did not "make a mistake" when you did it.

It is not possible to "unintentionally" fill out and sign credit applications in your brother's name, or to "inadvertently" identify yourself as your sister and steal her identity. There is no such thing.

You cannot sexually molest your child "by mistake." Yes, even if you're drunk or on drugs~ that is still no excuse. You did it because you *wanted* to do it.

If your adult child has already asked you to stop saying or doing something that is upsetting him or his wife, and you do it again after being warned, you cannot claim you "didn't know it would upset him," so you "made a mistake." You knew, because you were told. But you chose to do it anyway. That is not an "accident" or a "mistake." That is a deliberate choice on your part. You don't "accidentally" do something you have already been asked in plain English not to do.

Maybe you're defining a mistake as making a decision that turned out to be poor judgment. In that case, you are *admitting* that you made a deliberate decision. You intentionally chose to do something that would hurt someone else. You didn't do it "accidentally," and you didn't do it "by mistake." It might not have turned out to be the wisest decision on your part, but it was a *decision* nonetheless. The only thing that was unintentional on your part was that you got caught. You rolled the dice, knowing it was detrimental to your relative or friend, but you didn't care. And you didn't get away with it. You got found out. If no harm was intended, but harm resulted anyway, then you wouldn't hesitate to genuinely apologize and be remorseful. Only a sociopathic abuser would not admit she deliberately did wrong and got caught, because that would cause a power shift in the relationship. It would mean she screwed up and lost the game.

The "Everybody Makes Mistakes" premise presumes that the definition of a "mistake" includes deliberate malice, and that "everybody" maliciously abuses other people and then calls it a "mistake," which they most certainly do not. No matter how you slice it, abuse does not qualify as an innocent mistake. It is impossible to "accidentally" abuse someone. Abusers don't make "mistakes." They make *choices.*

Narcissists and psychopaths are hardly qualified to make sweeping statements about human nature. They are far too self-absorbed to observe others with an unbiased eye. They only observe you long enough to learn your weaknesses so they can exploit them. And, as we've already said, they assume that everyone else is just like them, only dumber. Just as selfish, just as manipulative, just as dishonest, and just as evil. Imagine if we *all* decided to behave the way they do~ because, after all, we're *all* "only human"~ and what's good for the goose is good for the gander, isn't it? Do you think they'd let *us* get away with it?

Evil always disguises itself as good. That's the only way it can continue to operate. Even Satan disguised himself as an angel of light.

Abusers use the "I'm Only Human" excuse to make their behavior sound as if it was *normal,* and *you're* the one who has something wrong with you because you didn't realize your abuser is no different than anybody else, including you. How stupid are you not to understand that *everybody* behaves this way and does these things? Yes, the implication is that *you,* too, are guilty of imperfection, selfishness and "mistakes" that cause *you* to abuse other people. When you confront your abuser and he uses the "I'm Only Human" excuse, he's telling you that you're no better than he is, because, after all, we're *all* "only human." You have no right to complain about his perfectly "normal" human behavior, because *you're* not perfect, either. You're just as selfish as everybody else, and you make mistakes, too.

He's also telling you that he can't help it and he's always going to act this way. *Because changing his behavior would mean going against human nature itself, you can never expect him to stop.* The "I'm Only Human" excuses are twisted, flawed logic, exactly the kind of convoluted, confusing, crazy-making mind-games narcissists and psychopaths play to allow them to continue getting away with abuse. They love to play innocent, and the pity ploy is one of their little tricks. They know that we *are* human, and human nature causes us to be inclined to give those we love the benefit of the doubt. We *want* to trust them, and we *want* to believe them. All they have to do is pretend they'd love to change if only they could, put on a good enough act, and *we'll* wind up feeling sorry for *them.*

If we continue to insist they change something they're not capable of changing, that would make *us* unreasonable and mean. *We* would be the bad guys, for making them feel bad about themselves. After all, it's not their fault. Nothing is ever their fault. They're only human. The next time your psychopathic abuser claims to be "only human," it might help to remind yourself that *no,* it's not.

PUT ON THE WHOLE ARMOUR OF GOD, THAT YE MAY BE ABLE TO STAND AGAINST THE WILES OF THE DEVIL. FOR WE WRESTLE NOT AGAINST FLESH AND BLOOD, BUT AGAINST PRINCIPALITIES, AGAINST POWERS, AGAINST THE RULERS OF THE DARKNESS OF THIS WORLD, AGAINST SPIRITUAL WICKEDNESS IN HIGH PLACES. WHEREFORE TAKE UNTO YOU THE WHOLE ARMOUR OF GOD, THAT YE MAY BE ABLE TO WITHSTAND IN THE EVIL DAY, AND HAVING DONE ALL, TO STAND....Ephesians 6:11-13 KJV.

CHAPTER 20

PRESUMPTUOUSNESS AND SPIRITUAL BULLYING

THEY ZEALOUSLY COURT YOU, BUT FOR NO GOOD; YES, THEY WANT TO EXCLUDE YOU, THAT YOU MAY BE ZEALOUS FOR THEM...Galatians 4:17 NKJV.

FOR IF A MAN THINK HIMSELF TO BE SOMETHING, WHEN HE IS NOTHING, HE DECEIVETH HIMSELF. BUT LET EVERY MAN PROVE HIS OWN WORK, AND THEN SHALL HE HAVE REJOICING IN HIMSELF ALONE, AND NOT IN ANOTHER... Galatians 6:3-4 KJV.

The Spiritual Bully is a subspecies of the Christian Abuser. The biggest difference is that a Christian Abuser is usually a main character in your life~ a sibling, a parent, an old friend~ who uses a phony façade of religion and pretends to be a Christian in order to get away with abusing you, to pressure you to forgive unconditionally and continue overlooking ongoing abuse, or to make excuses for evil people who cause pain for others. A Spiritual Bully, on the other hand, is usually a peripheral player in your life, someone you barely know and who doesn't really know you personally or well, but who blindsides you with an unprovoked attack. Spiritual Bullies are ignorant and in-error holier-than-thous who beat other people over the head with their version of the Bible, butting in where it's none of their business and telling them "what God wants them to do," to show off their own (incorrect) biblical knowledge. Church families are ripe breeding grounds for Spiritual Bullies, and there's usually at least one, if not several, in every church.

Spiritual Bullies are often people you don't even notice until they barge in and interrupt the private conversation you were having with someone else (that the Spiritual Bully was eavesdropping on) to insist you are wrong, you are sinning, you are not doing what God wants you to do, your faith is not strong enough, or some other similar judgment and criticism of your walk with the Lord. They will then take the floor, and smugly and forcefully proceed to lecture you on what you should or should not be doing, according to their usually completely fictional idea of what the Bible says and what God wants. And then they will often end their unprovoked attack on you by generously announcing to you and their audience that they will be praying for you!

SPIRITUAL BULLIES ARE VERY PRESUMPTUOUS

A FOOL FINDS NO PLEASURE IN UNDERSTANDING BUT DELIGHTS IN AIRING HIS OWN OPINIONS…Proverbs 18:2 NIV.

HE THAT ANSWERETH A MATTER BEFORE HE HEARETH IT, IT IS FOLLY AND SHAME UNTO HIM…Proverbs 18:13 KJV.

Presumptuousness is a very common narcissistic trait. Because narcissists have no real interest in others, they don't bother actually finding out the facts before jumping to conclusions and making assumptions that other people know less than they do. The narcissist is the center of the universe, and everybody else is merely an extension of her. Therefore, she knows you well, even if you just met. If she would have a certain opinion, then *you* must have the same opinion. If, given a certain set of circumstances, she would feel a particular way, then *you* have to feel the same way too.

When someone who doesn't know you well assumes something about you, or proceeds to tell you how you will feel, what you think, what you want to do, what you believe, etc., there's a pretty good chance that person is a narcissist. One time a woman I had just met insisted that I *had to* miss my old location and would want to move back someday, five years after I had very happily moved away. It is now years later and I'm still happy in my new location and never even think about my old one. I don't miss anything about it because I hated it there, which was no secret to everyone who *really* knew me. Because *she* still lived where I used to live, it was threatening to this woman's ego that anyone would dislike her choice of living area enough to move away. Another man I had just been introduced to kept insisting that I *had to* be Catholic, because I'm Italian~ as if I don't know what religion I am, but *he* does. More than once I have witnessed a "religious" narcissist prosthelytize to or lecture someone she recently met on the Bible, without knowing the stranger she was preaching to was a pastor, and far better versed in the Word of God than she was. Insanity plus ignorance equals one very nervy, rude and presumptuous narcissist.

One day I would love to ask a narcissist, "I know you are special and nobody else is, but when you lecture and educate strangers, how do you know what that person already knows? When you brag about your PhD or use it to win an argument, what if the other person has *two* PhDs and just didn't choose to share his personal information with you or didn't want to sound like he was bragging? Before you show off and try to impress, if you've only known the other person for fifteen minutes and didn't bother asking him anything about himself, just remember he might be a bigger expert than you are!" Ah, but I'm forgetting. There is no such thing as a bigger expert than the superior, know-it-all narcissist.

ROBERTA, BILL, TOM AND SUSAN VERSUS SPIRITUAL BULLY CHURCH HARPIES

THE THIEF COMES ONLY TO STEAL AND KILL AND DESTROY; I HAVE COME THAT THEY MAY HAVE LIFE, AND HAVE IT TO THE FULL…John 10:10 NIV.

BUT LET NONE OF YOU SUFFER AS A MURDERER, OR AS A THIEF, OR AS AN EVILDOER, OR AS A BUSYBODY IN OTHER MEN'S MATTERS…1 Peter 4:15 KJV.

Roberta and Bill had good friends Tom and Susan come to visit them for a few days. On Sunday, they all attended Roberta and Bill's church. Roberta and Bill introduced Tom and Susan to their pastor and several members of the congregation before the service started, and let them know that Tom and Susan were both ministers. At the beginning of the service, the pastor introduced them to the rest of the congregation and welcomed them, but the late arrivals did not hear this.

After the service, folks were chatting in the lobby. Tom and Susan were asked about their family and passed around photos of their new grandson. They were being congratulated by members of the church, and glowed with joy as they talked about him. When asked what the baby's name was, Susan's eyes welled with tears as she answered that his name was Thomas, and that their daughter had named her baby after her father to honor him. Everyone smiled and basked in this heartwarming moment, until a screechy voice from the other side of the lobby began raving.

Marching over to the group, two holier-than-thou nutjobs started lecturing everybody that it was unbiblical to name a baby after anyone, that no one should be honored but God, and that we should never name a child after our earthly father because the Bible says we should call no man on earth father, for we only have one Father and he is in heaven (Matthew 23:9). Tom and Susan's smiles faded and their faces reddened with embarrassment, and Roberta and Bill were mortified, as were the other folks in the lobby.

These two harpies had arrived late and never heard the introductions. They did not know Tom and Susan were pastors, and far better versed in the Bible than they were, although I'm not sure knowing that would have made any difference in their compulsion to judge, bully, and "educate" other people. Without knowing a single thing, they decided it was their place to criticize and lecture complete strangers by literally beating them over the head with the Bible and their ignorant and incorrect interpretation of scripture. The newcomers were getting attention and they were not, so they had to put a stop to that! Now the attention was on *them,* the know-it-all know-nothings. Filled with the devil's smug and gleeful spirit, they had stolen Tom and Susan's joy in their new little grandchild, and everyone else's joy as well.

JULIA VERSUS SPIRITUAL BULLY MARGE

EVEN A FOOL IS THOUGHT WISE IF HE KEEPS SILENT, AND DISCERNING IF HE HOLDS HIS TONGUE…Proverbs 17:28 NIV.

Julia and her family attended church with a woman named Marge. Marge is a holier-than-thou-type, always preaching to those she considers her religious "inferiors" without really knowing anything about them, and telling them what they should or should not do according to her sometimes quite preposterous religious beliefs.

Julia has a variety of health issues that make it potentially very dangerous for her to get sick. Because of this, she cannot be, and does not want to be, hugged, kissed or touched by sick people. You would think this would be a no-brainer, and people who are sick would have the courtesy and consideration to tell other people before contaminating them or to avoid contact altogether, but apparently not. Julia's medical issues are private and she does not believe she should have to tell people she barely knows about her personal medical history, because it's really none of their business. I agree with her wholeheartedly, and I also have underlying medical conditions that make getting sick especially dangerous for me. However, because most churches we've attended greet with hugs and kisses, she and I have both sacrificed our privacy to explain why we need sick people to not touch us. In fact, we need them not to touch or hug the members of our families either~ first, because our families do not want them to, and second, because if someone in our household gets sick, they will then expose us to illness as well.

Marge made it clear from the beginning that she thought Julia's boundaries were foolish, and she had no intention of respecting them. Julia was having a private conversation with another church member about this subject, and neither of them realized that Marge was eavesdropping until she barged in and interrupted. In a loud voice she informed Julia and the other person that *she* didn't mind it at all if sick people hugged her. Julia told her it didn't matter whether Marge minded or not, *Julia* minded. Marge then proceeded to state that Julia's faith was not strong enough, and that she needed to trust Jesus more because he loved her and would not let her get sick from hugging sick people in church. It took Julia a few seconds to recover from the sheer stupidity of such a statement. When she did, she asked Marge if she was actually saying that Jesus didn't let believers get sick, because, obviously, we all know plenty of devout Christians who have been sick. Marge evaded the question and merely ranted on about Julia's lack of faith until Julia finally chose not to engage her further and walked away, annoyed at her nerve in judging her walk with the Lord when she barely knew her, and wondering about her motives in trying to bully her, embarrass her, and make her seem foolish in front of other people.

Well, lo and behold, a few days later, *Marge* got so sick she missed six weeks of church and had to be hospitalized! Julia and I didn't know what to make of this, except that apparently Jesus must not love Marge as much as she thinks he does! Or maybe Jesus has an ironic sense of humor!

After this incident, Marge then targeted Julia for a "snubbing" campaign and embarked on a year-long period of totally ignoring her. Every time she saw Julia, she would walk right past her without a smile or even a glance. Once Julia was chatting with another church lady, and Marge walked up and interrupted their conversation to greet the other woman, and then turned and walked away without even looking at Julia. Julia was relieved not to have to deal with Marge's preaching and spiritual bullying anymore, and happy to stay as far away from her as she could.

But Marge wasn't satisfied with this at all. When Marge realized her snubbing and bullying were not getting to Julia, she remembered something she knew for sure would upset her nemesis. Trying to get her sick!

In the next few months, Marge twice tried to hug Julia while she was obviously sick~ coughing, nose running, and even complaining about running a fever. Both times she did it in front of other people, betting that Julia wouldn't have the nerve to stop her from such a "loving" gesture in front of witnesses, but both times Julia did stop her. Marge never tried to hug Julia when she was healthy, and in fact continued to completely ignore her. She only tried to hug her when she was sick. She was deliberately and maliciously trying to get Julia sick. And all this time, still no explanation for why Jesus was letting Marge get sick! Maybe *her* faith wasn't strong enough!

One day, after these two unsuccessful attempts to hug Julia and spending an entire year not speaking to her, Marge finally caught Julia off guard by grabbing her and giving her a huge bearhug. Then she stepped back, gleefully grinned at Julia, and announced "I have bronchitis!" When she saw the annoyance and concern cross Julia's face, she added, "Oh, don't worry, it's not contagious!" Julia realized that her boundaries had been violated once again by this "sister in Christ," who was now going so far as to endanger her health. Marge's juvenile nastiness would rival any eight-year-old schoolyard bully's. It was hard to believe this childish spitework was coming from a grandmother in her mid-fifties. In fact, some of Julia's friends told her that forcing unwanted touch on someone after being told not to touch was sexual assault, and maybe she should call the police. Marge set out to trample Julia's boundaries and upset her, and one way or the other she was going to succeed, even if it meant ambushing her and deliberately trying to infect her.

The next week, Marge made another move to hug Julia, but Julia stopped her cold by holding her hand out at arm's length and blocking her. In a clear, firm voice, she told Marge not to hug her ever again. Since the last time Marge hugged her, and *then* announced she was sick, Julia had no choice but to enforce her own boundaries against someone who did not respect them. Again Marge tried to hug Julia in front of witnesses, gambling that Julia would not have the nerve to stop her. But Julia surprised her by enforcing her boundaries even though people were watching. She also publicly stated very clearly what Marge had done to her in secret by ambushing her with a hug and *then* telling her with a big smile that she was sick. Marge could not gather her wits about her quickly enough to deny it, but only stammer that, fine, she would no longer hug Julia. Well, hallelujah! After a year of not speaking to her, why it was so important to hug Julia is a mystery. Unless, of course, it's just another example of Marge's spiritual bullying, and a deliberate ploy to upset Julia and make her look crazy or mean in front of other people for protesting an "innocent" hug.

VIOLET VERSUS SPIRITUAL BULLY LEAH

SURELY THE SERPENT WILL BITE WITHOUT ENCHANTMENT; AND A BABBLER IS NO BETTER. THE WORDS OF A WISE MAN'S MOUTH ARE GRACIOUS; BUT THE LIPS OF A FOOL WILL SWALLOW UP HIMSELF. THE BEGINNING OF THE WORDS OF HIS MOUTH IS FOOLISHNESS: AND THE END OF HIS TALK IS MISCHIEVOUS MADNESS. A FOOL ALSO IS FULL OF WORDS: A MAN CANNOT TELL WHAT SHALL BE; AND WHAT SHALL BE AFTER HIM, WHO CAN TELL HIM?...Ecclesiastes 10:11-14 KJV.

At Violet's church's annual picnic, several members of the congregation were having a conversation about letting go of relationships with toxic people or potentially damaging ones. Violet ran a well-known web ministry on this very subject from a Christian perspective and actively counseled other people. At first, Leah had not been aware of Violet's background. Because of her typical narcissistic disinterest in other people, she had never bothered finding out anything about Violet early on in their relationship, but she knew it now since it had been talked about in church.

During this particular discussion, Violet's adult son mentioned an old friendship he had to let go because the person was becoming very demanding and high-maintenance, getting involved with criminal activity and drugs, and being violent with women. Violet and her son had known this friend of his since his early adolescence and he had been through a lot, but was going down the wrong path and would no longer listen.

DO NOT BE MISLED: "BAD COMPANY CORRUPTS GOOD CHARACTER"...1 Corinthians 15:33 NIV.

Leah seized this opportunity as the perfect time to make Violet and her son look foolish. In front of several people, she tried to embarrass Violet's son by loudly criticizing him for "not being loyal to a friend" and staying in the relationship to preach Christ to him and save him. When she realized Violet had advised him to start backing off this relationship, she blurted that he was old enough to make his own decisions, and didn't he think he was too old to still be listening to his mother? Violet's son was very annoyed, and informed Leah that he respected his parents' opinions and often asked for them, but made his own decisions and did what he wanted to do. If he thought his parents were wrong, he would not do what they advised, but if he agreed with their opinions, then he would decide on his own to do what they suggested.

Violet pointed out the obvious to Leah~ "I counsel strangers about destructive relationships, so why wouldn't I counsel my own son?" But Leah continued to insist that Violet's son should have stuck with his friend and tried to save him. Violet said she disagreed, especially since the friend was getting into situations that could have caused problems for her son. She mentioned that in Proverbs it says not to speak to a fool, for he will not listen to the wisdom of your words (Proverbs 23:9). Leah immediately jumped to the conclusion that Violet was now talking about *her* (because with narcissists it's *always* about them) and not her son's friend, and angrily said, "I'm not a fool!" Violet had to clarify that she didn't say *Leah* was the fool (even though she was acting like a fool). She said her son's friend was the fool who wouldn't listen to the wisdom of her son's words, and the Bible tells us not to keep trying with fools. Leah grumbled something under her breath and turned away.

Leah had never been one to give godly counsel to her own children, and they did not lead righteous lives. Leah herself acted like a rowdy, loud-mouthed, low-class teenager, even though she was in her fifties. She didn't set a good example in many aspects of her life.

She was healthy and able-bodied, but didn't work. She complained about money, lived on the dole and freeloaded off others, but she didn't bother getting a job. She drove a luxury car, wore stylish new clothes, and had the money for travelling and social activities, but came empty-handed every week to the church potluck luncheon.

To add insult to injury, many times she helped herself to the food other people cooked for the luncheon, packing it up to take home for her dinner before anyone else had even gotten a taste, and hiding it in another room under her coat so no one else might see it or take it (or serve it for lunch, as it was meant to be served) until she was ready to go home. Leftovers are meant to be taken home *after* people have eaten, *not before*. That's why they're called *"left-overs,"* because they are what was *left over* when the meal was *done*. Leah would leave the service before it was over, while everyone else was still in church, and go into the lunchroom to grab as much food as she dared. By the time Leah was done loading up dinner for her family at other people's expense and effort, sometimes there wasn't enough left for everyone at the fellowship to have a helping. And yet, although she literally *stole* food from other people, Leah didn't seem to feel she should contribute so much as a plate of brownies from a dollar-store mix to share with her church family.

Leah maliciously gossiped, spied and listened in on private conversations, snuck around behind people's backs, was a thief who pilfered what wasn't hers, was too selfish and lazy to do her fair share, said hurtful things, tried to embarrass other people, and judged and bullied others. She was certainly not a paragon of godly womanhood or motherhood, and yet she arrogantly thought she had the right to judge and criticize another woman and her family. Was she trying to publicly embarrass Violet to take the focus off her own ill manners, dishonesty and socially inappropriate behavior? Or was she envious of Violet and her family? Did she feel they were "out of her league" and she had to bring them down a peg or two? Why was Violet's relationship with her son, or his relationship with an ex-friend, any of Leah's business? Why did she even care?

SPIRITUAL BULLIES ARE USUALLY WOMEN

Strangely enough, most of the Spiritual Bullies I have met or heard about have been women. Yes, that's right. Sweet little church ladies, and middle-aged church ladies seem to be more common Spiritual Bullies than the young or the elderly. I don't know why this is, although it certainly is interesting. Maybe men don't care all that much about giving the impression that they're some kind of religious expert, or, although I hate to perpetuate tired old clichés, maybe women have more trouble holding their tongues and butting out of other people's business. Or maybe there's a broader sociological dynamic at play here, and women who chafe at being relegated to subordinate positions in some churches feel an overwhelming need to show off their biblical knowledge (or lack of same) to bolster their status within the church. I don't know, but I do find it intriguing.

One of the few male Spiritual Bullies I've personally met was a "pastor" who didn't have his own church, but periodically showed up at other pastors' churches and surreptitiously passed out his business cards to the folks in the congregation. He claimed to be a "doctor" who had a "No-Divorce" counseling business~ even in cases of violence, danger and abuse. So of course he and I butted heads almost immediately. Not only is it inappropriate to try and "farm" other people's churches to drum up business for yourself, but it's offensive to assume that strangers are having marital problems and need your services, not to mention asking them personal questions about their private lives that are none of your business so you can "invite" them to come for counseling. And then to insist that a victim who is in danger of being killed by a violent spouse can never get away, even though the biblical marriage covenant has already been broken by the abuser, is just, well, spiritual bullying.

WHAT ON EARTH IS GOING ON HERE?

ANSWER A FOOL ACCORDING TO HIS FOLLY, LEST HE BE WISE IN HIS OWN CONCEIT...Proverbs 26:5 KJV.

IN THE MOUTH OF THE FOOLISH IS A ROD OF PRIDE: BUT THE LIPS OF THE WISE SHALL PRESERVE THEM...Proverbs 14:3 KJV.

IT IS AS SPORT TO A FOOL TO DO MISCHIEF: BUT A MAN OF UNDERSTANDING HATH WISDOM...Proverbs 10:23 KJV.

Spiritual Bullies are an interesting bunch and can be quite amusing. Their ignorance is startling, and their interpretations of the Bible are usually way off-base, if not downright insane. To say that it's a sin to name your child after your father, that Jesus would not let you get sick from hugging sick people, that God wants you to stay in relationships that have become risky and destructive, or that you are wrong if you believe illnesses are contagious and you simply need to have stronger faith to protect yourself from getting sick, is just nutty. Nowhere in the Bible does it say anything even remotely resembling such idiocy. And then to not only make such preposterous statements, but to continue to *insist* that they are accurate, as if your very life depended on embarrassing the other person and proving them wrong, points to a Spiritual Bully.

As abuse survivors, we are almost destined to run into the crackpot Spiritual Bully sooner or later. She will be the self-righteous, sanctimonious, holier-than-thou bigmouth who thinks she has the right to judge us for having boundaries concerning other people's behavior toward us, setting limits on our abuser or ending an abusive relationship. And she will spout all kinds of phony or out-of-context nonsense that the Bible never says, trying to convince us that she alone has a direct line to God, knows what he wants us to do, and is entitled to butt in where it's none of her business and ram it down our throats.

Now at this point, a rational person would be asking himself, "Why?" Why on earth is making another person look foolish so important to you that you would make a fool of yourself to do it? Well, for starters, Spiritual Bullies don't realize they're making fools of themselves. They think that by spouting off some obscure biblical "knowledge" that no one else possesses *(because it doesn't exist),* and stating it forcefully and repeatedly, they can convince onlookers that it's a fact. If they claim the position of an authority on God's Word, gullible people will actually believe they *are* an authority on God's Word and that they know what they're talking about.

Like all narcissists, Spiritual Bullies are petty, small-minded, close-minded, jealous, envious losers. It is hugely important to them to embarrass and humble other people, especially those they envy. If anyone else is getting any attention, they have to shift the attention back to themselves. If another person seems to be a good, righteous believer, a Spiritual Bully has to cast doubt on that person's walk with the Lord, to divert attention away from the fact that *his own walk* with the Lord is seriously deficient. If someone else is popular and people like that person, a Spiritual Bully has to make that person look bad so people won't like him as much. And what better way to sabotage or undercut someone than to use the ultimate authority to prove them wrong~ the Bible! God himself disapproves! If you're trying to make your argument seem believable, you can't get any more credibility than *God* agreeing with you.

THOU SHALT NOT LIVE; FOR THOU SPEAKEST LIES IN THE NAME OF THE LORD...Zechariah 13:3 KJV.

How to deal with the Spiritual Bullies in our lives? As with all abusive narcissists, the best and probably only solution is to stay as far away as you can. And that can be pretty far. I know one Spiritual Bully who was tuned in and eavesdropping on a private conversation being conducted in very low voices from over forty feet away, across a room full of other people who were also having conversations. The folks having the conversation were shocked to realize she could hear them and was listening in when she unthinkingly and reflexively responded to something they said. Spiritual Bullies just can't resist butting in, even if it's going to give them away. So be aware of your surroundings. If you really want to have a private conversation, close the door, go sit outside in your car, or call the person you want to converse with at home.

Spiritual Bullies are not only found in churches. Phony "Christian" narcissistic families have their share as well. They will be the enablers who are just chomping at the bit to judge and criticize you for having boundaries, standing up to the family abusers, or protecting your own children from them. But, interestingly enough, they will never say a word to the abusers themselves, the ones who are actually misbehaving. Spiritual Bullies will tell *you* what to do, but they won't tell the abuser what to do. Listen for the word "should, " as in "you *should* forgive and forget" and "you *shouldn't* say that to your mother." Also keep your antennae up for the sanctimonious bigmouths who think they have a direct line to God himself, and believe it's their job to tell you what he wants you to do. *The truly righteous stand up to evil, because **that** is what God wants us to do. They don't criticize those who stand up to it.* Anyone who blabs nonsense like God wants you to forgive ongoing crimes and allow them to continue, or God wants you to honor evil people, has no idea what she's talking about.

Once you know who the Spiritual Bullies are in your family, your church or your life, make sure you censor your interactions with them. Don't have them in your home, don't give them access to any personal information, never confide in them, especially not about any disagreements or problems you might be having with someone else, and make sure they cannot overhear any private conversations you might have, because they *will* be eavesdropping and they *will* be snooping. Do not give them any ammunition to use against you. The less they know, the better.

The insanity Spiritual Bullies spout is so ridiculous it's hardly worth responding to. If you want to have a little fun with it, you can try handing them a Bible and asking them to show you where it says that. But otherwise, there's little sense in getting into a prolonged discussion with them. If you're feeling feisty, feign surprise and say, "Oh my! Were you eavesdropping on my conversation?" Or you might want to glance at them and say, "Thanks for your input" and then go back to ignoring them. Again, you wouldn't bother arguing with the inmates at Bellevue, would you? So stay away and treat them like the petty, insignificant little losers they are~ not worthy of your time or attention.

HE THAT PASSETH BY, AND MEDDLETH WITH STRIFE BELONGING NOT TO HIM, IS LIKE ONE THAT TAKETH A DOG BY THE EARS...Proverbs 26:17 KJV.

THE LIPS OF THE RIGHTEOUS FEED MANY: BUT FOOLS DIE FOR WANT OF WISDOM...Proverbs 10:21 KJV.

CHAPTER 21

THE IMPOSSIBLE-TO-PREVENT NUCLEAR MELTDOWN

BEWARE OF FALSE PROPHETS, WHICH COME TO YOU IN SHEEP'S CLOTHING, BUT INWARDLY THEY ARE RAVENING WOLVES. YE SHALL KNOW THEM BY THEIR FRUITS. DO MEN GATHER GRAPES OF THORNS, OR FIGS OF THISTLES? EVEN SO EVERY GOOD TREE BRINGETH FORTH GOOD FRUIT; BUT A CORRUPT TREE BRINGETH FORTH EVIL FRUIT. A GOOD TREE CANNOT BRING FORTH EVIL FRUIT, NEITHER CAN A CORRUPT TREE BRING FORTH GOOD FRUIT. EVERY TREE THAT BRINGETH NOT FORTH GOOD FRUIT IS HEWN DOWN, AND CAST INTO THE FIRE. WHEREFORE BY THEIR FRUITS YE SHALL KNOW THEM.
NOT EVERY ONE THAT SAITH UNTO ME, LORD, LORD, SHALL ENTER INTO THE KINGDOM OF HEAVEN; BUT HE THAT DOETH THE WILL OF MY FATHER WHICH IS IN HEAVEN. MANY WILL SAY TO ME IN THAT DAY, LORD, LORD, HAVE WE NOT PROPHESIED IN THY NAME? AND IN THY NAME HAVE CAST OUT DEVILS? AND IN THY NAME DONE MANY WONDERFUL WORKS? AND THEN I WILL PROFESS UNTO THEM, I NEVER KNEW YOU: DEPART FROM ME, YE THAT WORK INIQUITY…Matthew 7:15-23 KJV.

Frances is a devoted Christian lady in her sixties who, along with her husband, adult sons, daughters and daughter-in-law are lifelong faithful churchgoers. Frances and her children play piano, guitar and drums and performed as a family band whenever they got the chance. In fact, they were the music ministry and band in two of the churches they attended for several years. They loved and played the old-time gospel music, from worship songs that brought tears to people's eyes to the hand-clapping, foot-stomping joyful standards that really let the Spirit move.

When Frances and her family started attending a new church, she introduced herself to the pastor and leaders and offered to play music whenever it was wanted or needed. This church was a family affair. The pastor's wife headed the women's ministry, his son headed the youth ministry, one of his sisters took care of children's church, and the youngest of his sisters, Edwina, was the worship leader in charge of playing the piano and singing every week with a small choir.

For the first year or so, no one asked Frances and her family to play music. They were invited to dinner at the pastor's house and treated to videos of Edwina playing and singing. But when Frances invited the pastor and his family back to her house, and after dinner asked if they'd like to see a couple of videos of her and her children playing and singing, she was shocked when they all said no! Not even, "No, thanks." Just "No," accompanied by shrugs and wrinkled noses, as if Frances had asked them if they wanted to do something disgusting. Frances and her husband thought the pastor's family would enjoy their videos after they had been gracious enough to sit through Edwina's videos and compliment her music, and it was surprising, awkward, and hurtful that Edwina and her relatives had the bad manners to turn them down flat. They weren't the least bit interested in hearing Frances and her family band play. After that, Frances, not wanting to step on Edwina's toes, did not offer to play in church or mention music again. She contented herself to sing along with the congregation to Edwina's music, and enjoyed not having the responsibility of planning and rehearsing music for church every week that she had had in her previous churches. She and her family had many musician friends, and got together to jam and play with them as often as they could.

Soon things started getting weirder, and it began to appear that Edwina was attracted to Frances' sons. Her main attraction seemed to be to Frances' youngest son, who was closer to her height than his brother. The only problem was that he was ten years younger than Edwina, in his mid-twenties, and certainly not looking to date someone with such an age difference. Edwina befriended both of Frances' sons, and occasionally they would go on an activity together, such as bowling, with Frances' sons considering Edwina to be just a friend from church.

Eventually Edwina started letting Frances and her children play music twice a year, during the church Christmas and Easter festivities. Their musical style was more casual and relaxed than Edwina's. Edwina rehearsed every detail and stuck to the script, whereas Frances and her family band were used to jamming and including other musicians. They always welcomed anyone who wanted to join in, and Frances' attitude was the more, the merrier, while Edwina seemed more comfortable keeping tighter control. Frances remembered and appreciated all the musicians who had given her and her sons and daughters a chance to enjoy playing with them, who were not competitive or threatened and were generous enough to share the stage and even allow newcomers to take center stage and play or sing solos. Frances didn't view other piano players as a threat to her superiority; in fact, she looked forward to seeing them play and always hoped to learn something new from them. She welcomed other musicians as well as the congregation to enjoy themselves by singing along, instead of just sitting there watching her and her family perform. Frances didn't mind not being the center of attention. She even encouraged Edwina to sing lead and cheerfully relinquished center stage and played back-up for her.

When Frances and her family played, the Spirit moved mightily. The congregation stood up, raised their hands, clapped and joyfully sang along. When one of the two occasions a year that Frances would be asked to play was approaching, church members began making requests to hear certain old favorites they hadn't heard in years, and Frances happily obliged. The first time Frances and her family were asked to play, they were only invited to play one song. They were very conscious of not wanting to seem as if they were trying to take over or steal the spotlight from Edwina. They got a standing ovation, and shouts of "Encore," but they did not just want to start playing another song without Edwina's okay, so they smiled and thanked everyone and returned to their seats. After the service, many folks said they wished Frances and her children had played more. The next time they were invited to play, Frances asked Edwina if they could play two songs, if Edwina could sing lead and the congregation could also have fun and sing along, and that's what they did.

THE BUILDUP TO THE COMING MELTDOWN: THINGS GO FROM SLIGHTLY ODD TO REALLY STRANGE

Edwina's older sister, sister-in-law and other relatives took Frances aside numerous times to confide in her and ask what she thought the chances were of either of her sons being interested in Edwina. Frances was uncomfortable being put on the spot and didn't know what to say. If her boys were interested, they would have asked Edwina out by now. But she was seven years older than one son and ten years older than the other. They wanted to date young women their own ages, and they wanted to be able to have children. Edwina was already pushing forty. She was decent looking, but her personality didn't seem to attract many men. She didn't seem to know how to flirt, or maybe she considered herself "too good" to flirt. Maybe she thought it was undignified, and the last thing it seemed Edwina wanted to appear was less than perfect. She didn't give the impression of being warm, funny, relaxed, down-to-earth or sexy. Instead, she seemed rather aloof, uptight and rigid, prim and proper, straight-laced, controlling and bossy, and a bit haughty and full of herself.

Socially, Edwina seemed to run hot and cold. Sometimes she would be friendly, and other times she would act aloof. At fellowship, Edwina often held herself apart from the others, sitting at the opposite end of the table, "observing" the interactions between church members as if she were a monitor in the school cafeteria, looking for somebody to slip up and "misbehave," instead of being warm and friendly, pulling up a chair in their midst and joining in. At non-church social occasions, she refused to sit or mingle with people her own age, her own educational and professional level, or even those who were in the same field she was and with whom she would have had plenty in common. Instead, she would request to sit with her relatives and the elderly people or children from the church, who could not be viewed as a threat to her superiority. When meeting new women in her age group, she seemed to view them as competition. She often acted cool or unfriendly, and could actually be seen standing back and giving them the once-over, looking them up and down with a disapproving expression, and then later on finding something critical to say about them. She usually had something critical to say about the men she met as well, and rarely did any make the grade and seem "good enough" for her. Edwina seemed to have an inflated sense of her own worth, and consider few people other than her own insular family to be worthy of her attention. She gave off the vibe of a conceited snob who thought she was too good for most, and even acted as if she was superior to the folks in church who were her elders and betters.

Whenever Edwina's relatives pressured Frances about the possibility of either of her sons dating Edwina, the only thing she could think of to say was that there was too much of an age difference, and hope that wouldn't be hurtful although it was at least partially the truth. Edwina seemed more like a mother, and a strict, controlling, stuck-up one at that, to Frances' sons, than wife and lover material. There was no way a romance was ever going to blossom because of Edwina's personality.

During this time, Edwina decided to go on a strict diet and exercise regime and managed to lose over a hundred pounds in a year. She started dating someone, but after they broke up three times the relationship finally ended for good. While she was involved in this on-again-off-again relationship, Frances' youngest son met a lovely young woman and fell in love.

As Edwina's doomed relationship went under for the third time, Frances' son's relationship was growing deeper. Eventually he brought his girlfriend to church and introduced her to everyone, and it seemed to take Edwina by surprise. After that, Frances sensed a new undercurrent of coolness toward her and her family.

Edwina and her relatives began asking Frances and her husband about their son and his girlfriend. It was almost as if Edwina was expecting his relationship to end after some time passed, just like hers had. But instead, the opposite was happening, and it was getting more and more serious.

At one point, Edwina casually asked Frances' husband how the young couple was doing, and he answered that they were doing great and even talking about getting engaged. Edwina appeared surprised at this unexpected news, and instead of saying, "Oh, how nice," she raised her eyebrows and said, with an incredulous and disapproving tone, "Oh, *really!* How long have they been going out?" Frances' husband replied, "I don't know. Eight or nine months." And Edwina immediately corrected him, "No! *Seven* months!" Frances' husband was shocked. He wanted to say, "Well, why are you asking me if you already know?" but he held his peace. He couldn't shake the creepy feeling of knowing that this inappropriately older woman was keeping track of his young son's romance and literally counting the time he had been with his girlfriend more than his own parents were counting. Edwina made it plain by her dubious attitude that she did not think seven months was long enough to be considering marriage. She acted as if the young man and his family were being foolish and could be making a big mistake that she, of course, would never make.

Although she kept up appearances by her "friendship" with Frances' sons and "befriended" their sisters and girlfriend as well, the cracks were beginning to show. Frances' son got engaged, and Edwina began gaining weight again. Within a short period of time, she looked as if she had gained back most if not all of the hundred pounds she had lost. She began posting depressing and desperate sounding comments on her blog about waiting for God to send her the right man, the perfect man being out there somewhere, how she wasn't in the mood for this or that, or just not feeling the holiday spirit. When the church had their Easter pageant that year, she did not invite Frances and her children to play.

The differences between Frances' music and Edwina's, and the congregation's response and participation, became more and more pronounced. Edwina was a fairly good pianist and vocalist, who could have played the same music Frances did, which everyone, including her own family, enjoyed. But, except for rare occasions, she didn't. Instead she focused on playing "modern" hymns to a congregation full of the older generation who knew and loved the old-time gospel music. She loudly banged the notes out as if she was taking her frustrations out on the keyboard, so much that she actually broke two electric keyboards before giving up and buying a real piano that could take the banging a computerized keyboard could not.

The songs she chose were repetitive and monotonous. She would drag the end of many of the hymns out for five or ten minutes or more of repeatedly playing the same couple of chords over and over again, talking, shouting and singing in her own words, which no one could follow or sing along with. She didn't seem to understand how to lower the volume and play softly in the background when backing up herself and the other vocalists, the prayer requests and praise reports, or the pastor's words, but instead continued to bang on the piano and drown out everything else. Instead of praise and worship that the whole congregation could participate in, her "performances" became one-woman shows which her captive audience could only listen to. It was as if she was trying to showcase her own vocal and piano skills rather than making it possible for anyone else to join in. Only two or three folks remained standing, raised their hands or tried to clap, but they couldn't follow her free-form vocalizations and sing along with her. If you looked around, you would see almost everybody else sitting down, doing puzzles in the bulletin, whispering to one another, dozing off, texting on their phones, or even going outside to smoke, get a cup of coffee, or chat and wait till the music was over and the sermon started. Some folks got headaches from the loud banging and wailing, and had to leave. Worst of all, the Spirit was stifled.

As Frances' son's wedding day drew near and it became obvious that the young couple were in love and really going through with it, Edwina's older sister and other relatives now turned their attention to Frances' other son. Edwina went with him to a couple of community events, but as far as he was concerned it was only as friends. There was still a seven year age gap here, and that was an obstacle that wasn't going away. Edwina's relatives continued to ask Frances about her son's interest in Edwina. But when Frances told them the difference in ages was too much of an obstacle, they laughed and said that wasn't so bad and shouldn't be a problem because they knew other couples who also had a big age gap. Except with the couples they knew, the *man* was the older one, and his biological clock wasn't a factor in being able to have children. Frances' son was not attracted or interested, but Frances didn't want to tell Edwina's relatives the unvarnished truth for fear of hurting Edwina. Frances had long since gotten the impression that both Edwina and her relatives were super-sensitive about anything that might sound even the slightest bit negative concerning Edwina, and she felt pressured to make excuses for why neither of her twenty-something sons wanted to date a woman who was pushing forty and in whom they just weren't interested. Even if Frances had any say in who her sons dated, she would not have encouraged them to date Edwina. It was getting tiresome to be continually put on the spot.

Frances' pastor was marrying her son and his fiancée, and they hired his sister Edwina to play and sing at their ceremony since it took place in the church where she was the music leader. Frances' older son was the best man, and at the reception, he made sure to ask all the single women to dance so they'd have some fun. When he danced with Edwina, her relatives were ecstatic. They thought it was romantic and read into it as if it meant he was interested in her. They didn't even notice that he also asked every other single woman who was there to dance. The wedding was lovely, the newlyweds began their life together, and Frances and her husband and the rest of their children continued going to church, with the newly married couple joining them on occasion, and the rest of the time attending a church closer to their home.

REACHING CRITICAL MASS: HERE COMES THE NUCLEAR REACTION

A couple of months later, Edwina performed music at yet another wedding. The very next day, which also happened to be the day before Christmas, Frances received an e-mail from Edwina out of the blue. Edwina informed Frances that she "just couldn't take" all of Frances' "negative and hateful" social media posts and had unsubscribed from seeing Frances' comments on her feed a couple of months ago (around the time of Frances' son's wedding). Now, she continued, she "heard" that Frances had posted mean things about people in church, so she had no choice but to unfriend Frances completely. She went on to say that Frances had also hurt other people in the church, and although she was one-hundred percent a person who believes in forgiveness and the love of Christ, she could not associate with the "unlovingness" and "hatred" Frances was "consumed with." She told Frances that she was "not looking for an argument" and "did not want to sit down and discuss anything." In other words, she wanted to be free to attack Frances, and not give Frances an opportunity to defend herself or even to find out who and what Edwina was talking about.

But Edwina wasn't done yet. *She then e-mailed all of Frances' children and her new daughter-in-law* to criticize Frances, and tell them she had unsubscribed to their mother's posts a couple of months earlier because they were too "negative" and "unloving" for her tastes and she was now unfriending Frances for "saying hurtful things" to people she knew, although it was with a "heavy heart." She added dramatically that she tried to ignore it for *so* long but just couldn't take it anymore. Then, even more insanely, she told them that she loved them all, and wished them a very merry Christmas.

Frances was bowled over. Edwina had never mentioned having a problem with her, and neither had anyone else. Why had no one in church come directly and privately to Frances if they had been hurt by her, and why had Edwina, who apparently considered herself to be church leadership, not counseled them to? Why did Edwina complain about Frances and try to embarrass her to her own family without first going to Frances in private? Jesus tells us when someone has offended us, to take it to that person first and try to resolve it, before involving third parties and gossiping about them:

MOREOVER IF THY BROTHER SHALL TRESPASS AGAINST THEE, GO AND TELL HIM HIS FAULT ***BETWEEN THEE AND HIM ALONE****: IF HE SHALL HEAR THEE, THOU HAST GAINED THY BROTHER. BUT IF HE WILL NOT HEAR THEE,* ***THEN*** *TAKE WITH THEE ONE OR TWO MORE, THAT IN THE MOUTH OF TWO OR THREE WITNESSES EVERY WORD SHALL BE ESTABLISHED. AND IF HE SHALL NEGLECT TO HEAR THEM, TELL IT UNTO THE CHURCH: BUT IF HE NEGLECT TO HEAR THE CHURCH, LET HIM BE UNTO THEE AS A HEATHEN MAN AND A PUBLICAN…Matthew 18:15-18 KJV.*

Frances hadn't changed anything about her social networking posts or her style of posting in recent months. She posted both negative and positive comments just like everyone else did. In fact, Edwina repeatedly posted about her own illnesses, not feeling well, not being in the mood for the holidays, her other various feelings and moods (both good *and* bad), her frustrations and the repeated failure of her on-again-off-again romantic relationship, and how she was still waiting and trusting for God to send her a husband, but for some reason she did not think her own posts were negative and depressing. Frances had been posting the same stuff for four years. The only thing she could think of that was different from what she usually posted in the time frame Edwina mentioned was that a couple of months ago, right around the time Edwina unsubscribed from her feed, she had posted some of her son's wedding pictures.

I "HEARD" YOU SAID SOMETHING I DON'T LIKE, SO NOW I'M MAD AT YOU~ AND I DON'T WANT TO TALK ABOUT IT!

DOTH OUR LAW JUDGE ANY MAN, BEFORE IT HEAR HIM, AND KNOW WHAT HE DOETH?...John 7:51 KJV.

Frances e-mailed Edwina back, but she didn't argue or "try to discuss" Edwina's criticism for several reasons. First, she didn't even know what she would have been discussing since Edwina was cryptic and vague in her accusations and did not say who was "hurt" or what exactly Frances supposedly said. Second, Edwina had only "heard" that Frances had posted hurtful comments, but she didn't bother reading them herself or she would have seen that the lies and hearsay she referred to were not what Frances had posted at all. Third, Edwina said she wasn't interested in hearing anything Frances had to say. And fourth, after talking to her family, Frances realized that she didn't have to answer to Edwina and she didn't owe her any explanations. No one had ever informed Frances that Edwina was any kind of pastor or elder or had any authority over her. There was nothing godly or biblical in the way she had confronted Frances. And dragging Frances' children into it was also *completely* unbiblical, seemed to Frances and her loved ones to be hypocritical, spiteful and evil, and appeared to be just a malicious attempt to hurt Frances and her family as much as possible.

Edwina was the only one who was being hurtful and hostile, and taking it over the top by not telling Frances what exactly she was talking about and giving a Frances a chance to resolve it, not to mention badmouthing her to her family, although of course that was with a "heavy heart" and "the best of intentions." Edwina was not Frances' contemporary or peer, and certainly not her better. Edwina needed to learn to respect her elders, not the other way around. She was twenty-five years younger than Frances, and was being rude, arrogant, insolent, ill-mannered and disrespectful to a woman old enough to be her mother, criticizing her, gossiping about her, and even trying to turn her own children against her. It would have been like Frances attacking an eighty-seven-year old woman, or a fifteen-year-old kid judging Edwina's behavior and calling her on the carpet. Frances did not have to explain herself to Edwina, and so she did not bother.

RISE IN THE PRESENCE OF THE AGED, SHOW RESPECT FOR THE ELDERLY AND REVERE YOUR GOD. I AM THE LORD... Leviticus 19:32 NIV.

LIKEWISE, YE YOUNGER, SUBMIT YOURSELVES UNTO THE ELDER. YEA, ALL OF YOU BE SUBJECT ONE TO ANOTHER, AND BE CLOTHED WITH HUMILITY: FOR GOD RESISTETH THE PROUD, AND GIVETH GRACE TO THE HUMBLE... 1Peter 5:5 KJV.

What Frances did do was to point out to Edwina that she should have actually *read* whatever Frances posted that got her all worked up instead of believing rumors and hearsay, just to make sure it didn't get misquoted, which it did. She pointed out that Edwina admitted to having "a problem" with her for months, and yet never said anything in all that time or gave Frances a chance to resolve the problem, whatever it was. She said she was never told that anybody in church was "hurt" by her and didn't know what Edwina was talking about, that Edwina believed and engaged in gossip about her without ever caring enough to ask her about it. Why had no one in the church approached Frances as Jesus instructs and let her know she "hurt" them? *Is it possible that no one was actually feeling hurt, and Edwina was just making it up?* What was Edwina doing meddling in an issue between two other people, anyway?

IT IS AN HONOUR FOR A MAN TO CEASE FROM STRIFE: BUT EVERY FOOL WILL BE MEDDLING...Proverbs 20:3 KJV.

LIKE ONE WHO SEIZES A DOG BY THE EARS IS A PASSER-BY WHO MEDDLES IN A QUARREL NOT HIS OWN... Proverbs 26:17 NIV.

What did Edwina want Frances to do? Was Frances expected to apologize *to Edwina* for something she supposedly did *to somebody else*, instead of apologizing directly to the person she "hurt?" How could she resolve a problem a third party supposedly had with her by placating "princess" Edwina? Over the next few weeks, Frances spoke with several different churches members and asked them if they or anyone they knew of had been hurt by her, and they had never heard of anyone who had a problem with Frances. They were stunned by Edwina's allegations. As far as they knew, the people in church loved Frances and her family. Who *were* these phantom "hurt" people? Did they even exist? Or was Edwina exaggerating, imagining things, or even lying to justify to her sudden irrational attack on Frances?

Frances pointed out to Edwina that although she was accusing Frances of being "consumed with hatred" and "unlovingness," *Edwina* was the one who picked *the day before Christmas* to e-mail Frances' children and daughter-in-law to criticize her and try to embarrass her and cause trouble in someone else's family, all under the pretense of having a "heavy heart" and being so sad about having to do it. She asked her if she didn't see anything hypocritical, hateful, unloving, or downright evil and malicious about *that*. She also asked if Edwina thought it would be appropriate for *Frances* to contact *Edwina's* relatives, especially those of the generation younger than Edwina~ her nieces and nephews~ and complain, criticize and gossip about Edwina? She asked if it wouldn't be selfish of her to upset them and make them feel bad about Edwina over something that had nothing to do with them, especially just as they were getting ready to celebrate the birth of our Savior?

Frances told Edwina that she just wanted to dump her own misery on Frances and did not want to hear that she might be wrong or give Frances a chance to speak, and that her judging without caring enough to ask, and then dragging her family into a dispute Frances didn't even know they had, spoke volumes about Edwina's own character and Christianity. What Edwina did was not the least bit righteous, godly, or God-pleasing. She told Edwina that none of this made sense and she believed there was something much deeper at work here, and that Edwina needed to remove the plank from her own eye, examine her own heart and not take her own issues and unhappiness out on Frances and her family, especially not just before Christmas.

Edwina's reply was short and sweet. She said, "Thanks for proving my point." It was the kind of silly nonsensical response you'd get from a ten-year-old who had nothing to say for herself. Frances and her family didn't even know what Edwina's point *was.* Did she mean that Frances proved her point by saying "hurtful" things to her~ after all the hurtful things *she* had just said to Frances? Why does it only go one-way? Narcissists can say anything they want to us, no matter how "unloving," hostile, malicious, hurtful or downright untrue, and that's okay. But let us even dare to answer them, and *we* are the ones who are wrong and are hurting *them!*

No one realized that Edwina had unsubscribed to Frances' posts two months before. She could have unfriended Frances if that's what she wanted to do, and not told anybody. Frances and her family would probably have never even noticed. It's not like they checked Edwina's page every day. If anyone had noticed and was all that interested in knowing why, they could easily have asked. Why did Edwina feel she had to "explain herself?" Was she trying to make herself look good to Frances' family by letting them know she had "noble" reasons for unfriending their mother? Or would it have been a blow to her ego if none of them noticed she had unfriended Frances or cared enough to ask her about it, *so she had to make sure they noticed* by telling them?

Was this colossal meltdown in which Edwina felt she had to not only lash out and "punish" Frances and break off communication with her, but try to upset and hurt her family as well, really just about "many months" of social media comments, which were perfectly fine and even amusing to all of Frances' other friends, but apparently too "negative" for the fragile sensitivities of a delicate little flower like Edwina? If so, it seemed like quite an overreaction. Was it really about Frances unknowingly saying something to hurt several mysterious, nameless other people, and Edwina, *as a third-party*, feeling that *she* "just couldn't take it anymore?" Was this an example of a narcissist viewing herself as the center of the universe and everyone else being merely extensions of her, so that by "hurting" someone she knew, it was the same as hurting her?

Since narcissists typically fail to differentiate between individuals, they often take a dislike to innocent bystanders who have the misfortune of reminding them of someone whose behavior offends the narcissist. This resemblance is usually quite superficial, and not an issue of character or personality. It could be a certain facial expression or gesture, or the sound of your voice. *If you are of the same generation as the narcissist's overbearing mother, play the piano like the narcissist's brother who fails to pay homage to her, or your laughter is similar to that of the narcissist's cheerful sister, who has the nerve to be enjoying her life, that is enough to trigger the narcissist's dislike.* And she will then take out her resentment toward her relatives or friends on *you,* with an unprovoked and irrational attack, simply because you subconsciously remind her of them. It appeared that Edwina had numerous boundary issues with her own interfering and domineering relatives. Was she displacing and transferring her anger with her own overbearing and intrusive older sister and sister-in-law onto another woman of their "generation" who was a safer target?

DO NOTHING OUT OF SELFISH AMBITION OR VAIN CONCEIT, BUT IN HUMILITY CONSIDER OTHERS BETTER THAN YOURSELVES...Philippians 2:3 NIV.

Or could all of this uproar have had anything to do with competing with Frances and her family musically, and knowing that other people enjoyed their music and they were getting attention for it, when Edwina felt that all the musical attention should belong to her? Or was it about Frances' son meeting his love and getting married, and Frances' other son showing no interest in Edwina, all while Edwina remained single? Edwina had performed at yet another wedding the day before she lambasted Frances~ did singing at one too many weddings for other people put her over the brink? Was Frances also somehow to blame for Edwina gaining back all that weight? Was *that* Frances' fault, too? Or was Edwina just a miserable, unhappy person taking out her frustrations, resentments and dissatisfactions with her own life on Frances and her happy family? Were Edwina's motives really pure and her behavior righteous, or were envy, jealousy, malice and bitterness at play behind the scenes?

A FROWARD HEART SHALL DEPART FROM ME: I WILL NOT KNOW A WICKED PERSON. WHOSO PRIVILY SLANDERETH HIS NEIGHBOUR, HIM WILL I CUT OFF: HIM THAT HATH A HIGH LOOK AND A PROUD HEART WILL NOT I SUFFER... Psalm 101:4-5 KJV.

As if Edwina's behavior wasn't disgraceful enough so far, Frances found out when she got her bank statement that month that *a mere four days before attacking her, Edwina had cashed the very generous check Frances gave her for Christmas.* Frances and her husband always gave personal checks to their pastors and church leaders as Christmas gifts. That year, not having the slightest idea that Edwina disapproved of her so much, Frances innocently mailed a nice check to Edwina's home in a Christmas card signed with love, just a few days before Edwina had her meltdown. Edwina had been judging Frances' integrity and had "a problem" with Frances for months, but had no problem with Frances' money. She had no ethical dilemma when it came to accepting money or gifts from people of whom she disapproved so strongly that she wouldn't even be "friends" with them on a social networking site anymore. A person of integrity would have been honest about her negative feelings toward someone who thought enough of her to remember her with a nice gift, and returned the check. As harshly as she judged Frances, Edwina saw no contradiction or hypocrisy in her own behavior, integrity, morality, ethics, or dishonesty. Since when would it be considered an honorable thing to take money or accept a gift from someone who has no idea you harbor such ill-will toward them, and whom you participate in gossiping and lying about? This little character flaw made the sanctimonious Edwina seem every bit as hypocritical as Jesus called the phony, two-faced Pharisees.

Needless to say, Frances and her family are now happily attending a different church, where they get to see old friends every week, the Spirit isn't suffocated, and the music is more their style. Now, instead of leaving church down and depressed because of the dismal and irritating music, Frances and her family leave church uplifted and praising the Lord, which is the way it should be! God is so good! He takes that which was meant for evil, and turns it to good for his children (Genesis 50:20; Romans 8:28).

AND WHOSOEVER WILL NOT RECEIVE YOU, WHEN YE GO OUT OF THAT CITY, SHAKE OFF THE VERY DUST FROM YOUR FEET FOR A TESTIMONY AGAINST THEM…Luke 9:5 KJV.

Edwina's relatives tried to protect her "perfect" reputation by lying to other church members about why Frances and her family left the church, but thankfully they were not listened to or believed by the godly ones who mattered to Frances. Edwina, emboldened by her success in getting rid of her "rival" Frances, and bolstered by the idolatry of her relatives, continued to be arrogant and haughty, acted disrespectfully toward several older church members, and alienated and offended still others. And through it all, the music still stank. People began leaving, and within a year Edwina's family's church could no longer function and closed its doors.

NO WEAPON THAT IS FORMED AGAINST THEE SHALL PROSPER; AND EVERY TONGUE THAT SHALL RISE AGAINST THEE IN JUDGMENT THOU SHALT CONDEMN. THIS IS THE HERITAGE OF THE SERVANTS OF THE LORD, AND THEIR RIGHTEOUSNESS IS OF ME, SAITH THE LORD...Isaiah 54:17 KJV.

GREEN-EYED MONSTERS PRODUCE RADIOACTIVE TOXIC WASTE

In my book *Breaking the Bonds of Adult Child Abuse*, there's a chapter entitled *Family Jealousy: The Shameful Secret Behind Abuse and Betrayal.* In it, I teach that when there is an unprovoked attack or anger that even the angry person can't explain adequately, it is almost always a sign of jealousy and envy. I talk about the first clue being that you thought everything was fine, until you got stabbed in the back and blindsided by an attack you never saw coming. After the initial ambush, you will remain confused and stunned, because there will be little or no explanation, and a refusal to clarify the accusations against you or to give you a chance to defend yourself is typical. The allegations against you will be vague or completely false, you will not be given details you can refute, and the people who supposedly passed around lies and rumors about you will remain anonymous.

Your attacker will insist you did something to hurt her, when you actually did nothing to her at all. This is because she has *felt* hurt by you all along, even though you did nothing wrong and were completely unaware of her feelings, because she is envious, jealous and resentful of you. Maybe you are more popular than she, or maybe you are better at something than she is, like cooking or music or conversation, and you didn't realize there was a one-sided competition going on.

Or maybe you were "hurting" her just by being happy, content, and fulfilled in your life, while unbeknownst to you, she was unhappy in *her* life. Just seeing you or your loved ones going about your business and enjoying your lives reminds her of her own dissatisfactions and bitterness. She has to take you down a peg or two and make you feel bad about yourself, just like you make her feel bad about herself, simply by going about your life without even realizing she feels this way toward you. Misery loves company. The only way a green-eyed narcissist can feel better about herself is to attack you, hurt you and eliminate you. Because you are a constant reminder of her own failures, disappointments and unhappiness, when she doesn't have to see you anymore, it's easier for her to stay on an even keel emotionally, stay in denial, and cling to her delusions of perfection and superiority.

THE NARCISSIST'S SLOW BURN

It's very common for narcissists to get offended over things that would not bother normal people, and then to simmer on a slow burn for months, until they finally boil over and spew their toxicity all over you. You usually have no clue that the narcissist is angry at you for some reason until the actual meltdown occurs. Many victims of Narcissistic Meltdowns, including myself, have been completely blindsided by irrational, unprovoked attacks and false accusations, when all along we thought everything was fine.

It is usually only in hindsight that you realize the narcissist was sending out signals for months that she was upset about something or other, but you never noticed. As the months passed, and you innocently went on laughing and having a nice time, enjoying your family gatherings or church fellowships, the narcissist was becoming more and more steamed that you were not paying attention to her and noticing her coolness, nastiness and snubs toward you.

After looking back, Frances and her family were able to recall several incidents of Edwina being aloof or rude to them or snubbing them in some way. It was only in retrospect that Frances realized Edwina was probably sending her a message by not inviting her and her family to play music at the church Easter pageant that year, but at the time Frances simply shrugged it off as an oversight. Edwina might have been waiting for Frances to ask about it, but she never did, and so Edwina was never given an opportunity to unload on Frances. This could have caused her to get even *more* offended at being ignored and not noticed, which is the worst thing you can do to a narcissist. The more time that passes without you noticing that she's stewing about something and making some effort to mollify her, the angrier and more agitated she gets. You are supposed to be in tune to her every mood and whim, and anything less is failure to pay proper homage to the Special Person she thinks she is. How dare we fail to notice that the narcissist is unhappy! How dare we not ask her, or *care,* for that matter, why she's pouting! Edwina had to continue steaming in silence until she finally, like she herself said, "couldn't take it anymore," and had a total meltdown all out of proportion to anything Frances did or didn't do.

If you have ever been the target of an insane, unprovoked attack that you never saw coming, think back to the weeks and months leading up to the big blowup. Was there anything different about the narcissist's behavior toward you? Any subtle little hints? If so, maybe she was doing the Slow Burn all that time, and you just didn't notice.

And by the way, even if you *do* notice, the best thing to do is to ignore it anyway. If you ask a narcissist what's wrong or if she's upset over something, I guarantee you'll regret it. Don't give her an opening.

EVIL DISGUISES ITSELF AS GOOD AND ALSO HATES GOOD

FOR SUCH ARE FALSE APOSTLES, DECEITFUL WORKERS, TRANSFORMING THEMSELVES INTO THE APOSTLES OF CHRIST. AND NO MARVEL; FOR SATAN HIMSELF IS TRANSFORMED INTO AN ANGEL OF LIGHT. THEREFORE IT IS NO GREAT THING IF HIS MINISTERS ALSO BE TRANSFORMED AS THE MINISTERS OF RIGHTEOUSNESS; WHOSE END SHALL BE ACCORDING TO THEIR WORKS...
2 Corinthians 11:13-15 KJV.

It often happens that the unrighteous in a church will gang up together to attack and eventually drive out the righteous. These evil "Christians" usually make a big show of being holy, but when you look at their fruit the truth about their nature becomes obvious.

IF A MAN PAYS BACK EVIL FOR GOOD, EVIL WILL NEVER LEAVE HIS HOUSE...Proverbs 17:13 NIV.

I have known numerous churches where the truly godly have been gossiped about, lied about, provoked for no reason, and made to feel unwelcome in the church, while the ungodly were catered to. This is especially noticeable in small churches where cliques and the dynamics between them are easier to see. The children of the devil will inevitably wind up sabotaging, undermining, attacking and driving out the prophets of God, who were given the gift of discernment and can see them for what they are.

I have known certain churches to go out of their way to make pedophiles and their co-conspirators feel welcome, while failing to support the children the pedophiles molested and their families, who were good, kind, godly, longstanding church members. The churches' solution to this awkward "problem" was to get the victims and their families to leave the church, instead of the perverts!

I have known churches to drive out entire families who made up their live bands, and who had been faithfully playing wonderful gospel music beloved by the congregation for twenty years or more, even though these churches are now left with nothing but recorded music. Maybe it's just me, because I'm a musician and I'm really into the music, but how does it make sense to get rid of a live band, and a great one at that, and then be stuck listening to canned music every week?

I have known churches that provided all sorts of support for abusive husbands and none at all for their abused wives. I have known churches whose pastors divorced their godly wives for their mistresses, and who then drove the ex-wives out of the churches where they had faithfully served for many years, while welcoming the adulterous pastors back and even allowing them to preach again. Ungodly churches give all of Christianity a bad name, even giving rise to old sayings like, "Christianity is the only religion that kills its own wounded." It's embarrassing for the rest of us, and we shouldn't tolerate it.

I have known very small churches to gang up on and attack the one or two families in the church who were actually making it possible for the church to exist~ by tithing, for instance~ while other people, who never contributed but managed to cause trouble on a regular basis, and were even *taking* money from the church for their rent or heating bills, were catered to.

I know of churches that drove off the people who cooked for the fellowships on a regular basis in favor of liars and gossips who ate the food they cooked and never even contributed a plate of cookies.

I've known churches who turned against the one or two people who always helped out with whatever was needed, whether it was money, music, hospital visits, small groups or committees, leaving themselves no one else but the "takers" who benefited from those good deeds but never pitched in themselves. Small groups and committees ended when there was no one left who was willing or able to run them, the "takers" who expected loans and other help from the church left when it was no longer available, and several of these churches eventually closed their doors when they could no longer pay their bills because they had foolishly bitten the hand that fed them.

ACQUITTING THE GUILTY AND CONDEMNING THE INNOCENT~ THE LORD DETESTS THEM BOTH...
Proverbs 17:15 NIV.

Do you think God is pleased with these ungodly churches and their evil leaders and unrighteous congregations? If we are disillusioned, disheartened and disappointed in them, I can assure you that God is disgusted with them! It is certainly not pleasing to the Lord to see *his* children being forced out of *his* church by the children of Satan, and weak or wicked leadership with false authority allowing it, when the ones who are *supposed* to be put out of the church are those who are doing evil:

AND YOU ARE PROUD! SHOULDN'T YOU RATHER HAVE BEEN FILLED WITH GRIEF AND HAVE PUT OUT OF YOUR FELLOWSHIP THE MAN WHO DID THIS?...WHEN YOU ARE ASSEMBLED IN THE NAME OF OUR LORD JESUS, AND I AM WITH YOU IN SPIRIT, AND THE POWER OF OUR LORD JESUS IS PRESENT, HAND THIS MAN OVER TO SATAN, SO THAT THE SINFUL NATURE MAY BE DESTROYED AND HIS

SPIRIT SAVED ON THE DAY OF THE LORD. YOUR BOASTING IS NOT GOOD. DON'T YOU KNOW THAT A LITTLE YEAST WORKS THROUGH THE WHOLE BATCH OF DOUGH? GET RID OF THE OLD YEAST THAT YOU MAY BE A NEW BATCH WITHOUT YEAST~ AS YOU REALLY ARE. FOR CHRIST, OUR PASSOVER LAMB, HAS BEEN SACRIFICED. THEREFORE, LET US KEEP THE FESTIVAL, NOT WITH THE OLD YEAST, THE YEAST OF MALICE AND WICKEDNESS, BUT WITH BREAD WITHOUT YEAST, THE BREAD OF SINCERITY AND TRUTH... 1Corinthians 5:2, 4-8 NIV.

One thing the shortsighted leadership in such churches usually fails to anticipate is that the few *real* Christians in the congregation love one another, consider each other family, and keep in touch outside of church. When a brother or sister in Christ, or a whole family, suddenly stops attending church, they don't just disappear. The people who love them call them to see if everything is okay and to find out what happened. And that's often how the true Christians in an ungodly church start comparing notes and receiving confirmation from the Lord that they are correct in the problems they thought they had been discerning. At this point it's common for other disillusioned and disheartened church members to leave as well for more righteous churches, or to follow their church family to the new churches they are attending. To hear the Spiritual Bullies and weak leadership tell it, there was a "split in the church" caused by the folks who originally left. *But the truth is the "split" was caused by the bullies and the unrighteous leaders, when they attacked and forced out the godly folks who left, and then compounded their sin by either never mentioning them again or lying about them.*

It makes absolutely no sense to attack and drive out the good, righteous Christians who help out, contribute and love others in favor of the Phony Christians, Pharisees and Spiritual Bullies who do nothing but cause problems and drain the church dry, at least to a normal, sane person. But to a narcissist, it makes perfect sense. *Evil cannot stand to be in the same room with good, so the good has got to go!*

In all the cases I've heard of, the people who were attacked were godly, righteous Christians, not troublemakers who were causing divisions. They were attacked by Jezebel Spirits whose job is to destroy the church, and the Jezebels won. But they would not have been able to win if there had been strong leadership who would do the righteous thing and put a stop to the narcissistic abuse, envy, gossip, lies and pettiness within the church. Where leadership is weak or corrupt itself, the devil gets a foothold and his children take over and destroy the church.

ACCUSATIONS WITH NO BASIS IN REALITY ARE FROM THE DEVIL

AND THE GREAT DRAGON WAS CAST OUT, THAT OLD SERPENT, CALLED THE DEVIL, AND SATAN, WHICH DECEIVETH THE WHOLE WORLD: HE WAS CAST OUT INTO THE EARTH, AND HIS ANGELS WERE CAST OUT WITH HIM. AND I HEARD A LOUD VOICE SAYING IN HEAVEN, NOW IS COME SALVATION, AND STRENGTH, AND THE KINGDOM OF OUR GOD, AND THE POWER OF HIS CHRIST: FOR THE ACCUSER OF OUR BRETHREN IS CAST DOWN, WHICH ACCUSED THEM BEFORE OUR GOD DAY AND NIGHT. AND THEY OVERCAME HIM BY THE BLOOD OF THE LAMB, AND BY THE WORD OF THEIR TESTIMONY; AND THEY LOVED NOT THEIR LIVES UNTO THE DEATH. THEREFORE REJOICE, YE HEAVENS, AND YE THAT DWELL IN THEM. WOE TO THE INHABITERS OF THE EARTH AND OF THE SEA! FOR THE DEVIL IS COME DOWN UNTO YOU, HAVING GREAT WRATH,

BECAUSE HE KNOWETH THAT HE HATH BUT A SHORT TIME...Revelation 12:9-12 KJV.

WHY DO YE NOT UNDERSTAND MY SPEECH? EVEN BECAUSE YE CANNOT HEAR MY WORD. YE ARE OF YOUR FATHER THE DEVIL, AND THE LUSTS OF YOUR FATHER YE WILL DO. HE WAS A MURDERER FROM THE BEGINNING, AND ABODE NOT IN THE TRUTH, BECAUSE THERE IS NO TRUTH IN HIM. WHEN HE SPEAKETH A LIE, HE SPEAKETH OF HIS OWN: FOR HE IS A LIAR, AND THE FATHER OF IT. AND BECAUSE I TELL YOU THE TRUTH, YE BELIEVE ME NOT. WHICH OF YOU CONVINCETH ME OF SIN? AND IF I SAY THE TRUTH, WHY DO YE NOT BELIEVE ME?...John 8:43-46 KJV.

Two of the most basic lessons the Bible teaches about the devil are that he is the accuser of the brethren, and that he is a liar and the father of lies. When you put those two things together and wind up with false accusations, and some so-called "Christian" who believes them, uses them to judge and condemn a child of God, and refuses to listen to the truth, you can be sure that Satan is at work, doing what he does best.

Social networking websites are relatively new but increasingly popular venues for family and church family "spying," troublemaking and misunderstanding, and I imagine they will only get more popular in the future. My family and I once attended a church where, although we had repeatedly explained that we needed to stay away from sick people because of underlying health conditions that made getting sick very dangerous for some of us, some people didn't seem to care. One day, without realizing it, we were horrified to wind up sitting and eating in a room full of sick children, who had been in that room for more than an hour before food was served, contaminating the air and every surface with airborne diseases. Right across from us children were sneezing and coughing without covering their mouths, and one child threw up at the table.

We left as quickly as we could, and were shocked the next day to read the Sunday school teacher Ursula's online blog saying that she was so proud of the children for being in church even though ninety-five percent of them were sick with everything from stuffy noses to laryngitis to pneumonia! No one warned us of so many illnesses or we could have stayed home, but it was already too late. I and my entire family were all sick by the next day, just in time for Christmas. We had to cancel some of our holiday plans, including a rare once-a-year family tradition, go on antibiotics, and were still sick and coughing eight weeks later. We later found out that other church members, some of whom also had underlying health conditions, had also gotten seriously ill, and one person had to be hospitalized for a week and now has to use oxygen.

Like just about everyone else who has a page on a social networking site, including other people in this particular church and Ursula herself, I posted about being sick. This was my post, word-for-word:

"We are all sick and so upset just in time for Christmas after being unknowingly exposed to others who were sick. Frank went to bed, Frankie and I are coughing our brains out and blowing our noses. Please pray we are better by Christmas and not worse. I'm totally disgusted right now ☹."

How terrible of me, right? How dare I mention that my family and I got sick because of being exposed to sick people and ask for prayer! Next thing you know, I received an angry e-mail from Ursula accusing me of saying things I never did and informing me that she unfriended me because *I* was "filled with hatred" and being "unloving" and she just couldn't read any more of *my* "hurtful" posts. Like Frances' attacker, she then sent the same slanderous accusations to each of my family members. Tattling seems to be a popular attack strategy among infantile narcissists. And just in case I had anything to say for myself or might point out that she was actually wrong, she also informed me that she would not discuss it with me. Shutting your victim up before she can defend herself is another common narcissistic battle strategy. As I've mentioned before, when a narcissist "disowns" you or refuses to speak to you, it isn't necessarily because *you* did something wrong. It's usually because *she* did something wrong or uncaring, like lying or gossiping about you, or failing to warn you about a danger. And now she's getting you out of the picture before you can confront her or expose her. It's called *neutralizing the target.*

Hmmm. Well, here we go again. It's like they're all following the same playbook. Let's see~ where do I begin? First of all, social media drama, tantrums, and writing poison-pen e-mails to online "friends" and their relatives, is the kind of thing you'd expect from a twelve-year old, not a normal adult. That's why it often takes us by surprise when someone who we *thought* possessed the same mental and emotional age as their chronological age turns out to be a case of arrested development who takes posts personally, uses public websites for attention and theatrics, and thinks nobody but her has the right to express themselves freely on their pages. These same people, who would censor everybody else, are the ones who post every boring, trivial, miserable little detail of their own various illnesses, depressions, moods, feelings and relationships, and even identify the people they're complaining about, especially their exes. All for sympathy and attention, which, of course, nobody else is entitled to.

Accusations of "unlovingness", "hatred," and "hurtfulness" seem to be the first weapons so-called "Christians" pull out of their arsenals when they are trying to inflict as much damage as possible and hurt us as deeply as they possibly can. Like Frances' narcissist, my accuser also claimed to have not bothered reading my post herself, but "heard" from a third party that I was posting "publicly" that I "was disgusted with everyone at church" for "unknowingly" exposing me and my family to contagious diseases. Then she took this gossip and ran with it, judging and condemning me without even checking it out for herself, which she could easily have done. And then she passed false accusations and gossip on about me to my loved ones and other people.

How do you respond to something that someone hasn't even read? No matter what I tell Ursula I *really* said, she'd believe the lies of the third party who got it wrong and reported it wrong. She even went so far as to tell me not to bother defending myself because she wouldn't discuss it. It's impossible to defend yourself from something you didn't do, anyway. Because she was not willing to read it for herself and find out the truth, she put me in the impossible position of *never* being able to prove to her what I did or didn't actually write, and very conveniently avoided having to admit she was wrong and apologize to me.

Ursula's refusal to read my post for herself, open her eyes and see the truth indicated someone who was *looking for an excuse* to pick a fight, because she had been jealous, envious, or stewing *about something else* for months, like maybe not getting enough narcissistic supply from me, but would not admit it. She did not want to risk that phony excuse for picking a fight being taken away, which would have happened if she read my actual post and saw what it *really* said, because there was nothing at all offensive about it. If she wanted to be fair and give me the benefit of the doubt, she would have read it herself, or *asked* me about it before assuming the other person was accurate and not mistaken or even lying. She would not have attacked me out of the blue and then refused to discuss it with me. That is not at all how Christ taught us to resolve differences among ourselves.

Some people appoint themselves to be the Online Social Network Gestapo, and think it's their place to judge us and "re-educate" us whenever something we post (or something they *think* we posted) doesn't meet with their approval. This woman was one of those people who posted details of her own illnesses whenever she was sick, but apparently I couldn't do the same and ask for prayer. Note that nowhere in my post did I identify anyone or say that my family and I got sick at church. We could have been at a birthday party or at the mall. I never make public the churches I attend, so even if I had mentioned church, no one who read my post could have known what church I was talking about. I didn't say they "unknowingly" exposed us; I said we "were unknowingly exposed." There's a difference. And I never said I was disgusted with *people* at all, in or out of church~ I was disgusted that we were all sick.

Note also that there wasn't the slightest care or concern about my family and me being sick, only defensiveness. And after finding out that other church members had also gotten sick at the same time and even had to be hospitalized, still no taking of responsibility, no apologizing, no offering to pray for us and our recovery, and no expressing any interest at all in how we were feeling or care for our health and safety. Just a nasty attack and an attempt to beat me to the punch, before I told my relatives and the other church members how we were exposed to a room full of illnesses without warning and all wound up getting sick just in time for the holidays, by discrediting me *as someone who had always been* "hurtful, negative and unloving," although she never mentioned it until now. How convenient. Narcissists in both families and churches waste no time in launching their smear campaigns against anyone who might make them look "bad" or careless or thoughtless just by telling the truth.

But by passing lies around about me to others, this "church lady" revealed her true character and made herself look far worse than I ever could have. It was all about damage-control. Preserving her image as "perfect," and someone who had the brains and thoughtfulness and consideration not to expose the entire congregation, which included frail and elderly people, many of whom also had underlying health conditions, to all of these highly contagious and potentially very serious illnesses without warning us, was more important than any empathy for us. So many people getting seriously ill within forty-eight hours of this exposure was making *her* look bad. So who is the "unloving" and "hurtful" one in this scenario, and who is the one who's projecting her own unrighteousness onto somebody else? Me? I don't think so.

HE THAT WORKETH DECEIT SHALL NOT DWELL WITHIN MY HOUSE: HE THAT TELLETH LIES SHALL NOT TARRY IN MY SIGHT. I WILL EARLY DESTROY ALL THE WICKED OF THE LAND; THAT I MAY CUT OFF ALL WICKED DOERS FROM THE CITY OF THE LORD...Proverbs 101:7-8 KJV.

Only the week before, Ursula and I had a discussion about parents who don't keep their sick children home from school, thereby infecting *her* children and causing sickness in *her* household, so it's not like she didn't grasp the science behind spreading around contagious diseases. In her e-mail, she made reference to "our poor sick babies" in Sunday school as if I was blaming *the children* for getting so many of us deathly ill and risking some folk's lives, instead of *her* carelessness. And yet "our poor babies," suffering from everything from colds to laryngitis to pneumonia, were taken out of their warm homes, driven miles on icy, snowy rural roads, and brought to church on one of the worst days of the year weather-wise, a miserable, raw, bitter-cold day filled with snow, sleet and freezing rain. They, too, were exposed to the serious diseases of the *other* children at a time when their own immunity was weakened because they were already sick with their own illnesses. Wasn't anyone worried about *them* picking up other illnesses or secondary infections, or having relapses? Why would anyone who loved "our poor babies" so much risk making all these sick little kids get even sicker? Is *that* being a caring, loving person, not to mention a responsible adult?

The reason Ursula was so "proud" of the children for soldiering on despite their illnesses was that they did a few-minute "play" for the congregation that could easily have been postponed until the next week, when the weather was better and the kids would have had another week to recover and feel better. Why not make an "executive decision," given the circumstances, and let the little children stay home, where they could sleep late, stay in their pajamas, rest, be warm and dry, and not get exposed to all those other sick children? I'm sure they felt tired, ill and miserable, and would have been much more comfortable staying home, especially the little guy who threw up. And yet, the person in charge and responsible for all this tried to twist it to sound like *I* was the one who wasn't being nice to "our poor sick babies," and to imply that I was blaming *them* for getting me and my family sick! News flash~ none of this was the kids' fault. In my opinion, anyone who was truly so concerned about the children and loved them so much would not have thought so highly of her own little stage production that it became an "idol"~ more important than, and given priority over, the comfort and welfare of so many "poor sick babies."

Like Frances and her family, in retrospect my family and I also recalled several hints that Ursula had been doing the Slow Burn toward us for a while, although we didn't notice it at the time, because our world didn't revolve around Ursula and her moods. For a few weeks before her hissy-fit, she had been walking past us in church without looking at us, whereas in the past she would make eye contact and smile. For the years we attended that church, she almost always sat directly across from us at the fellowship luncheons and conversed with us. But in the weeks leading up to her attack on me, she sat instead at the opposite end of the table, slumping in her chair and silently staring at us, observing from a distance our happy chatting and laughing with the other church members. I didn't think anything of it at the time, because we had done nothing wrong. I knew that no one had any reason to be upset with me or my family. No *normal* person, that is. But I wasn't factoring in what a *narcissist* might be thinking. Little did we know that Ursula was bent out of shape over something or other, and our failure to notice her pouting would lead to the steam building up in her until the pressure cooker blew its top!

But, not to worry. Like Frances, my family and I are happily attending a new church that we love, and where folks seem to have a basic understanding of hygiene and sanitary practices and how diseases spread through entire households or groups, and care enough about other people to take a few simple steps of prevention that might keep them safe. Thank you Lord!

As I write about these testimonies of contaminating and infecting other people in church with contagious diseases, and not taking the risking of children's and adults' health and the lives of those who are elderly or frail seriously, I can't help but wonder what's going on here and what on earth is wrong with people like this. Do they really have that much hatred and malice in their hearts for their fellow churchgoers? How can you claim to be a godly person when you won't even take responsibility for harming others through your carelessness, make an effort to improve your sanitary "procedures," or show any concern or love for the people you harmed or interest in their recovery? And what about Spiritual Bullies like the demented Marge, who *deliberately try* to get their "rivals" sick, and think they have the right to force themselves on another person by literally assaulting them with unwanted touch? Is *trying* to kill other people a godly way to act? Why does this seem to be such a popular type of church abuse? I don't know, but it seems particularly vicious and wicked to me, and I hope it's not a scary new weapon the devil is instructing his children to use against the children of God. We need to cover each other in prayer against this evil, and not hesitate to leave a church so lacking in love and common sense. Then we need to ask the Lord to lead us to a church that is not a health hazard, one that is truly righteous and godly, with folks who actually know what it means to show the love of Christ to one another, and *act on it* instead of just spouting empty words to impress other people with their phony "holiness."

THE TEN COMMANDMENTS DO NOT APPLY TO NARCISSISTS

We all know that rules never apply to narcissists, even the rules *they* make up for *us* to follow. But it's especially hypocritical when we realize that The Ten Commandments do not apply to church narcissists. These very same phony Christians who manage to throw Commandments at us whenever it suits them (like honoring evil parents) seem to be perfectly fine with breaking the Commandments themselves. Of course, we all know of church leaders and members who have committed adultery or stolen money from the church and congregation. But there are other commandments also, that they break without batting an eye.

Edwina's family *made an idol* of her, going so far as to tell other people, including potential boyfriends, point-blank that she was "perfect," when only *God* is perfect, and *she* was far from it. They also covered up her flaws and her wickedness toward Frances, instead of confronting her on them and being honest with the other church members about why Frances left the church. Edwina *made an idol* of her music and Ursula *made an idol* of her little children's play, putting them before God's children, their feelings and even their health and safety. Edwina and Ursula's few enablers *made idols* of both women, pretending that they could do no wrong and allowing them to harm, unjustly attack, gossip and lie about innocent people who had *really* done nothing wrong. All of these false idols were given priority over and treated as if they were more important than what the Lord would want done and the other children of God in their congregations. They were put before the Lord, and before doing the godly, righteous thing.

When narcissists envy us or want what we have, they are *coveting* what is ours. That might be a boyfriend, girlfriend, husband, wife, wedding, marriage, children, popularity, looks, friends, talent, musical ability, attention, success, or anything else we have that they are jealous of. We are not supposed to feel hatred and resentment toward a person or a family whose son married someone else, or whom we consider to be competition because they can play music that people enjoy more than the music we play, enough to maliciously hurt them all with poison-pen e-mails about themselves or the people they love~ especially not just before the celebration of Christ's birth. "Thou shalt not covet" is a commandment, too, and it says we are not to covet *anything* that is our neighbor's.

When Edwina wrote e-mails to Frances' children and Ursula complained about me to my relatives, making false accusations and spreading lies about us, claiming we said things we never said and did things we never did, they both *bore false witness* against us. When Edwina's relatives lied to other people about why Frances and her family left the church to protect Edwina's image, they *bore false witness* against Frances and her family. How come "Thou shalt not bear false witness against thy neighbor" doesn't apply to *them?*

And yes, when you never contribute anything of your own to your church fellowship luncheons, but leave the service early so you can sneak into the lunchroom while everybody else is still in church, help yourself to mounds of food that other people paid for and cooked before the meal it was meant for is even served, and pack it up to take home for several other meals for yourself, leaving too little for everyone at the luncheon to get a portion, and when you hide it in another room under your coat so nobody will see it until you leave, like Leah does, that is *stealing*. Doing it every week is downright disgraceful. Your fellow churchgoers are bringing food for *everyone* to share at the fellowship. They are *not* cooking *your dinner* for you. It would be one thing if you were destitute (although technically it's still stealing if you're taking it without permission), but it's a little hard to work up any sympathy for someone who does this although she wears nice new clothes, travels, drives a luxury car, and is able-bodied but doesn't bother getting a job. You can't be that hard up for money if you don't bother working. Maybe you're just too lazy to work *or* to cook dinner. Apparently "Thou shalt not steal" is another Commandment that doesn't count when it comes to our church narcissists.

BUT NOW I AM WRITING YOU THAT YOU MUST NOT ASSOCIATE WITH ANYONE WHO CALLS HIMSELF A BROTHER BUT IS SEXUALLY IMMORAL OR ***GREEDY, AN IDOLATER OR A SLANDERER****, A DRUNKARD OR* ***A SWINDLER.*** *WITH SUCH A MAN DO NOT EVEN EAT…*
1Corinthians 5:11 NIV.

NARCISSISTS ACT LIKE CHILDREN AND TREAT US AS IF WE WERE CHILDREN, TOO

ALL MY ENEMIES WILL BE ASHAMED AND DISMAYED; THEY WILL TURN BACK IN SUDDEN DISGRACE…Psalms 6:10 NIV.

It is often said that narcissists have the emotional maturity of two-year olds. Narcissists and psychopaths also have a grandiose authoritarian streak, where they imagine they are the tyrants who make all the rules and who must be obeyed. Nowhere is this more evident than in confrontations, in which they act like children, or, even more interesting, act like parent-figures who think they have authority over us, and treat *us* like children. Sitting down with goodwill and love and having a reasonable, rational discussion like mature adults, giving details of the supposed offense instead of vague generalities so the other person will know what they're actually being accused of and who they "insulted," being open-minded and fair and willing to listen to the other side, not having too much pride to admit you might actually be wrong, something might have been misquoted, or you might not have gotten the whole story, and approaching it in the spirit of resolving the problem instead of just attacking the other person and causing a *bigger* problem, are all signs of the way normal, functional, mature adults approach conflicts.

Leveling accusations, usually vague and often completely false, against someone while giving no details is a typical narcissistic battle tactic. They want to put you on the defensive, upset you, and take you down a peg or two, because they think you've gotten too big for your britches and you're threatening their superiority. Narcissists, bullies and abusers want to dominate and control and humble you, so they tend to lambast and attack, be punitive and vindictive, treat you like a child, and shut you up by refusing to let you speak or defend yourself. No back talk allowed!

Besides appointing themselves to be the Online Social Network Gestapo, controlling and bossy narcissists often think they have the right to supervise us, lecture and teach us as if we were naughty children, even if we're much older than they are and much more mature Christians, and make sure we "play nice" with them and their cronies according to their usually very faulty standards and arbitrary rules. *They believe it's their job and their business to police our interactions with other adults*, and to meddle in issues that don't concern them.

They do this to satisfy their addiction to power over us "lesser beings," to find something to criticize us about so they can make us look bad, and to curry favor and make themselves look like good "leaders" to their weak and submissive followers.

Some narcissists take on the role of schoolteacher to our naughty little child. As we've seen, some think it's their place to write "notes home" to our friends and relatives, explaining their reasons for "disciplining" and "punishing" us and describing our misbehavior. One narcissist, who actually *is* a preschool teacher and apparently has a problem separating her work from her personal life, treats the adults in her life as if they were children whom it is her place to supervise, discipline and "report on." She has written "notes home" also, tattling on other adults. But even more amusing, she publicly posts "behavior evaluations" of her occasional and sporadic boyfriend online. Perhaps to explain her desperate and embarrassing tendency to take him back repeatedly after he repeatedly mistreats and humiliates her, she either reports to "friends" on their personal pages for all *their* friends to see, or publicly posts on her own page for all *her* friends to see, that he is now a "completely different person" who "realizes the mistakes he made," and that she "hopes that it will continue in this pattern." Although she sounds exactly like a "superior" schoolteacher reporting on the behavior of a naughty little boy to his parents, she does not appear to understand how inappropriate this is, and how judgmental, controlling, and socially improper her *own* behavior is.

Theatrics are another favorite weapon in the narcissist's arsenal. They think that the more dramatic they are, the more believable they'll seem. Pretending that they've been heroically "holding it in" *till they just couldn't stand it anymore* and finally had to explode on you is an attempt to excuse their evil and make it look as if it is *your* fault they "couldn't help themselves" from having a meltdown. A narcissist's unacceptable bad behavior is never *his* fault. It's always someone else's fault. Narcissists want to vent the rage that has been building up in them all along toward you, usually due to their own intense envy and jealousy, and after they've dumped their toxic waste all over you, they feel better. They feel relieved. But if they let you speak, they might be proven wrong, or they might get drawn into a battle they really can't defend. Worse yet, it might turn out that *they* owe *you* an apology, and their pride can't stand for that.

A few years ago, my family and I attended a certain church. After we had been there a few weeks, one of the men called us at home and asked to speak to my husband. He then asked my husband if I was mad at his wife. My husband had no idea what he was talking about, and neither did I. I liked her just fine. Turns out I had not sought her out personally to greet her that day in church. I was involved in a conversation with other folks, and by the time we were finished, she had left. Notice, *she did not seek me out either.* If it meant so much to her to greet me, then why, instead of getting insulted and imagining I was "mad" for some reason, did she not just come up to me and say hello like a normal person would have done?

Narcissists act like babies. They also think they are Special People, family or church royalty, and you have to be the one to seek them out and approach them as a matter of respect. They don't have to "stoop" to find you and greet you, and they don't have to respect you, even if you are their elder and better. Bratty kids and bullies are looking for an excuse to take offense where none was meant, so you will knock yourself out trying to pacify them, apologizing for doing nothing wrong, and giving them attention. Even more infantile was the fact that the husband had to call my husband to ask about this, as if the men were our parents, responsible for our behavior and "training," instead of the wife calling me like a normal adult, or even like a real friend would have, and talking about it directly. How absurdly childish. Now maybe *I* should be the one who's offended.

Narcissists often use projection as a weapon. They project their own character flaws, rudeness and unacceptable behavior onto other people, usually their victims, and accuse us of doing, thinking and feeling exactly what *they* are doing, thinking and feeling. The "hurt" wife I mentioned above should have made sure to say hello (and goodbye) to me before she went home. *I* didn't leave. *She* did. In the world of normal people with halfway decent manners, the person who is leaving makes the rounds and says goodbye to those who are still there. She doesn't just disappear and then complain that someone else didn't notice in time to run across the room and catch her before she left.

Church members who accuse us of being "hurtful", "unloving" and "unforgiving," especially just for daring to complain about being mistreated by them, are the *real* hurtful, unloving and unforgiving ones. *Simply mentioning when they have harmed us or talking about it is not being hurtful, unloving or unforgiving.* That's absurd. And if it were true, then why is it okay for *them* to mention it when they think *we* have "hurt" *them?* Doesn't that make *them* just as hurtful, unloving and unforgiving as they accuse *us* of being? When you have caused harm to someone and they point it out or protest, the proper "loving" response is an apology and being accountable for what you did, *not pretending that your victim is being a bad Christian for even mentioning what you did to her. If we have to forgive them for causing us harm, then they have to forgive us for talking about it. Everybody* has to forgive *everything,* not just us. Why are they exempt from the same rules they force on us? "Christians" who are always looking for a lame excuse to get insulted and pick a fight are not being the least bit righteous or godly. The Bible warns us not to be quick to take offense:

BE NOT HASTY IN THY SPIRIT TO BE ANGRY: FOR ANGER RESTETH IN THE BOSOM OF FOOLS…Ecclesiastes 7:9 KJV.

A FOOL SHOWS HIS ANNOYANCE AT ONCE, BUT A PRUDENT MAN OVERLOOKS AN INSULT...Proverbs 12:16 NIV.

HE THAT IS SLOW TO WRATH IS OF GREAT UNDERSTANDING: BUT HE THAT IS HASTY OF SPIRIT EXALTETH FOLLY...Proverbs 14:29 KJV.

WHEREFORE, MY BELOVED BRETHREN, LET EVERY MAN BE SWIFT TO HEAR, SLOW TO SPEAK, SLOW TO WRATH: FOR THE WRATH OF MAN WORKETH NOT THE RIGHTEOUSNESS OF GOD...James 1:19-20 KJV.

Although narcissists have the mentality of spoiled bratty little babies, they are also bullies at heart. They often assume the bossy "parent" role in their relationships, treating other adults like foolish little children, believing they have the right to judge us, supervise us, teach us and tell us what to do, and we *have to* listen to them. They imagine that they have authority over us and assume the roles of schoolteacher, censor and dictator. The testimonies I've talked about in this chapter give numerous examples of childish behavior, not to mention narcissistic "logic" that would make most people think they were downright certifiable. Here are some elements of the juvenile and insane mentality apparent in these stories:

- "When *I'm* mad at you, I'm allowed to lash out, punish you, complain to you, and gossip about you to other people, but when *you* are mad, you have no right to say anything about it at all, to anyone. You just have to keep quiet."
- "My friend thinks you were mean to her, so now *I'm* mad at you and I'm going to take it upon myself to punish you." *Gang mentality against a common enemy (scapegoat) allows*

members of a dysfunctional family or church to vent their frustrations with each other at a "safe" target, someone who is not an "insider" in the group.

- "'I heard' you did something I don't like, so now I'm mad at you, *even if it's not true*. If you *had* done it, I wouldn't have liked it, so I'm justified in getting angry at you anyway, even though what 'I heard' was a lie. This makes perfect sense, because I'm crazy." *No details about what you supposedly did or who told her.*
- "When I do something wrong or even something that causes you harm, instead of apologizing and making amends, I'm going to turn it around, make *you* the villain instead of the injured party, and pretend to be mad at you so you are the one who has to apologize. You are not allowed to get angry, and your feelings will not be acknowledged. The only ones whose feelings count are me and my cronies. I am allowed to be unloving and hateful and hurt you and attack you, but you are not allowed to even mention it, or I will pretend that your perfectly legitimate protests are really *you* being hurtful and unloving to *me!*"
- *Lacking the maturity to deal with you in person, narcissistic nutjobs will often attack in a cowardly way~ by demented e-mail, letter, card or voicemail, or spitefully through a third party, again giving you no opportunity to respond.*
- "I'm gonna tell on you! Now I have to send a note home to your parents and tell them how naughty you were and why I had to discipline you, just like I was the strict old schoolmarm and you were a disobedient little kindergartener. And if you're too old to for me to involve your Mommy and Daddy, then I'll tattle to your siblings, your children, your friends, your neighbors, your boss or your coworkers. I'm going to try and ruin your reputation. I'm going to tattle-tale

on you to your relatives and other people who like you so they will understand my point of view, think I'm right, realize what a terrible person you are, get mad at you for being such a big old meanie, and turn against you." *Narcissists who are frustrated with their own families or their lack of power within their own families often make themselves feel better by instigating trouble in other people's families.*

- "You're always getting me mad, *but you can never be mad at me because I'm perfect.* You do all of these wrong things, but I never do anything wrong. *If you dare to get mad at me, I'll get mad at you right back,* for trying to make me look bad."
- "If you ever find out that I did something wrong, or even catch me red-handed doing something wrong, *I'll* get mad at *you* just for knowing about it."
- "I have no idea who you're talking about, but *if* it's me, I'm mad at you. And *if* it's somebody else I know, I'm mad at you. And just in case it's somebody I don't even know, I'm *still* mad at you. Actually, it really doesn't matter *who* you're talking about, because I'm just looking for any excuse to get mad at you so I can gossip and complain about you, and make you follow me around, giving me attention and trying to pacify me."
- "You posted that somebody did harm to you without identifying who, but you must be talking about me because what you described is exactly the kind of thing *I* do to people, only nobody is allowed to complain about it, so now I'm mad at you. Oh, and you are very unforgiving, too."
- "If you even mention anything I did that harmed you, I'll accuse you of being 'unforgiving.' And then *I* won't forgive *you* for having the nerve to mention it and making me sound less-than-perfect. But of course, that doesn't make *me* 'unforgiving.'"
- "I'm the only one allowed to talk, so don't try and defend yourself or even ask me what I'm talking about. You have

> to just shut up and listen! No back talk! It's my way or the highway! This is the way it's gonna be! I don't wanna hear it! Because I said so, that's why!"

AND IF THE HOUSE BE WORTHY, LET YOUR PEACE COME UPON IT: BUT IF IT BE NOT WORTHY, LET YOUR PEACE RETURN TO YOU. AND WHOSOEVER SHALL NOT RECEIVE YOU, NOR HEAR YOUR WORDS, WHEN YE DEPART OUT OF THAT HOUSE OR CITY, SHAKE OFF THE DUST OF YOUR FEET. VERILY I SAY UNTO YOU, IT SHALL BE MORE TOLERABLE FOR THE LAND OF SODOM AND GOMORRHA IN THE DAY OF JUDGMENT, THAN FOR THAT CITY...Matthew 10:13-15 KJV.

Nothing about this type of irrational, unreasonable, dictatorial, demanding attack on another person indicates a normally functioning adult, or, for that matter, a godly Christian who is following Christ's teachings for resolving differences among the brethren. Such over-the-top malice, insanity, hypocrisy and evil indicate mental or emotional instability at best, and at worst, a child of the devil.

There is no reasoning with someone who acts like this, no possibility of placating him and living in peace. It will only be a matter of time before he trumps up some more charges against you, refuses to speak to you again or to let you speak, or comes up with yet another asinine excuse to pick a fight with you. There will always be another problem, because he's just itching to tell you off, make you look bad to other people, humble you and make you feel bad, and then make you give him attention and beg him to forgive you and take you back without ever knowing exactly what it was you did. ***It's not about online blogs or posts, it's not about anything you supposedly said or didn't say to some third party, and it's not about not getting a chance to greet someone before they left.*** There's much more going on here and a whole other agenda you are not aware of. Welcome to the

Twilight Zone. You can never win, so don't even bother. The deck has been stacked against you for months, if not years, while the narcissist seethed in secret rage and laid in wait for his opportunity to attack you. And that's the way it will always be with miserable people who are consumed with envy and bitterness, and are just itching for a chance to turn on you and stab people who have always treated them well in the back. So just give up and get off the Crazy Train right here, at this stop, while you still can. It's the last stop before hell.

THANKS FOR PROVING *MY* POINT

I find it very interesting that a lot of narcissistic confrontations tend to take place in writing, rather than in person. Why would anyone literally *giftwrap* and hand to us the proof positive of their completely un-Christlike behavior, arrogance and sheer lunacy, so that when other relatives ask about the rift, or church members ask why we no longer attend that church, we can just hand them a copy and let them read the so-called "Christian's" malice, hostility and demented crackpot rantings for themselves? Nothing makes our case better than the toxic waste spewed directly from the horse's mouth in a deranged e-mail, card or letter.

I think there are two possibilities here. Either the narcissist thinks we will be so embarrassed by the things she accused us of that we would never let anybody else see what she wrote (while meantime, *she* will be taking advantage of our silence, getting the jump on us and spreading lies and rumors about us to anyone who will listen), or she is so delusional that she really doesn't see anything wrong with what she wrote, has no idea how bad and how insane it makes *her* look, and doesn't mind if we let other people read it.

Personally, I felt quite a bit better after the jaw-dropping that occurred when I showed other folks the nasty e-mail I got from Ursula, as well as the ones she sent to my relatives to badmouth me. The shocked and disapproving reactions of my sisters and brothers in Christ confirmed what the Holy Ghost was showing me about Ursula's own lack of love and defective "Christian walk," and validated my own feelings that the person who attacked me was way out of line, acted as spitefully and hurtfully as possible, and did not behave in a godly, "loving" or "forgiving" way in the least.

Bullies, abusers, and narcissists rely on our silence. It allows them to continue in their evil without fear of exposure. I see no reason to hesitate in passing around a poison-pen letter we get from a bully, especially if it's full of lies and false accusations, to people who would have an interest in knowing what happened that ended the relationship. If they care about us and we care about them, then our friends deserve to know the truth and to see the evidence for themselves. The only one who should be embarrassed about it and wind up looking like a fool is the person who wrote it. We have nothing to be ashamed of and nothing to hide.

THERE'S A FUNGUS AMONG US: SETTING A TRAP FOR THE SPY IN YOUR MIDST

WHERE NO WOOD IS, THERE THE FIRE GOETH OUT: SO WHERE THERE IS NO TALEBEARER, THE STRIFE CEASETH. AS COALS ARE TO BURNING COALS AND WOOD TO FIRE; SO IS A CONTENTIOUS MAN TO KINDLE STRIFE ...Proverbs 26:20-21 KJV.

AN UNGODLY MAN DIGGETH UP EVIL: AND IN HIS LIPS THERE IS AS A BURNING FIRE. A FROWARD MAN SOWETH STRIFE: AND A WHISPERER SEPARATETH CHIEF FRIENDS. A VIOLENT MAN ENTICETH HIS NEIGHBOUR, AND LEADETH HIM INTO THE WAY THAT IS NOT GOOD. HE SHUTTETH HIS EYES TO DEVISE FROWARD THINGS: MOVING HIS LIPS HE BRINGETH EVIL TO PASS...Proverbs 16:27-30 KJV.

One thing many of these testimonies have in common is that mysterious third party, who shall remain nameless. When narcissists unjustly attack, they will often state that they "heard" you said or did something, or that "somebody" told them, *but they will never tell you **who***, so you can face your accuser in person.

Most of these nameless busybodies exist only in the narcissist's imagination. They invent other people who are "mad at" us or "against" us so it will seem as if they have people on their side, who agree with them. This is another aspect of the juvenile "gang mentality" the childish narcissist has. A common bullying strategy is to isolate the target~ make you suspect your friends, think people are turning against you and talking behind your back, and the bully has allies but you don't. It's an intimidation tactic.

But in many cases, there really is a backstabber at work, busy currying favor with the powers-that-be by carrying tales about you back to them and then getting vicarious thrills when they "punish" you. Most toxic families and church families have at least one, if not several, two-faced phonies who will be sweet as sugar to your face and pretend to be your best friend, all while gathering information and spying on you for the Alpha Dog. Anything you reveal will be twisted, exaggerated and sensationalized to instigate as much trouble as possible. Watch for anyone who encourages you to reveal your opinions or feelings so that they can then be used against you. Remember, you are not actually allowed to have any opinions or feelings. Only the narcissist and her Silent Partners are allowed such luxuries. Even if you are asked a direct question and answer with the truth, it will be twisted so it looks like you hurt one of them, just by telling the truth. They are just looking for an excuse to criticize you and accuse you, to keep you in a one-down position in the power hierarchy, trying desperately to prove them wrong, make it up to them and please them. It's a sick little dynamic among petty, small-minded, ugly little people.

But who *is* this spy, who pretends to "love" you and then gives information about you to people who *don't* love you? Or who passes around lies and false rumors about you? Who is the nasty little troublemaking tattletale? In most groups, there are several possibilities. Thankfully, they are not usually the sharpest knives in the drawer, so they often wind up cooperating with us very nicely when we trick them into revealing themselves. Narcissists and their Silent Partners typically think they're quite clever, and underestimate everyone else. They think they're pulling the wool over our eyes by getting us to let down our guards, spying on us and reporting back, but it never occurs to them that maybe *they* are the ones who are being played. There is nothing wrong with exposing and eliminating a rat to protect yourself and your loved ones, just like Queen Esther did to the wicked Haman in the Book of Esther.

The old-school way of getting a spy to show her face is to plant a "red herring." Tell something to her, and *only* her, and then just wait. When it gets back to you, you'll know she's your man. If there is more than one suspect, tell each of them something totally different and wait to see which phony story of yours sees the light of day. It's possible that more than one of your red herrings will get passed around, and then you'll know you have more than one spy. And if you kept track of which story you told to whom, you'll also know who the culprits are.

With the popularity of online networking and other social media, old-school methods for catching a rat might have to be updated a bit, but they still work. The high-tech Red Herring Strategy goes like this: You post something controversial or sure to push somebody's buttons, and you use the website's tools to block everyone else in that particular group from seeing it except the person you suspect of being the spy, and then you wait again. Setting a trap for a spy requires patience, and your patience will be rewarded. After a few days, bait the trap with another post sure to get your spy and the head narcissist annoyed, and again allow only your suspected spy to view it while blocking everyone else in your family, church or group from seeing it.

If you have several possibilities among the people in a given group, you can set several traps at the same time, each one baited with a different red herring. Separate what each of the potential spies can see. Only allow one person in your family to see your first phony post, and block everyone else in the family. Then let another suspect see your next phony post, and block everyone else from seeing it including the first suspect. Keep track of each individual you do this with, and which phony post you made visible to her. Make the posts something you know will get a rise out of the narcissists in the group and provoke a reaction, so they will feel compelled to respond or confront you in some way. Whenever one of the phony comments you baited your traps with gets back to you, either through the grapevine or by an angry attack from one of the group narcissists, just refer to your little list and see who in the group you fed that particular story to. Voila! You have just uncovered your spy!

In my case, although the not-too-swift Ursula might have thought she was protecting her spy's identity by not naming names, I knew immediately who it was, because she was the only church member who could read any of my posts other than Ursula herself, and *she* had refused to read what I had actually posted. It didn't take a rocket scientist to put two and two together. In Frances' case, within a week she was able to flush out her rat by setting a Red Herring Trap. In narcissistic battles, it's always a good idea to know who your enemies are. Sometimes they're not who you would expect.

What to do once you know? Well, for starters, don't be hasty. Keep cool and act normal. Don't confront the spy or unfriend her or block her from seeing all your posts. Don't give her a clue that you know. *What you want to do now is turn her into a double-agent.* You want to use her to your advantage. Now you know enough to censor the information you let her have, so the risk to you has been neutralized. But besides keeping information *from* her, you can also feed her information you *want* her to pass on to the rest of the family or group. Just make sure the spy is the only person you tell.

Better yet, don't tell directly, just hint and imply and let the spy read into what you said and her imagination take over. You could really go to town on this~ the possibilities are endless. Each ridiculous comment you make to the spy or allow her to see will cause all kinds of drama and histrionics in the group when she blabs it to them. They will go crazy getting all worked up, trying to get more information, and passing rumors around. If the stories you hand-feed the spy are wacky enough and consistently prove to be untrue, eventually the Alpha Dog and the rest of the narcissistic group will think the spy is just lying or making stuff up, and turn on her. They will know she is no longer a trusted source and no longer useful, and their paranoia will make them suspect she's deliberately misleading them.

You can facilitate this by deleting or hiding the comment you fed to the spy whenever you know she will be in the presence of the group. For instance, if you feed a phony provocative comment to a church spy, make sure to use the social network website's filters to hide or delete it before she gets to church on Sunday, so if she tries to log on using a cell phone and show your comment to anyone else, it won't be there. Then "unhide" it that night or the next day so she can see it again once she's back home. See how long you can keep it up before anybody catches on, if they ever do. Outplay the rat, and then sit back and watch the show.

NO ONE WHOSE HOPE IS IN YOU WILL EVER BE PUT TO SHAME, BUT THEY WILL BE PUT TO SHAME WHO ARE TREACHEROUS WITHOUT EXCUSE...Psalms 25:3 NIV.

LET THEM BE CONFOUNDED AND PUT TO SHAME THAT SEEK AFTER MY SOUL: LET THEM BE TURNED BACK AND BROUGHT TO CONFUSION THAT DEVISE MY HURT...Psalms 35:4 KJV.

I DO NOT TRUST IN MY BOW, MY SWORD DOES NOT BRING ME VICTORY; BUT YOU GIVE US VICTORY OVER OUR ENEMIES, YOU PUT OUR ADVERSARIES TO SHAME...Psalms 44:6-7 NIV.

CHAPTER 22

"BUT I'VE CHANGED, SO YOU HAVE TO GIVE ME ANOTHER CHANCE"

THIS IS HOW WE KNOW WHO THE CHILDREN OF GOD ARE AND WHO THE CHILDREN OF THE DEVIL ARE: ANYONE WHO DOES NOT DO WHAT IS RIGHT IS NOT A CHILD OF GOD; NOR IS ANYONE WHO DOES NOT LOVE HIS BROTHER…1 John 3:10 NIV.

Sisters and Brothers, do any of these lines ring a bell with you?:

- "I've changed."
- "I'm a new person."
- "I don't do those things anymore."
- "I don't act like that anymore."
- "The Lord has worked a change in my heart."
- "I've turned over a new leaf."
- "I'm not like I was before."
- "I'm a different person than I once was."
- "That was in the past."
- "I promise I'm a changed man/woman."
- "I've learned my lesson."
- "That was the old me, this is the new me."
- "Things are different now."

Most of us have heard the above assurances at some time in our lives, usually in one of two situations:

1. Either we've gotten fed up with our abuser and he knows we are getting ready to end the relationship,

Or,

2. The relationship already ended some time previously, we haven't spoken to our abuser in a while and thought she was out of our lives. But meanwhile, she's getting impatient waiting for us to "come around," so she decided to try again.

When we fail to jump at the chance to have our abuser back in our lives, he will usually turn up the pressure with such statements as:

- "You *have to* believe me/ give me one more chance/ another shot/ the benefit of the doubt/ trust me/ let me prove it to you, etc."
- "You *have to* forgive and forget."
- "Let's move on."
- "Let's start fresh."
- "Everybody deserves another chance."
- "Just let bygones be bygones."
- "It's time to get over it."

Then, should we continue to hesitate, or ask for more details on exactly what changes he's made, he will change tactics and cop an attitude, turning the tables and becoming impatient and angry with us, as if we have some nerve for hurting or insulting him:

- "Why do you keep bringing up the past?"
- "You *have to* stop harping on it."
- "Why don't you believe me?"
- "I can see I'm never going to hear the end of this."
- "I worked very hard to get to this point and now you won't trust me."

- "Why are you so unreasonable?"
- "There's just no pleasing you."
- "You're *never* gonna let me forget it, are you?"
- "You'll never be satisfied until you see me beg."
- "What do you want from me?"
- "Look, I *told* you I changed! If you think I'm gonna kiss your butt, you can go to hell!"
- "Fine, *be* that way! If you're not gonna believe me, then just forget it! Some Christian *you* are!"

All of which proves he really didn't change at all, and we were right not to believe him or trust him.

Previously, I told part of the story of the breakup of my relationship with a friend who had become abusive, demanding, and controlling. The relationship ended over the course of a year and a half, during which a number of long e-mails were exchanged, containing several interesting recurring themes, which have been excellent examples of abusive reactions that we can all study and learn from.

One such recurring theme was this abuser's repetitive, but meaningless and ultimately untrue, declarations of change. Many times, when I held her accountable for her selfishness or nastiness, she would respond that she "no longer acted that way," the implication being that I was "blaming" her for the way *she used to act* in the past.

In the course of trying to convince me to give her yet another chance, after many, many chances, she told me *no less than eight times* that she "no longer does those things", "no longer reacts the way she used to", "has repented to God for what she was doing wrong", "finally pulled down those things that were strongholds for her in the past", and "God has shown her where she needed to make changes and she has made those changes."

However, here's the interesting part. Because her statements were vague and never specified exactly what changes she had made or what behavior she no longer did, I felt I needed some more details in order to discern whether or not she was being truthful. So each time she claimed she had changed, I asked her to tell me what the Lord had shown her, what she was now doing differently, and *how* she had changed. Whereupon she would again become just as rude, nasty and hostile as before, *and exhibit every one of the offensive behaviors which I had originally set limits on and which she claimed to no longer be doing.*

It actually only took very little prodding for her façade to drop and her true colors to come out once again. The simple act of asking for clarification exposed her lies, prevented me from wasting any more time giving her fifth and sixth and twelfth and twentieth chances, and protected me from getting involved again with a jealous, demanding, selfish narcissist.

Abusers think we should take their preposterous and often repetitive claims of repentance at face value. They don't get that trust cannot be turned on and off like a light switch, and that once they have damaged or destroyed our trust, they are going to have to put some time and effort into rebuilding it. They think if they simply repeat themselves enough times or raise their voices loud enough, it will make whatever hogwash they're trying to get us to buy more believable.

Control-freaks balk at the idea that they have to *earn* our trust. It rankles them that we are not going to reconcile with them until they have *proven* themselves, because this means that *we* are now in control, we are now making the rules, and we have taken the control away from them.

Narcissists think they are so wonderful that everyone should be grateful to be in their company. They believe they are entitled to anything they want. It is a foreign concept to them that they are *not* entitled to have a relationship with us unless they *deserve* it, and unless *we* want it, too.

DEAR FRIENDS, DO NOT BELIEVE EVERY SPIRIT, BUT TEST THE SPIRITS TO SEE WHETHER THEY ARE FROM GOD...
1 John 4:1 NIV.

Abusers become highly offended at the notion that we are testing them, and that we might not consider them a good risk or worthy of a relationship with us. But when they repeatedly fall back into their default mode of the same lame old empty promises and assurances, with never any actual concrete changes made, only to relapse time and again into their usual abusive behavior as soon as things don't go their way, we would have to be fools to believe their baloney without requiring proof of change. Like the old saying goes~ fool me once, shame on you; fool me twice, shame on me!

So when your abuser lavishes you with vows of repentance, no matter how convincing she may sound, stop and remind yourself that talk is cheap, and that actions speak louder than words. Take your time and feel free to question her. Ask her to be specific about exactly how she has changed, what she realizes she was doing wrong, what behaviors she has stopped, and what hurtful things she no longer does to other people.

When I asked my ex-friend for examples of how she had changed, one tactic she used was to ask *me* to give *her* examples of her own behaviors so she could answer. This is another nonsensical, crazy-making response so typical of abusers. First of all, how would I know what behavioral changes she had made? How could *I* tell *her* what the Lord had supposedly told her she needed to repent of? How on earth could I answer that question for her?

This response alone indicated that she was lying about really changing. She was just fishing for what I wanted to hear, so she could respond only to whatever she thought was important to me in deciding whether or not to reconcile with her. It brought to mind the way kids manipulate each other~ "You go first", "No, *you* go first." At the risk of sounding like one of those kids, "*I* asked her first!" I didn't want to give her the ability to merely pretend that whatever was important to me just happened to be the things she changed. I wanted to hear the *truth.* And that would not have happened had I let her maneuver me into answering my own question for her.

Obviously, if I gave her the examples of unacceptable behaviors which I had asked her to give to *me,* that would get her off the hook from actually having to do any introspection. Abusers are experts at taking the easy way out of being held responsible for their own behavior. She would have just pretended to agree with whatever I was saying, or she would have twisted what I was saying into another excuse to avoid accountability. But she would not have been required to back up her statement of change with anything of substance that would prove she really *had* changed.

So I simply told her I couldn't accommodate her and would have no way of knowing the answers to what she had learned from her own introspection. This caused her to drop her pretense of change and have another Narcissistic Meltdown. After several episodes of going around in circles like this, I was able to reach the decision to permanently cut off contact, knowing that I was only rewarding her narcissism by continuing to give her the attention she was manipulating me into giving her. At that point I realized she was a liar and I wasn't going to play her games anymore.

So when deciding whether or not to reconcile with an abuser, take your time and don't allow yourself to be pressured into making a hasty and premature decision. Don't settle for empty promises, vague assurances and evasive answers. Insist on details. Ask him to describe exactly how he has changed. Then listen and observe. Is he willing to put forth the effort needed to earn your trust? Is he being truthful? Does he agree that you have every right to question him, and that he can't blame you for not believing him right away? Does he respectfully answer your questions while remaining calm, sincere and remorseful? Or does he become angry, defensive, "insulted" or enraged? His responses will tell you whether he is genuinely remorseful and repentant, or just manipulating you, lying to you, and telling you whatever he thinks you want to hear so he can weasel his way back into your life. Do not allow yourself to be steamrolled back into a relationship that is not beneficial for *you*.

Here are some helpful guidelines for discerning whether your abuser has *really* turned over a new leaf, or if he's just trying to con you into taking him back without any real effort or commitment on his part to change his ways:

1. Don't be a fool and don't make it easy. Be skeptical and ask for details. When an abuser claims he's changed, don't just accept his statement with no further explanation. Say, "Really? *How* have you changed?", "What exactly do you mean by that?", "That's nice. What specific changes have you made?" or even, "I'm listening........" Then be quiet and let him explain. Let him put some effort into proving he's repented.

2. Ask open-ended questions and be careful not to answer them for the abuser. Some abusers are very clever at fishing for what we really want to hear and tricking us into giving them the answers which they then spoon-feed back to us. For example, in response to her statement that "I've changed," don't *you* say, "So you're going to stop criticizing me?", "So now you understand that I can't call you back right away all the time?", or, "Well, I'm glad you realize that lying upsets me and you're not going to do it anymore." If you do this, you just gave your abuser the opportunity to respond with a simple "yes" that will satisfy you while requiring no actual

introspection or thought from her. This is not a serious commitment to change on her part. In other words, when your abuser claims she's changed, don't *you* tell *her* how she's changed. Make *her* tell *you*. Make her justify and explain her statement of change so you can better determine how serious she is and how truthful she's being.

3. After you've heard what she has to say for herself, don't be afraid to ask more questions. Force your abuser to be very specific about the changes she's made in her life and her behavior towards you and others. If the only thing you get from her is evasive or vague answers, then say, "I really don't think you've given this enough thought. Get back to me when you have something more specific to tell me, and we'll discuss it then."

4. Make your "chat" short and sweet. Get right down to business, and don't get sidetracked. Don't allow your abuser to stay connected to you by keeping you talking and discussing when you have not yet decided whether or not to renew the relationship. If you let him involve you in a long talk at this point, you are *rewarding* him by talking to him before he *deserves* to be rewarded. Maintain the upper hand. If he cannot tell you precisely and in detail how he's changed himself, then end the conversation until such time as he can come back to you with the kinds of answers you're looking for.

5. If he has given real thought to making changes, and is able to give you details, don't hesitate to buy yourself time anyway. You don't have to forgive him on the spot, or take him back. You're allowed to have time to think it over. Tell him you appreciate his efforts at repentance, you need to think it over, and that you'll get back to him after you've made a decision.

6. Both during and after your discussion, keep your antennae up, observe closely, and consider carefully the abuser's words,

unspoken messages, attitude, facial expressions and body language. Did you see signs of genuine godly remorse? Or was she resentful that she was being forced to answer to you? Did she become impatient? Was there feeling behind her words, or was she cool, aloof, or detached? If she displayed feeling or emotion, did you get the impression it was sincere, or phony? Were her claims of repentance given grudgingly, or was she cooperative and eager to prove herself to you?

7. Make him work for it. Don't be a push-over. It's okay to make him squirm. If you make it too easy, he'll soon forget all his promises and go back to mistreating you. He'll learn that the next time he pushes you too far, all he has to do to con you is to *pretend* he's seen the error of his ways and make a few empty promises, and you'll take him back again. He'll know that he can keep repeating this cycle over and over again, forever, and always trick you into giving him another chance. This removes all incentive for *real,* genuine change. If he has to work for it, he'll appreciate your forgiveness more, and think twice before risking your goodwill and getting on your bad side again.

8. This little "dance," if done successfully, will result in a role-reversal of control and power in the relationship. Knowing that you are hesitant to give him another chance, and, indeed, might *not* give him another chance, upsets a narcissist's equilibrium. He thought you adored him so much that you'd put up with anything, but now he's not so sure. It's good to make him think that you're not all that eager to take him back. The next time he upsets you might be the last time, because obviously you're not as crazy about him as he thought. Seeing that you're willing to walk away from the relationship if he doesn't keep you happy puts a whole new spin on things.

> It shifts the power to you. He should be grateful to you for giving him one last chance. If he has really changed, then he'll have nothing to worry about. But if he's lying, he'll be more likely to at least make an effort to walk on eggshells, knowing that the next time he offends you, he just might get kicked to the curb permanently.

Many of us go through months and years of uncertainty before finally going strict No Contact. Unfortunately we have feelings for the narcissists and abusers in our lives, and it can take quite a while for us to be ready to stop wasting our lives and permanently let them go. When abusive family members or friends pop up again after a period of estrangement, it is not because they love us and miss us. *It's because they want something from us. In fact, it is often triggered by them losing one of their other sources of narcissistic supply* (another relationship they were feeding off of broke up), so they start looking up their old, already-housebroken victims and trying to resurrect them as targets again.

When a narcissist contacts us again after an estrangement, she will be on her best behavior and we might be tempted to believe her claims of change. But remember, first and foremost, *all narcissists are liars.* I have never known a narcissist to be able to keep up the "nice" act and the pretense of change for more than six months to a year without slipping up and letting you catch that telltale fleeting glimpse (yes, it will be quick, so keep your eyes open or you might miss it) of her true colors once again. Time is your friend here, so delay for a very long time before letting an abuser back into your life. Be patient, watch and wait. Buy all the time you need to be sure that any changes the narcissist claims to have made are real and permanent. By the time you realize you are still being played, maybe you will be ready to take that next big step, go strict No Contact, and move on forever to a narcissist-free life.

PART 3

SHOOTING THEMSELVES IN THE FOOT, AND BLESSINGS IN DISGUISE FOR US

CHAPTER 23

THE SILENT TREATMENT

BETTER A DRY CRUST WITH PEACE AND QUIET THAN A HOUSE FULL OF FEASTING, WITH STRIFE...Proverbs 17:1 NIV

THE HEART OF THE RIGHTEOUS STUDIETH TO ANSWER: BUT THE MOUTH OF THE WICKED POURETH OUT EVIL THINGS...Proverbs 15:28 KJV.

Probably one of the most amusing narcissistic reactions, at least to me, is the Silent Treatment. You have confronted your abuser, spoke up and told the truth, protested his treatment, exposed him, rebuked him, set limits on him. And he "punishes" you for having the nerve not to take his abuse anymore, by giving you the Silent Treatment. Instead of some honest communication aimed at resolving the problems between you, he pouts just like a defiant two-year-old, and stops speaking to you. Well, thank God for small favors.

The Silent Treatment is proof positive of the narcissist's awesome arrogance. Hilarious though it may be, he actually believes he is so special and so wonderful and so vital to your life that the worst thing he could do to you is to deprive you of himself. How will you ever be able to live without him?

Because they feed off our constant attention and the attention of everyone else, narcissists assume that *we* have the same craving for *their* attention as they have for ours. The only problem with that thinking is that when they focus *their* attention on *us,* it's rarely a good thing. It's a very negative thing~ stressful, annoying, upsetting, and aggravating.

My birth-father used the Silent Treatment on a regular basis~ with me, with birth-mother, and with other people. He would literally stick his lower lip out like a little brat, and if looks could kill, we'd have dropped on the spot. If you failed to notice and didn't try to make up with him, the dirty looks would get more and more hateful. It was ridiculous to the point of being comical. We used to joke that if he didn't knock it off, his face was going to freeze like that~ and sure enough, by the time he was in his seventies, it did! I learned early on to completely ignore him, go on chatting with the other people in the room, or just leave and go about my day. When he finally couldn't take it any longer and started talking to me again, usually in grudging monosyllables, I would smile at him and say, "Oh. I thought you weren't talking to me anymore." And then he'd get all indignant and ticked off again, and hopefully stop talking to me for another few hours.

I learned to get a few laughs out of the Silent Treatment and make the most of my "blessing in disguise," but Mommy Darling couldn't stand it. She hated it when he'd stop talking to her. She'd follow him around, repeatedly asking him what was the matter, what did she do wrong, what could she do to stop this argument, and could he please just tell her! And he would smugly turn his nose up at her, look the other way, and continue torturing her. No matter how many times she complained to me and I tried to enlighten her, she could not get it through her head that he *loved* toying with her and she was playing right into his hands.

Hey, let's look at this logically. When Daddy Darling *was* talking to you, it was only to abuse you. There was no such thing as a nice conversation. You had to watch every word out of your mouth for fear of setting him off. He was just itching to attack and upset you. Every time he opened his mouth, we got lectured, criticized, degraded, berated, screamed at or called names, and most of the time we had no idea why or what we had done wrong. He was an arrogant, sarcastic, sadistic, rude, belligerent, obnoxious, nasty bully who was always looking to pick a fight over something, no matter how trivial.

On the other hand, when he *wasn't* speaking to you, it was a blessed relief. It was great! You could relax a little. You could actually feel the mood in the room lighten. So why on earth would you want someone like this talking to you? Why look a gift horse in the mouth?

The biggest problem Mommy Darling had was that *she* was a gigantic narcissist herself. *She* thrived on attention, too. And, like all narcissists, the worst thing you could do to her was to withdraw and ignore her. That's why she kept hounding her psychopathic husband to start talking to her again, even though she was going to be a lot worse off when he did. To her, being criticized, arguing, and having to endure his sarcasm, lectures and nasty comments was still better than being ignored. *Any* attention was better than no attention. Despite her pity ploys, bids for sympathy from other people and complaints about his behavior, Mommy Darling didn't really want to "live in peace." She thrived on the drama.

What is the best way to handle the silly and infantile Silent Treatment? Consider it a gift and enjoy it while it lasts, because unfortunately, it won't last forever. Ignore your abuser right back. In fact, *out-ignore* him. Leave the room and let him sit there and stew. You don't have to sit around being bored and lonely because he's not speaking to you. Call up a friend and yak for a couple of hours. Or go out and meet her for lunch or dinner. Start cleaning out your closet or baking a cake for church. Go run a nice bubble bath, lock the door, relax in the tub and read a good book. Get online, go watch TV, take a nap or go to bed, go to the gym and have a nice workout, stroll next door and visit the neighbors, get in the car and go to the mall, the library, the beach or a movie. Don't sit around and stew.

If you look at the Silent Treatment as punishment, you are looking at it the wrong way, and actually *coming into agreement with* your immature bully of an abuser, who is *trying to* punish you. Start thinking of it as the blessing it is, and use it to your advantage. Distract yourself and get your mind off the narcissist with something you enjoy. In fact, make yourself a list right now of ideas for things to do the next time he is not speaking to you, and then *do* them. There is nothing wrong with quiet times and solitude. They are in fact quite desirable. Jesus himself often withdrew into solitude to pray and communicate with God. We cannot hear the voice of God if we are distracted by worldly, and especially devilish, things:

AND IN THE MORNING, RISING UP A GREAT WHILE BEFORE DAY, HE WENT OUT, AND DEPARTED INTO A SOLITARY PLACE, AND THERE PRAYED...Mark 1:35 KJV.

BUT THOU, WHEN THOU PRAYEST, ENTER INTO THY CLOSET, AND WHEN THOU HAST SHUT THY DOOR, PRAY TO THY FATHER WHICH IS IN SECRET; AND THY FATHER WHICH SEETH IN SECRET SHALL REWARD THEE OPENLY... Matthew 6:6 KJV.

AND HE WITHDREW HIMSELF INTO THE WILDERNESS, AND PRAYED...Luke 5:16 KJV.

AND IT CAME TO PASS IN THOSE DAYS, THAT HE WENT OUT INTO A MOUNTAIN TO PRAY, AND CONTINUED ALL NIGHT IN PRAYER TO GOD. AND WHEN IT WAS DAY, HE CALLED UNTO HIM HIS DISCIPLES; AND OF THEM HE CHOSE TWELVE, WHOM ALSO HE NAMED APOSTLES...Luke 6:12-13 KJV.

If you don't live with your abuser, ignoring his Silent Treatment is even easier. You don't even have to look at his sourpuss. If you are an Adult Child, and your abusive parents or siblings are punishing you by not speaking to you, consider it the best thing that ever happened to you. The first rule of playing hardball is, "*He who speaks first, loses.*" Don't let it bug you, don't make the first move, don't let them know they got to you or they'll never stop manipulating. Just ignore them.

Shift the power in the relationship. Make *them* call *you*. In fact, when they finally do break down and call, carry it one step further and don't call them back. Make them call you a few times before you'll agree to talk to them. Teach them that two can play the same game. Teach them that you don't have to play by their rules.

Why not have even more fun with it, play a little game with yourself, and see if you can *make* them stop talking to you? If you keep following them around like a little puppy dog, kissing up to them and being grateful for whatever crumbs they throw your way, they will never respect you. It is only when you take back your power, stop letting them walk all over you, start being a little unpredictable and stop letting them pull your strings, that you will stand a chance of being treated properly. And if you are never going to be treated properly, then the Silent Treatment is the best thing that will ever happen to you. Live it, embrace it, enjoy it, and don't mess it up by trying to change it.

BE STILL, AND KNOW THAT I AM GOD...Psalm 46:10 KJV.

FIND REST, O MY SOUL, IN GOD ALONE; MY HOPE COMES FROM HIM...Psalm 62:5 NIV.

CHAPTER 24

"YOU'D BETTER, OR ELSE!" THREATS, BLUFFS, AND ULTIMATUMS

"PUT YOUR SWORD BACK IN ITS PLACE," JESUS SAID TO HIM, "FOR ALL WHO DRAW THE SWORD WILL DIE BY THE SWORD"...Matthew 26:52 NIV.

When my husband and I were young newlyweds, most of our friends smoked, and we didn't. We entertained a lot, our guests blissfully puffed away, and the ashtrays got emptied and refilled all night long. I had not yet developed asthma, so I was able to tolerate the smoke even though it stunk up our house for days afterwards. When our guests would go home and my husband and I would go up to bed, the second floor of our home, including our bedroom, would be smoke-filled. We took to closing the bedroom doors while we had company, only to find that when we eventually opened them, the smoke that had been lingering in the hallway would waft into the bedrooms anyway. It got to the point that we had to take showers at 2:00 AM, after our company left, because our clothes and hair, and even our skin, reeked.

When we decided to start trying to have a baby, we wanted to give our child the healthiest head start possible. I immediately began eating healthier and stopped drinking coffee, diet drinks, and anything with artificial sweeteners. I wouldn't even take an aspirin when I had a headache. And we were the first in our social circle to make our home a smoke-free environment. If anyone wanted to smoke, they were free to go outside and stand on the covered stoop or in our screen porch.

Most of our friends had no problem at all adapting, and were more than happy to be invited for an evening out, even if it meant standing outside a couple of times during the night to have a cigarette. They appreciated that we were hosting them in our home, and didn't mind abiding by the new house rules. In fact, within five or six years after that, almost every one of our friends quit smoking anyhow.

But, as usual, there has to be one obnoxious narcissist in every crowd. My husband and I typically invited all of our cousins to our get-togethers, even the ones we weren't all that close to. There was one particular cousin and her husband whom we only saw once or twice a year. They rarely invited us to their home when they entertained, they never called to chat, and they didn't socialize with us other than to come to our house for parties. The main reason we continued to invite them was that we were very close to the wife's siblings, and since we were inviting her sister and brother, we didn't want to leave this last sibling out. However, it certainly didn't matter at all to us whether or not they actually came. We just invited them to be nice, not because we craved their company. The party would go on either way, with or without them.

When we started our no-smoking rule, most of the folks who had bothered to keep in touch during the year leading up to our annual Christmas party already knew about it. But there were a couple of people, including this cousin and her husband, who didn't know yet because they never kept in touch other than to accept our invitations. So when I sent out the invitations to that year's Christmas party at our home, I included a light-hearted little note advising everyone who hadn't already heard that our house was now a smoke-free zone, and that we appreciated their understanding. I didn't want anyone to be embarrassed or unpleasantly surprised when they got there and unknowingly tried to light up inside.

Well, the next thing you know, I get a call from the husband of the cousin who rarely bothered with us. He said he was RSVPing to our invitation. I thought something was up, because *he* was replying to the invitation instead of his wife, so I just said, "Okay....." He then curtly informed me that they would not be coming to our party, because he would not be able to smoke in our home. I reminded him that there were sheltered areas outside where he could smoke, but he said no, he wasn't going to get up in the middle of the party and go outside to smoke. Apparently he was too good for that.

I don't know what he expected. Was I supposed to make an exception for him, because he was a Special Person, and tell everybody else but him that they couldn't smoke inside? Or were we supposed to rescind our own rule and go back to having our home stunk up and exposing our future child to harmful fumes? After all, we were trying to have a baby, and I could have already been pregnant and not known it (back then there were no home pregnancy tests~ you had to wait a few weeks to find out).

Whatever, I didn't really care. Because, contrary to what Mr. Obnoxious might have thought, I was just as happy to be let off the hook and not have to invite them anymore. Fewer people, less work, and less food to buy and prepare. We never saw them for months on end anyway, and, quite frankly, he was a conceited, know-it-all, pompous jackass whose company we weren't going to miss all that much. I tried to keep from laughing out loud as I responded, "Oh well, sorry to hear that. We'll see you some other time, then," hung up the phone and jumped for joy. So much for *that* obligatory invitation! I never invited them to another party. Because, after all, he wouldn't be able to come anyway. Thank *you!* They sat home from then on while the rest of their relatives got together and enjoyed themselves at our house on a regular basis. It was no skin off *my* teeth not to have Mr. and Mrs. Obnoxious there, and nobody else seemed to miss them, either.

THE CRAZY IN-LAWS' TURN FOR GIVING ULTIMATUMS

Fast forward a year or so. My husband and I had our first baby, and, like all first-time parents, we were super careful about exposing him to germs or people who could possibly be sick. My husband's father was a very abusive narcissist who had already caused many problems in our family. He always managed to raise my husband's blood pressure, and my husband avoided him as much as possible. If it wasn't for me trying to smooth over disagreements and keep them in our lives, the relationship with my in-laws would have ended long ago. I had been raised to be the problem-solver in my own family and to take on the full responsibility for overlooking abuse and keeping the family together no matter what. So in the early years of our marriage, I tried to do this with my husband's family, and all I got for my efforts was them fighting and stabbing each other in the back, and then everyone would blame *me*. Now I know better. I was one hundred percent wrong. I should have just let them work it out, or not, among themselves. But it took me many years to go against my own dysfunctional upbringing and learn that keeping the peace was not my job.

When our baby was born, my husband and his father started speaking again after a three-year estrangement. When our firstborn was about six months old, he was at the stage of always putting his hands in his mouth. My husband very nicely and politely asked his stepmother to please not kiss the baby on the hands since he was constantly putting his hands in his mouth. She seemed fine with it, and we had no idea that she had taken offense until they started driving by our house (they lived down the block) and refusing to wave or even look at us. I called my father-in-law to see if something was wrong, and he proceeded to read me the riot act about how my husband had insulted his wife. I was bowled over. I knew that an insult was never my husband's intention. I explained to his father that my husband had been very nice about it, never meant it as an insult, and that we were the baby's parents, and *we* didn't even kiss his hands, because we didn't want him putting *our* germs in his mouth.

Father-In-law Darling demanded that my husband apologize and told me to tell him. I said I would pass it along, but I didn't know if he would apologize because he didn't do anything wrong. He said that if my husband didn't apologize to them, "you stay in your backyard, and we'll stay in our backyard." I reminded him that we had all just started speaking again after three years and that he now had a new grandchild. I said, "Are you sure that's what you want? You mean, you'd really give up your new grandchild and your son over something like this, after you only just got back together?" His answer was a curt yes. At that point, I just shrugged and said, "Okay, I'll tell him."

Well, needless to say, my husband did not apologize. In fact, he was livid when I repeated the conversation to him. That was the last time his father spoke to us for the next three years, until our next baby was born. Then *that* reconciliation lasted a mere ten months, until I caught Father-In-Law Darling trying to pour wine down my new infant's throat at our Christmas dinner table, and he got insulted at me for stopping him. I didn't raise my voice or do anything to embarrass him. I just asked him nicely to please not give the baby wine. This time, when we finally realized they weren't talking to us *again,* I again tried to make amends, but Father-In-Law-Darling was having none of it. He demanded an apology, and I wasn't giving it to him. I had done nothing wrong, and I wanted something from him instead~ a promise not to give my baby or my older son alcohol or anything else potentially dangerous without checking with my husband or me. Again I reminded him that we were only just back in touch after years of not speaking and now he had *another* grandchild whom he would be cutting out of his life. I patiently tried to explain why he couldn't give wine to the baby, but I was talking to a brick wall. Once more I said, "Are you *sure* you want to break up our relationship *again?* Over *this?*" His cold reply? "We can wait as long as you can."

Well, okay. That's probably not the smartest thing to say to me, because I can wait a *very* long time. In fact, with me, it's pretty much out of sight, out of mind. You see, I'm a creature of habit. I tend to adapt to whatever the status quo happens to be, I like routine and order and don't do well with unpredictability, and I also tend to be uneasy with and resistant to change. So, if we got off on the right foot right from the beginning, you're an important part of my life, and we have a relationship on a certain level of mutuality and caring, I tend to foster it staying that way. But if you're really not much of a factor in my life to begin with and we really never had much of a relationship, I tend to be satisfied with leaving well enough alone and finding my close, caring relationships elsewhere. In fact, it makes me very *un*comfortable to try and change an already established relationship dynamic. And if you think you're going to be in and out of my life like it was a revolving door, well, in *my* world, once you're gone, you're gone. I forget all about you and move on with my life. I'm in absolutely no hurry to let narcissists and sociopaths back into my life. I can outwait an abuser any day. I can wait forever.

Father-In-Law Darling waited eleven years before any of us spoke again, and that was only because my mother-in-law, whom we had always liked, made the first move, and we didn't want to hurt her. Granddad-from-hell missed out on both of his grandsons' entire childhoods, even though he only lived two blocks away. But boy, he sure showed *us* a thing or two!

MY BIRTH-MOTHER'S TURN FOR GIVING ULTIMATUMS

Fast forward again to some years later~ this time to Mommy Darling disowning me. It was Homecoming Weekend at our sons' high school, and the entire weekend was full of social activities for our kids~ parades, bonfires, dances, and of course, two football games, including the big varsity game in which our older son was playing. But hold the phone! It was also birth-mother's birthday that day, and she was angry because we would have to wait until the next weekend for all of us to be able to get together for her birthday cake. Our relationship had been deteriorating for some time, and she knew it. We had been withdrawing more and more to protect ourselves and our children from my birth-parents' abuse, and anyone with a shred of sensitivity would have backed off and not caused a major scene over something so silly. But Mommy Darling just had to push it all the way to the last straw.

She gave me this ultimatum: either make my son cancel his plans and celebrate her birthday on the exact day on which it fell, or she would disown me. Taken aback, I asked her if she was sure about that, after all I had done for her, including saving her life a couple of years earlier. She haughtily replied that she was sure, and in fact, if we did not give in to her demands, from then on she would pretend I lived two hundred and fifty miles away, the exact distance birth-sis, her *other* daughter, had moved from her twenty years prior. A little resentment there, perhaps?

I was stunned and hurt, and could not believe how selfish and childish she was being. But, after forty-seven years of being a devoted daughter who did everything possible to please her, even though my only reward had been a lifetime of being repeatedly used, abused and stabbed in the back, when she gave me that nasty ultimatum, a little switch inside me clicked. Probably the biggest miscalculation she could ever have made was to force me to choose between her and one of my children. It was no contest, a power-play she was doomed to lose. There was a moment of dead silence, and then I quietly replied, "Well, okay, if that's the way you want it. Goodbye, mother," hung up the phone, and started crying. I was devastated for weeks, but I got over it. And I have gone on to live a happy, abuser-free life without her, praise God.

We never spoke another word to each other, nor did she ever speak to her grandsons or her son-in-law again, for the rest of her life. To avoid sounding like I'm gloating, I would say there were no winners in this situation, but the fact is, there *were* winners~ and losers. Mine and my family's lives were vastly improved. We could finally live in peace, and never had to deal with her drama or her husband's abuse again. And *her* life was pretty much ruined. Because she was so unreasonable and so unwilling to postpone for a few days one birthday celebration that she would actually disown me over it, now she'd be spending the rest of her birthdays and holidays without us forever. She lost her family, all because she pushed too far, gave me an ultimatum she was bound to lose, and then had too much pride to apologize and make amends.

BEFORE YOU TRY TO FORCE SOMEONE ELSE'S HAND WITH AN ULTIMATUM, YOU'D BETTER BE DARN SURE IT'S WHAT YOU REALLY WANT IF THEY CALL YOUR BLUFF

Ultimatums have a funny way of backfiring on those who make them. They are power-plays that often end in the abuser cutting off his own nose to spite his face. They originate from the narcissist's over-inflated opinion of his own importance, his arrogance in assuming he knows what makes us tick and how to manipulate us, and his misinterpreting the fact that we have politely tolerated him for years to mean that he is so indispensable to us we would choose him over our own kids. It's really not too bright to give ultimatums or make threats to people you don't know as well as you think you do, and take a chance that they will react the way you want them to. You might win, and then again, you might just lose.

Each time I was on the receiving end of a threat or ultimatum from a family member, my feelings ranged from bewildered to astounded. My abusive relatives' battle tactics were completely illogical for two reasons.

First of all, each abuser was showing how little he cared about me and my family, by being perfectly willing to walk away from us forever over something so completely stupid and trivial. The concept of "picking your battles" wasn't something that computed in their brains. The overreactions to imagined slights were all out of proportion to the supposed offenses. Only crazy people would end family relationships over such idiotic stuff.

And second, *by carrying out their threats, each of my abusive relatives stood to lose far more than **I** did.* Mr. and Mrs. Obnoxious were left out of all future social gatherings at my house. They missed out on parties that their own sister, brother and cousins enjoyed for many years to come, which was fine by me. I couldn't have cared less that they weren't there, and nobody else missed them, either. Father-In-Law Darling and Mommy Darling lost their children and grandchildren because they were stubborn, prideful and unreasonable, and missed out on every holiday and family occasion for years, all precious time and lost memories that they could never get back. But my family and I didn't miss a beat. All of these nice occasions continued on just fine without them. It wasn't by *our* choice that they weren't there. It was *their* choice to carry out their threats. But without meaning to and without even realizing it, they did me and my family a huge favor. They set us free.

THE DOGS MAY BARK, BUT THE CARAVAN MARCHES ON

It was also astounding to me that none of these abusers had the slightest sensitivity concerning my feelings, or lack of same, toward them, or realistic estimate of their value to me and my family. They actually thought they were so important to me that I would kowtow to their blackmail in order to keep them in my life, just so they could abuse me and my family some more. They miscalculated and overestimated their importance to my husband and our children as well. Their absences were blessings to my family, and enabled us to enjoy pleasant and stress-free get-togethers from then on. Even our children never mentioned them again.

I have no idea how Mr. Obnoxious ever got the notion that I cared all that much about him either way. I barely knew him. And both toxic grandparents somehow believed that if my husband and I were forced to make a choice between them and one of our children, *they* actually stood a chance of winning. Their egomaniacal assessments of their own importance in our lives was contrary to everything we had ever felt for them, and showed they had no sensitivity whatsoever to the true state of our toxic relationships.

These were not loving, caring, mutually beneficial relationships. These relatives had never shown love in their relationships with me and my family. They had done nothing but torture us for years. And yet, they still smugly thought we would panic over losing them and would do anything to keep them in our lives, even if it meant sacrificing our own children. After all, *they* wouldn't hesitate for a second to sacrifice their children whenever it suited them, so I guess they thought we'd betray *our* kids just like they would (and *did*, many times). They failed to read the hundreds of signals we had sent out over the years making it clear that *we* did not consider our relationships to be good, and that they were certainly not indispensable. They should have been grateful that we had been willing to overlook so much of their mistreatment for so long and allow them to continue being a part of our family, but instead they kept pushing and pushing, because they read our endless patience with them as *weakness*. They were blind to the fact that we were reaching the end of our rope and had been getting fed up with them for a long time, or that they had never meant all that much to us in the first place, and that we would be relieved and glad to be rid of them. They never expected us to call their bluffs and *let them* walk away.

One day, I would just love to ask one of these raging egomaniacs, "What *exactly* is so wonderful about you? What am I missing here? Are you kind, loving, thoughtful, generous and helpful? Are you a fascinating conversationalist? Do you have a great sense of humor? Is your company really so enjoyable? *Why* would anybody want to keep you around so badly that they would allow you to blackmail them by holding over their heads the threat of losing you if they don't do what you demand? What exactly are you bringing to the party that makes you worth it? Worth more than other people, worth more than your victims, worth more than your victims' children?"

The answer from a narcissist would be, "Yes, I *am* worth it. Because I'm *special.* My character, my personality, my accomplishments~ none of these are in line with my inflated sense of my own worth. In fact, by the standards of the common people, in most respects I would be considered a delusional, dysfunctional failure, a complete loser. But I'm *still* special. *You're* the one who has something wrong with her, because you just can't understand that."

TAKE THE MONEY AND RUN

Much like The Silent Treatment and always being Second Fiddle, ultimatums are one of those battle tactics that can completely backfire on those who give them and be huge blessings in disguise for their targets. Narcissists can be very theatrical when it comes to getting narcissistic supply, and ultimatums are the ultimate in drama. I have found the best way to deal with an ultimatum is not to add to the theatrics or reward the big dramatic gesture, but instead, to simply shrug and say, "Okay, if that's the way you want it," and let it play itself out. Let it go. Let *them* go.

Especially when a narcissist is forcing us to make a choice between him and our own well-being or our own spouse and children, it is brutally obvious that we are dealing with an unreasonable, toxic, selfish bully who doesn't care about anybody but himself, who will insist on winning no matter what the cost to us or him, and who has lost his grip on reality. *Narcissists will willingly and smugly lose everybody who ever loved them rather than lose the game.* It's the principle of the thing! There is no way to argue or reason with such a person, and no way to even work out a compromise. An ultimatum indicates a bully with a take-no-prisoners attitude, someone who is willing *to lose everything* as long as he can dominate you. As long as you continue trying to reason with him, you are teaching him that you are *afraid* of losing him, and that his threat actually matters to you, enough to keep you trying to calm him down and work it out. You are teaching him that his ultimatums work. So withdraw from the battle and let him carry out his threats. Then breathe a sigh of relief and enjoy the peace and freedom he has just inflicted on you, before he changes his mind and comes back.

CHAPTER 25

YOU'RE ONLY AS GOOD AS YOUR LAST PICTURE: THE IDEALIZATION AND DEVALUATION/DISCARD CYCLE

FAITHFUL ARE THE WOUNDS OF A FRIEND; BUT THE KISSES OF AN ENEMY ARE DECEITFUL…Proverbs 27:6 KJV.

Narcissists and psychopaths have a pattern of relating to other people called the Idealization and Devaluation/ Discard Cycle. As long as you are useful to them, or *might be* useful to them, they love you. As soon as you start not being so useful or protesting their behavior, they hate you. There is no middle ground. They go from lavish greetings, showering you with attention, and big theatrical performances of being your best friend, to not speaking to you anymore and unceremoniously dumping you in the blink of an eye~ and then going around lying about what happened between you and badmouthing you to anyone who will listen. There is usually no explanation, and chances are you will never know exactly why you got demoted from best friend to persona-non-grata.

In narcissistic families, this pattern can play out repeatedly over decades with the same cast of characters. When your narcissistic sister wants something from you, she'll butter you up with flattery and smiles. After she gets what she wants, or if you fail to provide it, she'll stop taking your calls and walk right by you in the street. Until the next time she wants something from you~ and then she'll call you up as sweet as pie, like nothing ever happened.

In non-family situations where you'll be meeting new people regularly, such as work or church, the dynamic might be a little different. It's also not so easy to recognize when it's someone you don't know well and haven't seen do it many times before.

An interesting example which I've seen in churches is a narcissist who thinks she's not just holier-than-thou, but holier-than-*everybody*. When a new person starts coming to church, the narcissist, under the guise of "welcoming" him, immediately finds and singles him out like a heat-seeking missile, and then gloms onto him and starts preaching every chance she gets, showing off her "superior" biblical knowledge. If the new person asks for prayer, the narcissist will corner him and preach that he shouldn't worry, just trust Jesus, Jesus will take care of everything, his faith needs to be stronger, and so on. She will often ask personal questions of the new person, fishing for information which she can then use to "judge" his walk with the Lord and tell him what he should or should not be doing. The words "*should*" and "*shouldn't*" are very popular in the vocabulary of holier-than-thou narcissists.

When this happens, the narcissist is not necessarily grooming the new person for future favors or money. The narcissistic-supply payoff here for the narcissist is attention, respect and admiration. The new person, and everyone else within earshot, is supposed to be impressed with her scriptural knowledge and walk with the Lord. She is showing off for all to see. It's like a competition to see whose faith is stronger. She is being prideful, and we all know the Bible says she *shouldn't* do that!

I have seen the above scenario played out quite a few times, and things *really* started getting interesting when it turned out the new person was an ordained minister. In each of these situations, the ministers were not pastors of their own churches but ministered in other capacities~ prison ministries, abuse recovery ministries, hospital ministries, military chaplains, etc. A couple were retired from their own churches or had relocated. They were looking for a church to attend with their families and did not introduce themselves as pastors when visiting new churches for a variety of personal reasons. Some were just humble, others did not want to step on the toes of the pastor of the church, and still others just preferred to keep a low profile until they got to know the church better.

Some of them attended the new churches alone, and some went with their spouses and children. They were both male and female pastors, so apparently gender had nothing to do with it. *Yet every single one of them had the experience of being approached and glommed onto by the resident narcissist in every new church they checked out.*

But, get this. *As soon as they let it be known that they were ordained ministers, every single one of those resident narcissists disappeared!* Just ducked and ran for cover, and then fizzled away into a little puddle of grease, like a vampire who got hit by the sunlight! Some of the pastors introduced themselves and mentioned their credentials right after the first service they attended, and others waited a few weeks. Either way, when the church narcissist found out who he was talking to, he suddenly made himself scarce. I could almost imagine him throwing his cape over his face and snarling, "Curses! Foiled again!" Some of the ministers are still attending some of these churches after several months or years, and the narcissists who originally glommed onto them are still avoiding them like the plague.

I find this example of the Idealization/Devaluation Cycle absolutely fascinating. The visiting ministers were not direct sources of narcissistic supply to the church narcissists. Instead, they were *indirect sources* of supply, serving as foils to bounce the narcissists' preaching off of. Just by being there, they gave the narcissists an excuse and an opportunity to show off, not just to them, but to the entire congregation. The narcissists focused on the visitors, but made sure their holier-than-thou, judgmental and preachy comments were overheard by an audience of everyone within earshot.

They pretended to welcome and care about the new people, but they were actually ***using them*** *to get the attention and admiration of the people they already knew.*

As soon as they realized the visitors were actually ministers whose biblical knowledge was *way* better than theirs, they lost their confidence and slunk off into a corner. Remember the musically-challenged Edwina and her unprovoked attack on and elimination of her "rival" Frances? Narcissists must be the superior ones. It's the only thing their egos will allow. They cannot be equal to you, and they definitely cannot tolerate being inferior. They have to be the know-it-alls, the experts, the teachers, the lecturers sharing their pearls of wisdom with all the dummies. They will not be caught in close proximity to someone who is superior to them for fear that comparisons will be made and they will come up short and be embarrassed. If the resident narcissists in these churches could no longer lord it over the newcomers, then they were not going to waste any more time being nice to them. They simply discarded them and went in search of more desirable prey, someone who would look up to them, feed their egos, and make them look good by comparison.

DONNA VERSUS CHURCH NARCISSIST CAROL

NOW I BESEECH YOU, BRETHREN, MARK THEM WHICH CAUSE DIVISIONS AND OFFENCES CONTRARY TO THE DOCTRINE WHICH YE HAVE LEARNED; AND AVOID THEM. FOR THEY THAT ARE SUCH SERVE NOT OUR LORD JESUS CHRIST, BUT THEIR OWN BELLY; AND BY GOOD WORDS AND FAIR SPEECHES DECEIVE THE HEARTS OF THE SIMPLE. FOR YOUR OBEDIENCE IS COME ABROAD UNTO ALL MEN. I AM GLAD THEREFORE ON YOUR BEHALF: BUT YET I WOULD HAVE YOU WISE UNTO THAT WHICH IS GOOD, AND SIMPLE CONCERNING EVIL. AND THE GOD OF PEACE SHALL BRUISE SATAN UNDER YOUR FEET SHORTLY...Romans 16:17-20 KJV.

Donna and Carol attended the same church, and Carol is your typical holier-than-thou church lady who is always judging others and preaching to other people about what Jesus wants them to do. For two years Carol was playing the "snub you" game and ignoring Donna. She did not speak to her in church, not even to say hello or goodbye, unless a new person whom she was trying to impress happened to be watching.

It was during this two-year Devaluation/Discard period that Donna's internationally-known Christian website won a prestigious award and she published her first book, and not one word of congratulations or any acknowledgment at all of such exciting achievements came from Carol. Donna was also interviewed on a Christian radio station, and again not a word from Carol. Carol's child won a contest in school, and Donna, despite being ignored for years, generously congratulated her. Then Donna's daughter got married, and again, Carol didn't utter a word. She seemed to be stinging from Donna getting any attention from the other church members. Her envy was becoming very apparent as she bent over backwards to show no interest at all. There were only two times she spoke to Donna during this two-year-plus Devaluation/Discard period, and both times it was to publicly criticize her and her family and try to embarrass her in front of other people.

Then Donna had a health crisis and was diagnosed with cancer. For several weeks, she and her family lived with fear, stress and exhaustion as she went through multiple tests and doctor's appointments, surgery and radiation. The Lord told Donna and her family from the beginning to trust him and that he would heal her, and their faith was very strong as he was faithful to his promises. There were many tests~ the doctors had to find out what kind of cancer it was, how big it was, and if it had spread. One by one the tests came back with good results. Donna did not need chemotherapy, and the Lord healed her completely, just as he promised. Her journey was shared step by step with her brothers and sisters in the congregation, who prayed for her and her family constantly and called often to see how she was doing, since she missed several weeks of church while recovering and undergoing treatment. During this time, the Lord blessed her and her family with the love of their sisters and brothers in Christ. Many people were calling and praying for them, checking to see if they needed anything and helping, encouraging and comforting them. Old friends, new friends, friends of friends~ the Lord continued to put many wonderful and kind folks in their lives who let them know they were cared about and loved.

But guess what? As I write this it is a year and a half since Donna's diagnosis, *and the only person who never once in all that time said one single word to her or her family about her illness* is~ you guessed it~ holier-than-thou, self-righteous, wonderful "Christian" church-lady *Carol!* Not one word of care or concern or even interest. To this day, she has never even asked Donna how she is or how she's feeling.

Carol refused to acknowledge *either good news or bad news* in Donna's life. The point she was trying to make was that Donna was unimportant, and not worth her time or attention. The only time Donna was worth not ignoring was when Carol saw an opportunity to criticize or embarrass her. Big accomplishments did not elicit congratulations or good wishes, and serious illnesses did not elicit sympathy or caring. It was more important to send Donna a message, which she received loud and clear~ you don't matter, you have no value, I don't care about you, I don't wish you well, I don't even *like* you (and in fact I'm secretly thrilled if something bad happens to you)!

Carol couldn't have cared less if Donna lived or died, but strangely enough, there was something she *did* care about as Donna fought her battle with cancer. *Online games!* Donna had accepted Carol's friend request on a social networking site a few years earlier, during the Idealization part of the cycle, before she knew Carol well enough to realize what she was. Now, after ignoring her for two years every time she saw her, suddenly Carol wanted to be Donna's "neighbor" in one of the website's games, which she and Donna both played.

Still trying to recover from her surgery, Donna would come home from two radiation treatments a day and a sixty-mile car trip so drained she could barely walk, sleep for three hours, log on to the computer to relax for a few minutes, and find as many as five requests a day from Carol to be her neighbor or help her play the game by sending her game gifts or fulfilling other requests. Too exhausted to deal with Carol's selfish narcissism at this point, Donna deleted all her requests. She certainly did not wish to be any more connected to Carol than she already unfortunately was.

The topper on the cake was when Carol, apparently testing to see if Donna was deliberately ignoring her requests, changed her name on her profile and sent Donna game requests using a different name, and then changed her name back again after sending the phony requests. At this point, Donna had had more than enough of Carol's hounding and harassing her, and finally unfriended her altogether. And during all this time, still not a single inquiry about Donna's health or expression of care or concern from Carol.

Carol had a cousin, Carla, who also attended the same church. The two of them often stuck to themselves and chatted. Around the time Carol began ignoring Donna, Carla changed her online social network page to block Donna from posting on it or reading the posts. Donna logged on to wish her a happy birthday and found out she couldn't. So Donna then blocked Carla too, so that although they remained "friends," she could not post on Donna's page or read her posts either. Donna was not comfortable allowing someone full access and the ability to post on her page when she did not have the same privileges on theirs.

Once, after Donna unfriended Carol, Carol and Carla were engaged in a conversation, talking in hushed tones, and not realizing that Donna's husband was in the next room. He opened the door just in time to hear Carla say, "Let's see what she's up to" as the two of them accessed the internet on the cousin's cell phone. When Donna's husband opened the door and came face to face with them, they became very flustered, stuttering and stammering and putting the phone behind their backs to hide what they were looking at. Since Carol no longer had any access to Donna's page on that particular social networking site, apparently they were trying to see whatever they could by using Carla's account. Thankfully, there wasn't very much information, since Donna had already censored what the cousin could see as well.

Since Carol had to keep up Donna's "punishment" by continuing not to speak to her, it became Carla's job to fish for information about Donna and her family. At every opportunity, Carla would pigeonhole Donna with a big, phony, overly cheerful smile, follow her around and hound her with one personal question after another about herself and her family. She'd ask "So what's new?", "So how's everything?", "So what have you been up to?", "So what are your kids doing lately?", "So how's work?" all while barely taking a breath in between. But she was no match for Donna, who deftly changed the subject, gave evasive answers, or gave monosyllabic responses before turning it around and asking Carla what was new with her. No way was Donna going to give her nosy "enemies" Carol and Carla any information about herself or her family.

Once Donna turned the tables and started ignoring the narcissistic Carol right back, things got even sillier. Not only was Carol cut off online, but Donna had not spoken to *her* either, for most of the time she was snubbing Donna. Donna wasn't going to chase Carol around to greet her or chat with her. Apparently, at some point Carol started noticing that Donna wasn't bothering with *her,* either. So she began upping the ante.

Every Sunday after the service there was a fellowship breakfast and the congregation all sat around a big table and chatted for a while. As it usually seems to happen in many groups, people take the same seats week after week. For a few years, Donna and her family took certain seats toward the end of the table that allowed them to sit together without intruding on anyone else's seats. Now Carol and Carla started hurrying to the table first, and putting their big, dirty pocketbooks right on the table at Donna and her husband's usual places, so they could not sit there. It was hard not to notice their infantile schoolyard bully tactics. Donna and her family had a good laugh every time they did it, and simply moved to other seats. They loved all their fellow churchgoers and really didn't care who they sat with or talked to. Eventually Carol and Carla were the ones who would become uncomfortable sitting in seats they weren't used to, and give up and go back to their normal places. Until jealous Carol got bent out of shape at Donna again for some reason, and then their purses would be back on the table to "punish" her again.

Believe it or not, after two years of not speaking to Donna, Carol has cycled around to speaking to her again. Just like when she stopped speaking to her, there is no reason and no explanation for this about-face. Is it just to put on a phony show for other people, who by now are noticing Carol's rudeness toward Donna? Or is it trying to get attention and narcissistic supply from Donna after being ignored right back? Or is it pretending to be Donna's friend again, because she had been "kicked out of" Donna's social network, blocked from seeing Donna's page, and was now an "outsider?" Maybe if she started being nice to Donna, Donna would "friend" her again, and she would once again have access to information about Donna and her life. *Gathering information about us gives the nosy narcissist something to feed her envy, and it also gives her ammunition to use against us..*

We'll probably never know, but for now Donna is content to keep the narcissistic bully Carol and her Flying Monkey cousin Carla at arm's length. Narcissists think they control everything, including whether we speak to them or not. It is often an eyeopener for them when we take the choice out of their hands and make our *own* decisions about whom we choose to socialize with. Donna prefers to socialize with *nice* people, and the bottom line is that Carol and Carla just aren't very nice.

When a narcissist devalues and discards us, the best strategy is to count your blessings and go with it. It's really one of the greatest things they could do for us, but unfortunately it's rarely permanent. Remember, the Idealization/ Devaluation and Discard Cycle is just that~ *a cycle*. Being discarded is usually only temporary, and the narcissist will be back when he wants something from us. This is often nothing more than narcissistic supply, and it is common for narcissists to pop up again in our lives when someone else dumps them and they have lost one of their other sources of supply. That's when they'll try to resurrect us as a source, and that's when we need to take the decision out of their hands and refuse to get sucked back in. I know how tempting it is to say, "Oh. I thought you weren't talking to me anymore!" and watch the narcissist go into his act, feigning innocence and spouting all kinds of denial. So if you'd like to have a little fun with it, be my guest!

CHAPTER 26

"ADOPTING" ANOTHER KID TO REPLACE YOU

BUT IF ANY PROVIDE NOT FOR HIS OWN, AND SPECIALLY FOR THOSE OF HIS OWN HOUSE, HE HATH DENIED THE FAITH, AND IS WORSE THAN AN INFIDEL…1 Timothy 5:8 KJV.

One of a narcissistic parent's favorite devaluing tactics is to "adopt" another child to replace you. She is trying to make you jealous, so you will try harder to please her and give her more narcissistic supply. The message is that if you don't toe the line, your narcissistic parents will give their love and attention (and maybe even money) to your replacement~ a distant relative, neighbor, church acquaintance, or even your own child who they are trying to woo away from you, thereby killing two birds with one stone. The message is that you are not good enough to have the honor of being their child. You will notice this dynamic in other narcissistic relationships as well, such as when a former "friend" of yours makes a point of flaunting his new "friend" in your face.

My in-laws were famous for this, "adopting" one young couple after another who lived in the neighborhood, and then having them for holidays, bringing them dinners, babysitting their kids for free while they went to work, even making their kids call them "grandma and grandpa." Meanwhile, we lived down the street and they snubbed us, going so far as to drive past their *real* grandchildren without so much as a wave. More than once I had to explain to our little boys why their mean grandfather wouldn't even wave at them when he passed by. On the rare occasion that we were invited to dinner at their house, my narcissistic father-in-law would sit a male guest at his right instead of my husband, his only son. Translation in old-school Italian~ This is the place of honor that is rightfully yours as my son, but you don't deserve it so I'm giving it to this replacement son. *He's* my son now, and he's more important than you.

My borderline grandmother lavished love, gifts, and attention on people she barely knew, while neglecting and abusing her real family. She loved telling us that "friends are better than family." Secondary message~ *You* are not good enough, you're not pleasing me and kissing my butt enough, or you had the nerve to stand up to me, so I'll show you! I'll get my narcissistic supply from strangers and demote you to a lower position of importance.

The underlying message which hurts the most, *and is meant to hurt*, is that they don't love us. Because obviously, if they did, we wouldn't be disposable and we wouldn't be replaceable. Now this very same parental love and devotion which God meant for us has been tainted and rendered meaningless, given away cheaply to strangers who are now in the position of Golden Child in *our* families. The narcissist's "love" is no longer of any value to us, certainly not worth striving so hard to merit. It is completely worthless, used as a bargaining chip to buy attention and given to people the narcissist barely knows. So why are we knocking ourselves out to earn it?

Way to deal~ again, count your blessings and let it happen. Consider yourself off-the-hook. The day will come, as it did with my in-laws, grandmother, and numerous other smug narcissistic relatives and friends I'm aware of, that the "adopted children" will unceremoniously dump *them*. *It usually turns out that the adoptees are also narcissists,* so they feed off each other for a while, and then get on one another's nerves with too many demands for supply. And mark my words~ when your narcissistic parents get old enough to start needing help, their "adopted children" will be nowhere to be found. Hopefully, neither will the "good-for-nothing" *real* children, who got the message long ago that they weren't good enough to be considered a son or a daughter, so they were replaced. *At this point, what the narcissistic parent has in effect created for himself is* ***two sets of non-children***, neither of whom has any obligation to be there for him when he needs someone to take on the responsibilities of an adult child toward an elderly parent. Because one isn't his child anymore, and the other one was never his child to begin with.

CHAPTER 27

A LESSON LEARNED: NARCISSISTS USE US TO DO FAVORS FOR OTHERS, SO THEY CAN TAKE THE CREDIT

GIVE NOT THAT WHICH IS HOLY UNTO THE DOGS, NEITHER CAST YE YOUR PEARLS BEFORE SWINE, LEST THEY TRAMPLE THEM UNDER THEIR FEET, AND TURN AGAIN AND RENT YOU...Matthew 7:6 KJV.

Sometimes the Lord has surprising and hard lessons for us to learn. In a narcissistic family, you eventually learn that, unless you want to be repeatedly targeted and taken advantage of, it doesn't pay to be the considerate, helpful, generous, tolerant and loving person. You will wind up being used and abused because you're perceived as "weak" and the family "patsy," while the one who never does anything for anybody and causes all the trouble (the Golden Child) gets kissed up to. If there is ever a conflict between you and her, the rest of the family will only care about *her* feelings and keeping *her* happy. Your feelings do not matter. If you have the nerve to even protest her mistreatment of you, they will get mad at *you,* not her. She will get pussyfooted around and never confronted, and you will get taken for granted and expected to suck it up, no matter what she does to you, or *you* will be accused of being the "troublemaker," instead of the *real* troublemaker.

Narcissistic families will often *use you* to do nice things for the Golden Child, like giving her a gift you bought for them. Even if you and she aren't on speaking terms, you just might find out that she is benefiting from your generosity, while still treating you like an "enemy." Breaking the old patterns and learning to go against our own natures, withhold the "niceness," and stand up for ourselves is a hard lesson to learn, but crucial in getting some relatives to think about *our* feelings once in a while, too.

NO GOOD DEED GOES UNPUNISHED

Instead of donating her very nice maternity clothes to the thrift shop, Autumn spent money having them all cleaned and then handed them down to her sister Jolene, who was planning on getting pregnant in the future and wanted them. Jolene then turned around and gave them to Autumn's *estranged* sister-in-law Marla, their brother's wife. Jolene *used* Autumn to get credit for a favor that cost her nothing (while making her sister spend money to clean the clothes), and "gave aid and comfort to the enemy" on her sister's dime. Why would she think her nice, generous sister would appreciate knowing that her clothes were being worn around town by someone who wasn't even speaking to her? And as if *that* wasn't bad enough, clueless Jolene, with a big idiotic grin, actually *told* Autumn she gave her clothes to Marla. It was almost as if she was mocking Autumn.

What upset Autumn even more was that she had other friends who could have used the clothes, and it would have been her choice to make sure they got them if her sister was honest about not wanting them. They would not have gone to waste. She also could have donated them to the charity of her choice and gotten a tax deduction. Or she could have kept them herself for her next pregnancy instead of having to buy new ones. She gave them to her sister because Jolene claimed to want and need them, so she thought she was helping *her sister*, and then Jolene turned around and gave them to someone Autumn would never have wanted to have them. Plus, she spent money cleaning them, which then benefited her enemy, so when you think about it, something was actually taken away from her for a purpose she would not have chosen if she had not been misled and lied to by her sister. Not only did it cost her to clean the clothes for the wrong person, but now she will have to buy all new clothes for herself the next time she gets pregnant, so there was a tangible loss to her besides just hurt feelings and betrayal. In actuality, *her sister stole from her.* Autumn did wind up helping Jolene, but not by giving her maternity clothes to wear. She helped her look good to other people, impress their sister-in-law, and obligate the sister-in-law to her, all at Autumn's expense, when that was never Autumn's intention.

A big part of what bothers me here is the taking away of the victim's freedom of choice. If I was Autumn, and I had something that meant something to me or that I had spent time or money or effort on, and I wanted to give it away, *I* should be able to decide who I'm going to give it to and who will benefit from it. If Autumn wanted to give her clothes to her sister-in-law, she could have and would have. That should have been *her* decision. The choice should not have been taken away from her. The clothes she wore when she was expecting her first child meant a lot to Autumn. They had emotional significance to her. Giving them away was done out of love, when she thought her sister would be the one who benefited. She was trying to make her sister's life easier, not her enemy's.

But then her sister thought so little of her caring gesture that she pretty much spit in Autumn's eye, and highjacked the good deed Autumn did for her to get the credit for doing a favor for their nasty sister-in-law. Autumn was deceived and forced against her will to do something nice for someone who doesn't like her and treats her like dirt. *If the person I want to give something to doesn't need it or can't use it, then they should turn it down and let me give it to someone else of my choice.* They shouldn't take it anyway, and then turn around and give it to someone who doesn't even like me. That's just rude.

And worse than rude, it's a betrayal. You do a favor for a relative, and they use your own nice gesture to betray you and stab you in the back. And even more upsetting is that they don't even see anything wrong with this. Many of them are stupid enough to actually *tell you* what they did.

Autumn learned that it doesn't pay to be nice and generous and helpful to some people. Again, fool me once, shame on you; fool me twice, shame on me. She now has some very nice furniture she no longer wants, and is donating it to the thrift shop instead of asking her sister if she could use it. She figures if she offers it to Jolene, it will only wind up in her enemy's home with Marla's narcissistic butt sitting on it. Lesson learned. Nobody likes being made a fool of.

EVERY MAN ACCORDING AS HE PURPOSETH IN HIS HEART, SO LET HIM GIVE; NOT GRUDGINGLY, OR OF NECESSITY: FOR GOD LOVETH A CHEERFUL GIVER…2 Corinthians 9:7 KJV.

In the Bible, it says we are supposed to be *cheerful* givers, and we are not supposed to give reluctantly or grudgingly or if forced to. *It is impossible for normal human beings to feel happy about doing something nice for ingrates and users like our narcissistic relatives.* That's just the way God created us~ to *not* feel joy about being used, betrayed, taken advantage of and stabbed in the back. *Once the narcissists take the joy out of giving for us, it's time to* ***stop***. No more good deeds for people who don't appreciate them. We need to save our generosity and kindness for those who deserve it. *We are supposed to be good stewards of the resources God has given us, not squander them on the children of the devil.*

It's a sad state of affairs when you have to stop and think before doing something nice for your family. In toxic families, the nice ones always seem to get sacrificed, and the problem relatives get catered to. When narcissists are involved, it's truer than ever that no good deed goes unpunished. It makes no sense, but then what can we expect? It's just another reason to stay far away from the dysfunction of toxic people and save the niceness for people who appreciate it, normal people who we can relax and be ourselves around. When we stop being so helpful and so accommodating, a strange side-effect we often see in abusive families is that our narcissistic relatives will suddenly start having a little respect for us.

CHAPTER 28

EMBRACING SECOND FIDDLE: THOUGHTS ON BEING THE SCAPEGOAT VERSUS THE GOLDEN CHILD

FOR UNTO WHOMSOEVER MUCH IS GIVEN, OF HIM SHALL MUCH BE REQUIRED; AND TO WHOM MEN HAVE COMMITTED MUCH, OF HIM THEY WILL ASK THE MORE ...Luke 12:48 KJV.

In my narcissistic family, everything was expected of me~ all the holidays, favors, help, birthdays, entertaining, etc.~ and nothing was ever expected of my birth-sister, who made it a point to stay as far away from our parents as possible. There were numerous times when Mommy Darling asked something big and expensive of me, something that would have been huge amounts of work and taken tremendous amounts of time and money, something that there was no way I could do all by myself, like throwing major parties for my abusive parents. But when I asked her what her *other* daughter was going to do to contribute, she'd look at me like I had two heads. I had children and a full time job, which the Golden Child didn't, but the thought of imposing on daughter #2 to even pitch in a little never entered birth-mother's mind. But paradoxically, whenever there was a choice to be made between their two children, whenever there was a disagreement between us or hurt feelings, even caused completely by her, the Golden Child would always be favored by our narcissistic parents. She would be kissed up to, and I would be told to get over it. However, God forbid *I* did something to upset *her*~ boy, would I ever get handed my head by our parents.

I have seen this paradox repeatedly over the years, in many families and churches, including my own. The Scapegoat who treats his family like gold always loses out to the Golden Child who does nothing for them, or even treats them like dirt. But in Luke 12:48, *Jesus says that the one who* ***is given much*** *is the one who should be required* ***to do much.*** Since the Golden Child is consistently favored, then shouldn't *he* be the one required to do all the work, buy all the nice gifts, and be at the narcissistic family's beck and call whenever they want something? And, conversely, doesn't that mean the one who is given little~ or nothing, or even abused~ should have little or nothing required of him? *We are only second fiddle when it comes to favoritism, mistreatment and unfairness, but we are sure first violin when it comes to responsibilities, favors, and keeping the family happy.* In fact, *we are the only ones* trying to keep the family happy. The Golden Child doesn't even bother, and yet he gets treated like a king. Plus, if he picks a fight with us, the entire family will side with him and gang up on us. He is favored, and we are taken for granted. There always was, and always will be, a double-standard in a narcissistic family.

NARCISSISTIC FAMILY LESSONS: THE EQUAL VERSUS FAIR PARADIGM

Not all narcissistic families treat the Golden Child obviously better than the Scapegoat. Some families like to boast about how *"fair"* they are, because they treat everyone *equally. But is* ***"equal"*** *always* ***"fair?"*** Take this quiz and think about it:

Two brothers, one set of parents. Normal brother treats parents like gold, narcissist brother treats parents like garbage, yet parents insist they must treat both sons, not fairly, but *equally*. They will not do anything for their normal son (invitations, visits, gifts, money, love, attention) unless they can do the exact same thing for their narcissistic son. If they don't want to do it for the narcissist, because he has hurt or upset them with his selfishness and abuse, then the nice, normal son, who treats them with love and respect and tries his best to please them, has to do without, too.

Quiz question~ Who is the genius here, and who is the sucker?

NARCISSISTIC FAMILY LESSONS: THE SQUEAKY WHEEL PARADIGM

In narcissistic families, being the nice guy doesn't always pay, but being the troublemaker does. Here's another little quiz to illustrate this point:

Three married adult children, two sets of grandparents, one normal set and one set of narcissists. Normal grandparents are loving, sweet and helpful to all the kids, including paying some major expenses for them, like college and down payments on houses. Narcissistic grandparents do not help the kids out, cause nothing but trouble, start arguments, pit one relative against another, have temper-tantrums, break promises, con the kids out of money, freeload, impose, lie, backstab, gossip, and in general leave a trail of upset and chaos wherever they go. But the abusive grandparents get catered to and pussy-footed around, and the family is very careful not to "hurt their feelings" or upset them in any way, while the normal grandparents get their feelings hurt on a regular basis and can't even ask for small favors. Even when the narcissist grandparents do something to hurt the normal grandparents, like lying about them, there are no consequences. The normal grandparents just have to suck it up, and had better not even complain about it or the family will get mad at *them*. So we have normal grandparents who treat the kids like gold and get treated like crap in return, and we have narcissistic grandparents, who treat the kids and everyone else like crap, and get treated like gold in return. Quiz follows~

Question#1~ Who are the geniuses here, and who are the suckers?

Question #2~ What do the normal grandparents need to do to start being treated at least as good as the narcissistic grandparents get treated?

When nice, loving, generous relatives get treated the same as narcissists and bullies, or when the family is constantly trying to placate the Squeaky Wheels so there won't be any "trouble," that cannot be considered "fair." *What's **fair** is that each individual gets treated **the way they deserve** to be treated.* If there is an unspoken (or spoken) family rule that everyone has to be treated equally regardless of how they treat everyone else, then the relatives who treat you with respect, consideration, thoughtfulness, generosity and love *are literally being punished* for the selfishness, disrespect, thoughtlessness and nastiness of the narcissists. Why should the nice relatives be nice all the time, go out of their way for others, do favors, not complain about mistreatment or "unfairness" or cause a big blowup over it, often at an emotional, financial, mental, physical or time cost to themselves, when they are never going to be treated any nicer or with any more consideration than the problem relatives who get away with never doing anything for anybody but instigating trouble?

WHAT CAN WE LEARN FROM THE GOLDEN CHILD'S SELF-CENTERED ATTITUDE?

It occurs to me that we are complicit in our own lack of favoritism or even fairness. We are the people-pleasers, and the Golden Child (I use the term loosely here~ the Golden Child could be a child, a parent, a grandparent, or even a church "insider") is not. I think we can learn a lot from him, and take a page out of his book. He is always looking out for Number One~ *him*~ and so is everyone else. And no one gives a hoot about us. Obviously he's doing something right to earn this favored treatment, and we are doing something wrong. Next time the opportunity arises to do something nice for our ungrateful and unfair families, or something they have come to expect, why not ask ourselves, *"What would the Golden Child do?"* before we jump in~ and then do what *he* would do?

Jesus said much is expected of those who are given much. The Second Fiddle is given less or nothing, so it follows that the upside should be that less or nothing is expected of him. We can't change being second-class citizens in our families, but we *can* change running ourselves ragged to please disloyal relatives who are going to turn on us and enable the narcissistic Golden Child to abuse us and rule everybody's lives. One hand washes the other. It's time for the Golden Child to start earning his favored status, and the one who always winds up with the leftovers to stop lavishing his best on a family full of ingrates.

In the second part of Luke 12:48, Jesus clarifies even further when he says that *when people give much to a particular person, of that person* ***they*** *should ask and expect more* (than they do of people they haven't given much to). Our narcissistic families, who have always shown favoritism toward the Golden Child, *need to start asking and expecting the Golden Child to cater to their needs,* and we need to step back and stop allowing ourselves to be exploited and taken advantage of so that this can happen. We need to stay out of it, not get sucked into the middle, and force the people who kiss the butt of the Golden Child to *ask him themselves* for whatever they want or need, with no help from us. *Do not help them handle the monster* ***they*** *created.*

So let's start looking at this with a new attitude and embrace being Second Fiddle. Our second-class, bottom-of-the-barrel position is set in stone and is never going to change anyway. Whether we kill ourselves to make our relatives happy or don't bother, we will still never be as important as the Golden Child, much less the favorite. Either way, they will always treat us like they always have, and we will always lose. So why are we knocking ourselves out? Every cloud has a silver lining, and if we play it right, the Scapegoat position could be a *good* thing. It could start working to our advantage.

Let's take a step back, *stop* doing for our narcissistic families, and let the Golden Child pick up the slack. Just say "No," and tell them that *Jesus said* they need to tell the Golden Child to do it! No more throwing our pearls before swine. This will result in much less time, energy, money, stress, work and responsibility for us. Any time of year is a good time to start, and by all means don't wait, but the holiday season is the perfect occasion for breaking old habits and starting to love our Second Fiddle position. Ahhh, I can feel the relief already. Time for the Golden Child to step up to the plate and earn his favored status. And if he doesn't, oh well, I guess it just doesn't get done, and the family can take it up with him. Meanwhile, we can make ourselves a nice cup of tea, ignore the drama, and relax while *they* figure it out. Before you cook another huge holiday meal or buy all those expensive Christmas presents, remember to embrace being Second Fiddle.

DO NOT GIVE WHAT IS HOLY TO DOGS, AND DO NOT THROW YOUR PEARLS BEFORE SWINE, OR THEY WILL TRAMPLE THEM UNDER THEIR FEET, AND TURN AND TEAR YOU TO PIECES...Matthew 7:6 NASB.

CHAPTER 29

GETTING DISOWNED: THE BEST PUNISHMENT EVER

BUT IF THE UNBELIEVING DEPART, LET HIM DEPART. A BROTHER OR A SISTER IS NOT UNDER BONDAGE IN SUCH CASES: BUT GOD HATH CALLED US TO PEACE...
1 Corinthians 7:15 KJV.

I often hear from victims who have been disowned by their narcissistic parents and families and are wondering if they still have to go to the funeral, or what their obligations are for care, emergencies, money-lending, family events or whatever else the narcissist wants from us when she decides to *un*-disown us.

For starters, let's define exactly what disowning means. According to numerous sources, some dating back over a century, "disown" has been defined to mean: *to deny any connection with, to refuse to acknowledge, to decline to accept as one's own, to reject a relationship with, to repudiate, to renounce, to disclaim any connection with, to disavow any identification with, to refuse to own, to renounce all connection with, to deny, to refuse to recognize as belonging to one's self,* and *to refuse to be associated with.*

Okay, then. From over a hundred years ago (and no doubt a lot further back than that) until modern times, disowning has meant ***The End***~ *no* relationship, not even a connection anymore, done, over, kaput. When you have been disowned, you are no longer related to the narcissist. She severed your connection and *it no longer exists.* The same principle applies if *you* were the one who had to disown *her* because her ongoing abuse forced you to go No Contact.

Regardless of who disowned whom, if a "disowning" has taken place, that's the *end* of the relationship.

And it's also the end of doing things for the narcissist. She's nobody to you now. You are like total strangers, as if she were just some random person at the supermarket. You wouldn't go to a total stranger's funeral, would you? You wouldn't let a total stranger use you or freeload off you or drain you dry, would you? You wouldn't get involved in a prolonged personal conversation if a total stranger upped and called you, would you?

If you get fired from your job, do you still have an obligation to go back a year or so later and do more work for them? Of course not! When a narcissist disowns you, she is telling you she has no further use for you and no further obligation to you. You're fired! You have been dismissed! What this also means, even though the narcissist may not realize it at the time, is that *you* have no further obligation to her, either. So stop looking for a reason to get dragged back in. You don't need to wait for the funeral. She's already dead to you, just like you are dead to her.

Disowning you is the biggest favor a narcissist can do for you. You're off the hook! You're finally *free!* It'll hurt (maybe) for a week or two, and then you'll start seeing the bright side. Your biggest problem in the future is going to be *staying* disowned when the narcissist decides she wants you back so she can use you again. Maintaining strict No Contact is the way to handle it. Your responsibility to her is over forever, so go in peace and enjoy your narcissist-free life.

FORMERLY, WHEN YOU DID NOT KNOW GOD, YOU WERE SLAVES TO THOSE WHO BY NATURE ARE NOT GODS. BUT NOW THAT YOU KNOW GOD~ OR RATHER ARE KNOWN BY GOD~ HOW IS IT THAT YOU ARE TURNING BACK TO THOSE WEAK AND MISERABLE PRINCIPLES? DO YOU WISH TO BE ENSLAVED BY THEM ALL OVER AGAIN?...Galatians 4:8-9 NIV..

PART 4

VICTORY FOR THE CHILDREN OF THE KING

CHAPTER 30

THE DECLINE AND FALL OF OUR ABUSIVE RELATIONSHIPS

FATHERS, DO NOT EXASPERATE YOUR CHILDREN...
Ephesians 6:4 NIV.

When our abusive relationship really starts circling the drain, there will typically be a series of confrontations, getting progressively worse and more frustrating, as the narcissist digs in his heels and becomes spiteful instead of just apologizing and knocking off his unacceptable behavior. These confrontations can go on for months or years, but they are leading up to the final confrontation, our very own family Armageddon. The pattern that The End and the countdown to it typically follow goes something like this:

1. We approach the narcissist with hope, never thinking a polite request for change will be a problem, *because it shouldn't be.*
2. The narcissist responds with denial, projection, anger, guilt-mongering, pity-ploys, lies, tears, getting "offended," and other diversionary tactics. In other words, everything *but* a sincere apology and a promise to change. What should have been a cooperative dialogue has now become confrontational and adversarial. *And so the battle begins...*
3. The abuse continues.
4. We are confused about what is going on.
5. We think maybe we didn't express ourselves clearly.

6. We continue to hope, because we don't get it yet. We assume the narcissist loves us and is acting in goodwill like we are. We do not yet comprehend the actual malice in the abuser's heart towards us.
7. We confront again.
8. More denial, projection, rage, tears, etc.
9. Numbers 1 through 8 repeat indefinitely, going around in circles with nothing constructive ever getting accomplished.
10. The abuse continues and even escalates.
11. We become hurt and start to get angry.
12. We start reading self-help books and websites or go into counseling.
13. We start learning how to set limits.
14. We set limits. *To the narcissist, war has now been declared...*
15. The abuser gets angry at us for setting limits and becomes spiteful and vindictive.
16. The abuse continues and escalates. The abuser is daring us to enforce our boundaries.
17. A maturation process begins for us, a time of starting to see reality instead of deluding ourselves with hopeless hopefulness.
18. We finally start enforcing consequences for disrespecting our boundaries.
19. The abuser becomes enraged at our enforced consequences.
20. We start to feel hopeless and realize the abuser does not want a nice resolution and *is* acting out of spite and malice.
21. The situation becomes very hurtful, toxic, upsetting and stressful. We feel overwhelmed and near our breaking point.
22. We begin to distance ourselves, pulling away and shutting down emotionally, and possibly beginning to limit our exposure to the abuser and our time together.

23. The abuser senses our withdrawal and ups the ante, acting even *more* outrageously, challenging us to take a stand, forcing our hand.
24. We realize that it has now become critical to our well-being to protect ourselves.
25. At this point, either we dump the abuser or he dumps us.
26. If he dumps us, we feel hurt and angry, maybe even devastated. But if we let it be, eventually we feel relief and begin to enjoy our freedom
27. No matter who dumps whom, the abuser will~
    A. Be angry and seek revenge.
    B. Lie, badmouth us, and try to turn other people against us.
    C. Not accept that the relationship is over and he lost control of us.
28. After some time passes (the amount of time varies), the abuser will contact us again as if nothing had ever happened, possibly through a third party. He may or may not offer a phony apology to get us to relent, but will not change his ways (repent).
29. We will forgive without requiring repentance, and the whole thing will start all over.
30. This pattern will continue indefinitely until we learn to require repentance (true remorse and *change*) before forgiving.
31. When we begin requiring repentance, the pattern will be broken and relationship will end because the abuser will refuse to change his ways.
32. We will now be at peace with ending the relationship, knowing we have given him many more chances to behave properly and start treating us nicely than he ever deserved.
33. The abuser will periodically pop up to test the waters, often around the holidays, but possibly at other times such as birthdays, weddings, funerals or hospitalizations. He will not

be able to accept that his behavior backfired on him and he has lost control of us for real this time. Because he was always able to lure us back in the past, it might take many years before he finally accepts defeat and gives up for good. (This is why it's better to end it permanently a lot sooner, before this on-again-off-again pattern gets established and he learns we are weak and he can weasel his way back in.)

34. When he contacts us again, we will not respond, having moved on with our lives. At some point, it might become necessary to show the narcissist we mean business so he will start taking us seriously and leave us alone. This may include sending him a cease and desist letter from a lawyer, getting a restraining order, or having him arrested for stalking, aggravated harassment, trespassing, etc. But we will not break No Contact and talk to him personally, or send messages back and forth with Flying Monkeys. All communication must be through lawyers or the police.
35. Eventually our stress and anger will lessen and subside. Biblically, we are relieved of the burden of forgiving an unrepentant abuser, but we may feel like praying for him. We will come to understand that we can feel better about him or even forgive him, and yet still not reconcile. We will accept that he is what he is and will never change. Many years later, we might even have some happy memories of our time together or feel some fondness for him, from a safe distance, without having him be a part of our lives. We will internalize that he is in our past, and will never again be a part of our present or our future.
36. The abuser will take out his frustrations on others. When we are out of the picture, he will move on to other targets which he will use and abuse until those relationships end also. Without repentance and change, he will continue to alienate

everyone in his life except his enablers. But one day, even they will be gone. Eventually he will drive everyone away and be lonely and miserable, but will take solace in blaming us or everyone else, and never himself.

37. We will continue to grow and blossom and go on to have joyful, healthy lives. We will be at peace. Having learned many valuable lessons, we will make every effort to keep all narcissists out of our lives and only get involved with normal people from now on.

CHAPTER 31

DEFINING "HONOR"

THEN THE KING BECAME FURIOUS. HE SENT OUT HIS ARMY TO DESTROY THE MURDERERS AND BURN THEIR CITY. AND HE SAID TO HIS SERVANTS, "THE WEDDING FEAST IS READY, AND THE GUESTS I INVITED AREN'T WORTHY OF THE HONOR"...Matthew 22:7-8 NLT.

Yes, Sisters and Brothers. *Some people are not worthy of honor*, even if they happen to be parents. I think we need to give ourselves permission to be the ones to define "honor," and not let evil people or outsiders define it for us and then force us to live by *their* definition.

First of all, "honoring" is not "obeying." As adults, we do not obey other adults. We have become children of God and we only obey God.

If we set boundaries on our parents' behavior toward us, how is that "dishonoring" them? We are treating them honorably by expecting them to live *up* to a certain standard of correct and acceptable behavior, not *down* to a low, base, primitive level of behavior.

If we need to go No Contact, how is that dishonoring anybody? All we are doing is giving up trying to change them, honoring their choice to be the kind of person they want to be and live as they wish to live, and helping them not to sin anymore by removing ourselves from the picture so they cannot inflict their evil upon us. Having contact with us contributes to causing them to sin by giving them a target. *We **are not doing anything** at all to a narcissist by simply staying away from her.* If we live in the truth as the Bible instructs us to do, bring evil deeds into the light, and tell the truth about our abusive parents, how is that dishonoring them? Wouldn't it be much more dishonoring to lie about them and hide what they do as if we were ashamed of them? I really think we need to stop equating "honoring" with "obeying" or "submitting" or "overlooking" or "covering up for." It is none of those things.

Where does it say to honor abusers and forgive the unrepentant who fully intend to continue doing evil and hurting others? When abusers and their Silent Partners use God's Word against us, it helps to remember that the Bible was never written to benefit abusers or to facilitate their evil and unrepentance, and to suggest that it was is to defy logic. The Bible is the Lord's instructions for *godly* people in *godly* families and *godly* churches, *not* the ungodly. It is his teachings for *his* children to live in peace and love with one another, *not* with the children of Satan. Jesus never ignored wrongdoing or overlooked evil. From overturning the money-changers' tables in the temple (Matthew 21:12-13) to the Seven Woes of the Scribes and Pharisees (Matthew 23:1-36), he always spoke the truth, stood up to wrongdoing and publicly rebuked those who did evil, even though it might embarrass them. We are never to honor the evil, nor are we to overlook and tolerate evil behavior, and certainly not to cover it up and keep it secret. To believe that *that* is what God wants us to do is simply preposterous.

CHAPTER 32

WHAT'S THE POINT OF CONFRONTING?

You might be asking yourself what exactly is the point of confronting a narcissist, when you know the response you're going to get (denial, tantrums, lies, drama, gaslighting, turning it around on you~ you misunderstood, you're too sensitive, etc.) will only make it seem like you didn't accomplish anything at all. Well, on the surface it might seem like you didn't accomplish anything, but actually you did. You showed the narcissist that you're not an idiot, you know exactly what he's doing, and you're not just going to keep quiet and let him get away with it. And better yet, you're going to expose him and tell other people what he did. After all, if he says he didn't do anything wrong, then he shouldn't mind if the whole world knows. Narcissists hate exposure more than anything, but Jesus tells us that whatever is whispered in our ear we should shout from the rooftops:

SO DO NOT BE AFRAID OF THEM. THERE IS NOTHING CONCEALED THAT WILL NOT BE DISCLOSED, OR HIDDEN THAT WILL NOT BE MADE KNOWN. WHAT I TELL YOU IN THE DARK, SPEAK IN THE DAYLIGHT; WHAT IS WHISPERED IN YOUR EAR, PROCLAIM FROM THE ROOFS...
Matthew 10:26-27 NIV.

We are never taught to cover up evil, but we *are* taught to publicly expose it:

THOSE WHO SIN ARE TO BE REBUKED PUBLICLY, SO THAT THE OTHERS MAY TAKE WARNING…1 Timothy 5:20 NIV.

Again, it might not seem like you accomplished much by speaking up, but look at it this way~ by *not* speaking up and just suffering in silence, *you haven't accomplished anything at all* in all these years. You have just been letting the narcissist get away with it. In fact, I'm willing to bet over time his abuse has gotten worse and worse. The more you let an abuser know he can get away with it, the more he views you as weak and vulnerable~ the perfect prey. And the more outrageous his behavior gets, until somebody finally stops him. There are only two ways to do that.

One way to stop *some* narcissists from abusing you is to just refuse to take it anymore. Nobody is handing out gold medals for suffering in silence, so quit being a martyr. The long-term effect of calling out a narcissist on his bad behavior is that he might start to think twice before doing it again, or at least before doing it *to you.* Don't give him the satisfaction of thinking he's upsetting you because that's what he feeds off of. Instead, make it plain that you consider him disgraceful and lacking the class or intelligence to behave properly, and that you're not going to cover up for him anymore. Hopefully, your confrontations will become so uncomfortable for him that he will eventually start trying to avoid them and move on to easier targets. Unfortunately, this doesn't work with all narcissists and there are no guarantees that it will work with yours.

The only other way to stop a narcissist from abusing you is to go No Contact. You might not be ready for that yet, but you probably will be after you waste another few years trying to change your narcissist. If you really want to *stop* him, this is the only pretty much foolproof way to do it. He cannot target you if you move yourself out of range. If you are looking for a permanent solution, strict No Contact is the only way to win the war.

CHAPTER 33

FOUR SECRET WAYS TO "CHANGE" A NARCISSIST

We all know that narcissists never change. No amount of reasoning, nicely asking, "understanding," tolerating, arguing, yelling, crying (although they *do* love to see us do all of those things, because it's a power trip for them), therapy, medication, anger management, etc., etc., ever works. However, although they will never *truly* change, and their character will always remain disgustingly deficient, there are four tactics we can use that have been known to convince them to modify their behavior, at least around us. You might think they're worth a try, especially if you are not yet ready to kick your narcissist to the curb permanently:

*One caveat~ Since these battle strategies tend to antagonize the narcissist, I do not suggest using them on a violent abuser. If your narcissist is or might be physically violent, call your nearest Domestic Violence hotline for help instead.

1. *Withhold Narcissistic Supply* (attention, admiration, respect, sympathy, favors, etc.), but first tell the narcissist *why* you are doing it. From now on, whenever he does____, you will do ____. As long as he does ____, you will not do ____. The next time he raises his voice, you will leave the room. The next time he badmouths you to your aunt, you will not speak to him until he goes to your aunt and undoes the damage he did. Then start ignoring him and distancing from him, *before* he acts up again. Act like you're mad at him, and *stay* mad

for a while (you know, like *he* does to *you*). Thinking you are serious about withholding his supply will send him into a panic of reasonably decent behavior, at least for a little while.

2. *Always speak the truth about him* and his manipulation, bullying, lying and other bad behavior. Never protect him with silence and secrecy. Blab everything he does wrong to all those people he tries to impress, to the whole world, and if he tries to get you to keep something he did a secret, tell him absolutely not~ that you are going to tell *everybody,* and the next time he isn't going to want people to know what he did, then he shouldn't do it. Darkness hates the light, and evil hates being brought out into the open for all to see. Exposure and the threat of exposure is a very powerful deterrent to narcissistic behavior: "*AND THIS IS THE CONDEMNATION, THAT LIGHT IS COME INTO THE WORLD, AND MEN LOVED DARKNESS RATHER THAN LIGHT, BECAUSE THEIR DEEDS WERE EVIL. FOR EVERY ONE THAT DOETH EVIL HATETH THE LIGHT, NEITHER COMETH TO THE LIGHT, LEST HIS DEEDS SHOULD BE REPROVED*" *...John 3:19-20 KJV.*

3. The key to confronting a narcissist is in *how* you do it. *You* have to control the confrontation and not let him take over or divert you from your point. Since he feeds off upsetting you and is titillated and excited by getting your goat, you can't let him see that you're upset, or he wins. You have to stay deadly calm and state firmly that you don't approve of or appreciate his behavior. Even if you're quaking on the inside, don't let it show on the outside. Don't be intimidated~ look him right in the eye. Don't argue, just firmly but casually repeat whatever it was he did. If he lied, say "Everybody knows you're a liar, and nobody believes you" right to his face. If he lied about

you, look down your nose at him and say "Well, we all know you've always been a troublemaker." If he abused someone, say "You're just a little bully," with a look of disgust. When he acts out like an immature little brat, look at him with repugnance and say, "How *old* are you, anyway? Five?" *Guilt never works on narcissists, but* ***shame*** *does.* Narcissists want to be superior, and they can't stand it when you think they're petty, silly little dirtbags who aren't even worth your time to argue with. Mock him, laugh at him, belittle him, show disgust and revulsion, shake your head at him, roll your eyes, sneer at him like he does to you, tell him he's pathetic.

Narcissists can also be quite paranoid, so when you make it seem as if other people are talking about him and agreeing with you ("*Everybody* knows...," "*Nobody* believes you...," "*We all* know..."), you are pushing the right buttons. You are turning the tables on him. Instead of *him* isolating *you*, you are making it seem as if he is the subject of disapproval and tittering behind his back, other people think he's wrong and don't like him, and you're turning people against him by telling them the truth about him, all of which means *he* is the one being isolated. When he responds to your rebuke with his usual nonsense, shrug and say, "Well, I'm going to tell _____ and _____ and _____, and see what *they* think about what you did," and watch him start twitching. Then *ignore* him and leave the room. Don't give him any more attention. Let him sit there and stew.

4. *Very* strong shouting down and standing up to a narcissist will often make him back down. It takes some skill and experience to develop the right technique for doing this. You must never appear vulnerable or out-of-control in any way. No crying or signs of weakness. Angry shouting is good, but enraged

screaming is not, because it makes you seem as if you've lost control. You have to take the emotion out of it and depersonalize it. You need to be righteously angry, powerful, forceful and authoritative. You need to not respond to his efforts to get you to back down with tears, "hurt feelings," or his own fake outrage. Just ignore it all and keep hammering him.

When cornered, most narcissists will switch to diversionary tactics. You need to insist on direct answers to direct questions and not let the narcissist get away with any of his usual avoidance tactics, such as lying, being evasive, asking *you* questions, or diverting the conversation. Instead, just steamroll right over him. For instance, if the narcissist insults you or says something he should not have and you confront him, his typical response would be to tell you that you took it the wrong way or that upsetting you wasn't his intention. Upon hearing this, many victims get side-tracked and drop it, but that's the wrong way to deal with it and nothing will get resolved. What you need to do is throw it back in his lap and demand a straight answer to a straight question~ "Oh really? *I* took it the wrong way? Well then, what *was* your intention? I want to know what, in your mind, would make that an acceptable thing to say to me!" Don't accept anything less than a non-evasive answer, one that actually makes sense. No matter what lame response he comes up with, keep repeating the question until you back him down and he either tells the truth or apologizes.

At the same time, you have to be cool and detached, not caring about his reactions. It's critical that *he* winds up being the one who feels flustered and attacked, and not you~ so never let him get the upper hand or take control, and do *not* answer his questions. Just keep talking right over him while systematically laying out all his misbehavior, one thing after another. Overwhelm him, interrupt him and wear him down. Make him never want to get stuck in another argument with you again.

This technique, done correctly, has been known to back down many a narcissist, and even get them to start minding their Ps and Qs around us for fear of being lambasted again. We are training them here, making every offense backfire and be so unpleasant for them that they will start trying to avoid confrontations with us, and wind up walking on eggshells themselves instead of making *us* walk on eggshells. You will raise the narcissist's blood pressure here, and probably your own as well. But afterwards, when you've had a chance to calm down, you will feel pretty good. I have been successful in getting a couple of family narcissists to modify their behavior around me using this technique, and I know several other former targets who have perfected it as well. Consistency helps to change some narcissists' bad behaviors~ not letting the narcissist get away with even the slightest offense without letting him have it with both barrels.

These are a few ways to get a narcissist to think twice before abusing us. They require a lot of repetition and a long-term commitment to being willing and able to engage in confrontations for the foreseeable future, with the potential for only a limited amount of success. Before you bother, you might find it valuable to do a little cost/benefit analysis to determine if it's worth it or not. Only you can decide if staying in contact with your particular narcissist is worth all this effort to get him to grudgingly, and possibly only slightly, improve his behavior, although not his heart.

CHAPTER 34

IS IT "UN-CHRISTIAN" OR POLITICALLY INCORRECT TO CALL A DIRTBAG A DIRTBAG?

You may have noticed something about my writing by now. I tend to be pretty unsympathetic in the way I refer to the abusers and psychopaths I write about. A little graphic, perhaps even a bit harsh, you might say. When you deal with the havoc wreaked on innocents by "human" garbage that I deal with every day, you start to get a little testy about it~ and yes, a little *angry.* I sometimes use names that you might not hear too many other Christians use. I tend to call a snake a snake, if you will. And my attitude is pretty much this: if a pervert doesn't want to be called a pervert, then maybe he ought to stop molesting children. Till then, I'm gonna call him a pervert, because that's what he *is.*

If you knew me personally, you'd know that I'm a little rough around the edges. I make no apologies for this. It's probably a product of my Brooklyn upbringing, to a great extent. We old-school Brooklynites have a certain colorful way of expressing ourselves. But more to the point, I'm a product of my own abusive upbringing. When you live with a predator, you learn never to appear weak. You learn to act tough, even if you don't always feel tough, because any sign of vulnerability or softness will be seen as weakness and an invitation to an attack. After decades of living under siege, it's pretty much ingrained.

Along the way, I also developed an "advocate/activist" mentality. My birth-mother used to say I always defended the underdog, even if that meant taking the brunt of the attack upon myself. In our toxic household, the "underdog" was *her,* according to her, and it was my job to protect her, diverting my birth-father's rage away from her and onto me. That, too, became an ingrained part of my personality, and I went on to spend twenty years of my life advocating for Vietnam veterans. Another layer of toughness, standing up for justice, and telling it like it is, added to the previous ones. And then, the Lord took the sum of all these life-experiences and led me in another direction~ to advocate for those who are being abused by the families, and church-families, they love~ children and adult children alike.

Does it seem harsh or un-Christian-like to you to refer to a child rapist as a pervert and a dirtbag? Or to call someone who would terrorize her own two-year-old to the point that he can't catch his breath and is gasping for air, and then laugh at his panic, a sadist and a sociopath? Or to call a mother who stays married to the pedophile who raped her child, fails to do anything to protect that child, *and then tops it all off by babysitting other people's children* and leaving them alone with the pervert so he can (and did) rape *them* too, a lowlife who belongs in the prison cell next to him? Is calling a baby-killer a "murderer" going to hurt his poor widdle feelings? Well, too bad.

Is there even a name bad enough, or should I say "descriptive" enough, to refer to a mother who would set up her own child to be raped repeatedly by her husband, to keep him from focusing his attention on *her?* What about a father who pimps out his children to his friends for money and beer? Or the jackass who has a fight with his girlfriend and then beats their five-week-old baby to death for spite, to get back at *her?* Or the psychopathic parents who lock their child in a room for seven years, make her use a litter box for a bathroom, and starve her so badly that she weighs only thirty-five pounds when she finally dies? Or the dirtbags (not teenagers, mind you, adults who were almost thirty years old) who claim they can't afford a baby (because they'd rather spend their money on cigarettes and alcohol), and decide to get rid of their hours-old newborn by dropping a cinderblock on her?

Hey, they are what they are. I'm not here to help them feel good about themselves. Seriously, what else would you call them? What would be the politically correct way to refer to scum like this? "Slightly irresponsible"? "Child torture-challenged"? "Having low self-esteem which results in unintentionally acting out their frustrations and beating the baby to death"? "Having boundary issues about sexually touching children"? "Being a little temperamental~ sometimes resulting in accidentally going too far and killing a child?" Oh, pull-eeze. Enough, already.

Someone who *likes* to see pain and gets their jollies by making a helpless victim suffer *is* a sadist. That's the definition of the word "sadist." A person who remorselessly and brutally inflicts his malice and violence on an innocent target, has absolutely no conscience or compassion about it, and in fact often then tries to use what he did to elicit sympathy for *himself, is* a psychopath. That's what a psychopath *is.* No, really. Look it up. Let's not disrespect the victims and minimize their experiences and pain by making up more pleasant sounding euphemisms to cover up their abusers' true natures. That sends a false message to victims and to the rest of the world~ that what was done to them wasn't really so bad. But it *was*, so let's stop beating around the bush. Let's stand up and make our disapproval of and contempt for their abusers loud and clear. Tell it like it is.

Jesus certainly didn't pull any punches when he called the Pharisees just about every name there was in the book at the time. Hypocrites, snakes, a brood of vipers, unclean, greedy, whitewashed tombs full of dead men's bones and all kinds of filth on the inside, blind fools, full of wickedness, sons of hell (Matthew 23:13-33). He used the strongest possible language of his day to denounce them. He made an example of them. He spoke, not just directly to the

Pharisees, *but for the benefit of everyone else within earshot.* Do you think the people who heard him got his point? Evil is evil. It is never un-Christian-like to tell the truth, nor is it un-Christian-like to use strong language when you tell it.

This is not a subject we need to be wishy-washy, calm, or easy-going about. We don't need to phrase it kindly lest we insult a dirtbag or offend his partners-in-crime. Using strong language to describe abusers and their enablers serves a purpose. It gets people's attention. It underscores for them just how disgusting, shameful, and yes, *evil,* the behavior of these so-called "parents" is, and how disgusting, shameful, and *evil* the parents themselves are.

It says if you protect an abuser by tolerating or minimizing abuse, *then there is something wrong* ***with you,*** too. You are just as guilty as he is, and just as much of a dirtbag. It brings things that are often hushed-up or whispered about out into the open, and gives other people the courage to stand up and tell it like it is. It makes a big deal out of something that many people would just as soon pretend isn't happening or isn't really that bad. It makes it *unacceptable* to accept abuse. It drives home the point that abuse, and enabling abuse, is *not* "accidental." It is *not* something "they can't help." It is *not* a "mistake" or a "misunderstanding." It is *despicable.* It is *intentional, deliberate,* and supremely *selfish.*

To those who think I'm being "too harsh" on bullies, abusers, pedophiles and their enablers, and that I need to be "understanding" of psychopaths, liars, thieves, backstabbers, tyrants and baby-murderers and their enablers in order to be more "Christ-like," I would say there is nothing heroic or "Christian" about overlooking or tolerating evil and abuse, and Jesus certainly never did.

We also have no right and no authority to "forgive" a dirtbag for damaging another person. That's up to the person he harmed, not us. It does not make anyone a "good Christian" to "forgive" or tolerate an unrepentant abuser, especially not an abuser who abused or is abusing *somebody else.*

It also does not make anyone a "good Christian" to "live in peace" with the children of the devil, and *no,* God never, ever told us to do that. If this is what you do and what you preach, then you need to stop trying to make yourself look "saintly" for not standing up, shunning and proclaiming righteous anger toward these dirtbags, instead of what you *really* are, which is an abuse-colluder and an abuse-enabler. Oh, and a coward, too. Don't criticize outspoken people who have the courage that you lack, to call a spade a spade and call attention to and condemn evil and the children of Satan in explicit and unambiguous terms. They are the prophets of God. Grow a backbone, open your mouth, and take a stand, too.

Abusers victimize others to get their own needs met, and their colluders/enablers allow it, and even encourage it, to make their own lives easier and to get *their* own needs met. It's a sick, twisted dynamic. And they continue until they are exposed, or better yet, arrested. They continue until the silence is broken. They continue until we stop circumventing the issues, molly-coddling them, walking on eggshells around them, and talking about them in nice, mild, smiley-face terms~ terms that are vague, deceptive, and fail to present the *true* picture and emphasize the gravity of it to the listener. It's not *our* fault if the truth is ugly.

Evil always tries to hide in the darkness and minimize its sin. It thrives in silence, and in meek, "inoffensive" whispers. Do you think Jesus whispered meekly when he threw the money-changers out of the temple (Matthew 21:12), or do you think he raised his voice? There are many times that taking authority over evil, public rebuke, and a show of righteous anger are the only correct and appropriate reactions. If we *really* want to be "Christ-like," then we need to use common sense, open our eyes, read the Bible and do what Christ actually *did,* instead of deluding ourselves into believing that he was always "gentle" and "meek," never rebuked evil, and let the wicked get away with anything they wanted to do while he remained silent or pussyfooted around them for fear of upsetting them or making a scene. Honestly, where do people get these wacky ideas about Jesus, when the truth about his true nature and personality, authority and outspokenness is right in front of them in black and white in the Bible they claim to follow so carefully?

Abusers and their colluders/enablers continue until they are embarrassed and shamed. Until someone stands up and shouts the truth about them from the rooftops. They continue until the people who know them stop sugar-coating their behavior, sweeping it under the rug and making excuses for them, and start looking at them with the appropriate revulsion and loathing. They continue until nobody wants to be associated with them anymore, until others start avoiding them like the plague, and warning everybody else to stay away, too. In the Bible, this is referred to as "shunning," and it's meant to produce shame and repentance. They continue until it gets through, not just to them, but to everyone around them, that what they are doing is *wrong,* wicked, evil and bad. They continue until we make our opinions of their behavior so crystal clear that there can be no mistaking our repulsion and condemnation of them and their behavior for any reaction even slightly milder. They continue until we start forcing them to own what they are~ degenerate, disgusting, sadistic, psychopathic, perverted, lowlife *dirtbags.*

As for me, believe it or not, I do try to tone it down a bit. Imagine what my ramblings would sound like if I didn't! But I am what I am, too. I don't believe in pussy-footing around with stuff like this. My calling is to minister to the *victims,* not the abusers. Victims need to know that other people support them and agree that what was done to them was terrible, and that the lowlifes who did it are terrible. Survivors need to know that we validate them and their experiences, and stand together with them against bullying and abuse. I'm here to help victims heal and to give them a voice~ a nice, *big* voice~ not to help abusers gloss over, justify and feel okay with, or even good about, what they've done.

A bully's main goal is to be regarded with respect and fear, so one of the best lessons we can teach him is that his behavior produces just the opposite effect, and causes others to regard him with contempt and scorn instead. I believe in drawing lots of public attention to abusers and the things they do so they can no longer operate in secret, and condemning them with the word "dirtbag" or other strong language gets people's attention and empowers others to openly disapprove of bullying and abuse, too. Abusers don't deserve the privilege of being able to walk among the rest of us with their heads held high. I believe in letting dirtbags live with the consequences of their own actions, including shame, embarrassment, and the disgust of good people everywhere. That's the way God made *me.* And I believe in keeping it up, relentlessly, until they start thinking twice before raping a child or beating a baby, or bullying, stealing from, sabotaging, lying about, or otherwise doing deliberate harm to an innocent person. Who knows? If we make the social consequences of their actions uncomfortable enough for them, then maybe, just maybe, they'll repent of their evil ways, turn to the Lord, and be saved.

AND YE SHALL KNOW THE TRUTH, AND THE TRUTH SHALL MAKE YOU FREE…John 8:32 KJV.

CHAPTER 35

WE DO NOT NEED THERAPY

Surprise, surprise. We do not need therapy. *There is nothing wrong with us.* Our depression, anger, PTSD, anxiety, headaches, stress, nightmares, physical symptoms, etc. *are normal reactions that healthy people have* to being abused, manipulated, unjustly accused and attacked, gaslighted, stalked, lied about, used, exploited, betrayed, bullied and victimized long-term. We would be emotionally disturbed if we were *not* upset and affected by such mistreatment.

When we begin taking a stand and rocking the boat, our abusers and their Silent Partners will be befuddled and angry, and often accuse us of "going crazy." But finally beginning to protest their abuse and to quit just lying down and being a doormat are signs of emotional growth and getting healthy. These are *good* things, not something that has to be "fixed" so we will go back to being compliant victims again.

How can therapy cure a perfectly normal person? Getting toxic people out of our lives is the only way to lead healthy lives. As long as the toxic ones are still there, we will be in therapy indefinitely, just playing catch-up. It's only a temporary band-aid, and it can't possibly fix anything permanently because the person who causes all our problems, and who there *is* something wrong with, isn't going, and wouldn't go in good faith if he was forced to.

You can't keep going back and forth to the doctor for pain medication forever. Sooner or later you have to schedule surgery and let him cut the tumor out. Then, and only then, can you truly heal and get better. I know dozens of folks, including myself, who never went to therapy. They just went No Contact with their abusers, and after the passage of some time are leading happy, healthy, well-adjusted lives.

Now don't get me wrong. That is not to say that therapy can't help us, as long as it's approached from the right angle. It just can't *cure* us, because we are not sick. There is nothing to cure. *Any therapy we get should be with the goal of giving us the tools and courage we need to walk away from the narcissists, never to "handle" them or live "peacefully" with them (impossible goals), and to have some standards for our future relationships (only two-way, mutually caring and beneficial relationships with respectful, kind, loving, rational,* ***normal*** *people).* We might need a little help and guidance in claiming our freedom and reprogramming ourselves to be repulsed by narcissists instead of attracted to the familiar in our future relationships, and that's great. But we do not need to be "cured," because you can't cure normal.

CHAPTER 36

FROM NOW ON, HEALTHY RELATIONSHIPS ONLY

DO NOT BE MISLED: "BAD COMPANY CORRUPTS GOOD CHARACTER"...1 Corinthians 15:33 NIV.

A big part of recovering from abuse is deciding how we are going to spend the rest of our lives. Are we going to allow ourselves to be doomed to repeat history in our future relationships, or are we going to take the bull by the horns and change things? Are we going to allow our lives and our characters to become corrupted~ spoiled, depraved, contaminated, and perverted~ by the company we keep? Or are we going to live life on a higher plane, with people of integrity, honor, kindness, love, godliness and good character, instead of down in the gutter with the dirtbags? The choice is ours.

This might surprise a lot of people, *but yes, we do have a choice.* We have a choice over what kinds of relationships we are going to permit ourselves to get involved in from now on. We have a choice over the kinds of people we're going to socialize with. We have a choice to get into therapy so that we will be capable of making healthy decisions for ourselves.

We have the choice to accept mistreatment or to refuse to accept it. We have the choice, and the *right,* to say *no.* We have the choice, and the *right,* to walk away from a relationship that is unhealthy for us. And if we are going to live healthy lives and claim our God-given peace and joy, that is what we will have to do.

Therapy can be helpful for some of us because, having been raised by abusers and indoctrinated into believing that abuse, control and betrayal are just normal parts of life and relationships, we might have a problem internalizing the fact that *they are not.* Many of us even have trouble recognizing when we're being abused, controlled or betrayed, because we have accepted this toxic behavior all of our lives. If you opt to go for some therapy, I cannot say enough about the importance of finding a counselor who specializes in abuse recovery. Not every counselor has what it takes to help recovering victims heal and go on to happier and abuse-free futures. Keep searching until you find one who truly understands.

A big obstacle to having a healthy future and a healthy life is understanding and accepting that you have the *right* to decide who will share that life with you. You have the right to only associate with people who make you happy and bring out the best in you. You have the right to set limits and boundaries and to have them respected. You have the right to be treated with kindness and consideration. You have the right to be cared for and unconditionally loved. You have the right to say no, and to end relationships that do not provide you with these basic human needs.

Some people cannot conceive of the fact that it is okay to end a relationship that is no longer healthy for them, even if it is a lifelong friendship or a birth-family relationship. Sometimes we do grow apart from people we love and our lives go off in different directions, but because we love each other, we still keep the relationship going even though we no longer have much in common. Our differences are celebrated, and add richness to our lives. A particular long-term relationship may no longer be meeting all of our needs, but if it isn't damaging to us either, then we can still continue this relationship in love, and have the rest of our needs met with other relationships.

But when there is abuse involved, it's a different story. An unhealthy, toxic relationship is not one that we should stay enmeshed in for old time's sake. Such relationships are devoid of kindness, love and caring, at least towards *us*. Just because someone is in our lives, often by no choice of our own, it doesn't mean they have to stay there forever. When a relationship has run its course and not only ceases to be beneficial to us, but becomes upsetting, stressful, draining or harmful, then we have to give ourselves permission to say goodbye~ for our own good, if not for our own survival.

Frequently this will involve cutting ties with a parent, sibling, or other relative. But it can also mean breaking it off with an unhealthy friend, keeping a phony "Christian" at church at arm's length, or not allowing ourselves to get any more deeply involved with an acquaintance whose negative side is showing more and more as we get to know him better. Sometimes it's as simple as learning to keep our distance from people who are giving off the wrong vibe, and we need to ask the Holy Spirit to sharpen our discernment so we can recognize such people and stay away from them. It is easier and a lot less complicated to not even get involved with problem people in the first place than it is to break it off after a relationship has developed.

What are some traits of a healthy relationship? How can we know what to look for and what to run from? What promises can we make to ourselves that will protect us from getting involved with narcissists and help us recognize and choose relationships that are good for us?

1. **I WILL REFUSE TO BE INVOLVED IN A RELATIONSHIP WHERE I AM NOT CONSIDERED EQUAL TO THE OTHER PERSON.** A healthy adult relationship is one between *equals*. Neither party is "the boss." One is not the leader while the other is the follower, one is not the domineering parent-figure or rude, pushy "schoolmarm" while the other is the helpless or incompetent child. One is not the know-it-all lecturer or big-shot expert while the other is the one who

can't function without his "advice" and supervision. Neither dominates, criticizes, judges or controls the other.

2. **I WILL REFUSE TO BE IN A RELATIONSHIP THAT RESTRICTS MY FREEDOM.** Freedom is an integral part of a healthy relationship. Each person feels free to relax and be himself with the other. Each is free to express his honest feelings and opinions, to have his own interests and friends, and to make decisions, all without fearing criticism and disapproval from the other. Support, help and favors are not demanded, but freely given out of love. And each person also feels free to turn down a request without having to fear losing the approval or love of the other person. There is no need to pretend to be someone we're not just to please the other person. Each person feels secure in the knowledge that the other loves and accepts him for who he is.

3. **I WILL REFUSE TO BE IN A ONE-WAY RELATIONSHIP AND I WILL NOT ALLOW MYSELF TO BE USED OR EXPLOITED.** Healthy relationships are balanced relationships. There is give-and-take. A good relationship is a two-way street. One person does not do all or most of the giving, while the other sits back and relaxes, or does all or most of the taking. For instance, one person does not do all the inviting, while the other is the perpetual guest. When you realize you never get to talk to someone unless *you* do the calling, then you are in an unbalanced, unequal relationship. The phone goes both ways. When you consistently make the time to be there for your friend whenever she needs to talk, but she never seems to have the time for you when *you* need to talk, then your relationship is one-way. If you are the one doing all the favors, and never getting anything in return, you are in a relationship with a *user,* and that is not good

for you. *If you are not benefiting from the relationship just as much as the other person is, then it is not a healthy relationship for you to be in.*

4. **I WILL REFUSE TO HAVE A RELATIONSHIP WITH ANYONE I CAN'T TRUST.** Trust is a key element of a healthy relationship. If there has been betrayal, treachery, gossip or passing around false rumors, dishonesty, lies, deceit, scheming, backstabbing, manipulation, conniving, broken promises, exploitation, passive aggression, gaslighting, ulterior motives, hidden agendas, or sneaking around behind the other person's back, not to mention stealing, cheating or outright sabotage, then there can be no trust. Everyone is entitled to some degree of privacy, but if someone is keeping a secret or hiding something that rightfully concerns the other person or the relationship, then there can be no trust. In new relationships, it takes time to build trust. You need to learn a lot about the other person first. If someone is pushy and overly familiar, and pressures you for more intimacy quicker than you are comfortable with, that is a red flag. Take the time to get to know new people before becoming too involved. *Most narcissists cannot keep up the phony façade of pretending to be a charming, lovable, nice* ***normal*** *person for more than six months to a year without slipping up and showing their true colors, so be alert and take note when the mask drops for that split-second and you catch that little glimpse of a warning.*

5. **I WILL NOT HAVE A RELATIONSHIP WITH A NARCISSIST (AND I WILL MOST DEFINITELY NOT HAVE ONE WITH A PSYCHOPATH, NO MATTER HOW CHARMING HE MIGHT SEEM AT FIRST).** If you are in a relationship with a narcissist, it is not going to be

healthy for you. Relationships with people who think it's all about them, and that other people don't matter, do not work. By definition, a relationship is about *both* people, not just one. If one person is selfish and self-centered, thoughtless and inconsiderate, he is not relationship material. A person who demands the lion's share of the attention, respect, admiration, sympathy or favors, who is high-maintenance, who constantly manages to direct the conversation back to her and her issues, who has little or no interest in your issues, barely listens when you try to talk to her, and doesn't seem to care about what anyone else may be going through, is not relationship material. Do you know someone who complains about everyone and everything? Who always seems to have a problem, and has a history of broken friendships, consecutive short-term employments or *no* employment, not "getting along" with people, and romantic failures? Who always claims to be depressed, upset, worried, hurt or angry over something? Who always has some sort of vague physical ache or pain to whine about, but who ignores the genuine, serious, life-threatening illnesses of others? Narcissists are not simply people who think they are better than everybody else. *They are people who want to be the center of attention~ good, bad, or otherwise. It doesn't matter whether they are getting your admiration, your pity, or your anger, as long as they are the focus of your attention.* This will never be a good relationship for you.

6. **I WILL REFUSE TO HAVE A RELATIONSHIP WITH SOMEONE WHO DOES NOT RESPECT ME.** Respect is critical to a healthy relationship. Respect for each other's feelings, needs, desires and dreams. Respect for each other's hurts, disappointments, heartaches and sore points. Respect for each other's likes and dislikes, respect for each other's

boundaries and limits, respect for each other as a person. This means when you tell your friend that he has hurt you, he apologizes and doesn't do it again, because he cares for you and respects your feelings. This means that when someone is doing something that upsets you on an ongoing basis, and you tell her, she respects your wishes and *stops it.*

7. **I WILL NOT ALLOW MYSELF TO BE ABUSED.** Disagreements are bound to happen in every relationship. That does not make the relationship unhealthy. But *how* the disagreements are handled and resolved will tell whether the relationship is ultimately good for you or not. Behaviors such as name-calling, screaming, raging, vengefulness, lying, denial, aggression and hostility are destructive. Resolving things with cooperation and goodwill is constructive. Losing one's temper and then sincerely apologizing and promising not to do it again might be acceptable once. But losing one's temper on a regular basis, causing one to be nasty and hurtful to the other person, is not acceptable. Physical or sexual abuse is *never* acceptable, not even once. Ongoing patterns of temper tantrums, rage, mistreatment, spitefulness, hostility, cruelty or passive aggression are *abuse.* If this characterizes your relationship, then it is not healthy for you.

8. **I WILL NOT ALLOW MYSELF TO BE CONTROLLED BY ANOTHER PERSON.** In a healthy adult relationship, no one controls anybody else. No one uses guilt, pressure, manipulation, tears, anger, emotional blackmail, ultimatums, mocking, sarcasm, or the threatened or implied withdrawal of approval or love to get their own way or to force the other person into doing something she doesn't want to do. If you are only "loved" when you are doing what the other person wants you to do, and that love is withdrawn when you fail to

do what the other person wants, then you are being emotionally blackmailed.

9. **I WILL NOT HAVE RELATIONSHIPS WITH PEOPLE WHO REFUSE TO APOLOGIZE WHEN THEY'RE WRONG AND TO CHANGE OFFENSIVE BEHAVIOR.** People who are healthy to have relationships with have no trouble sincerely apologizing and expressing remorse if they've upset or hurt the other person. Because they *care* about the other's feelings, and don't want to upset her, they will make every effort to avoid repeating the offense and to modify their behavior so as not to hurt their loved one again. When offensive behavior becomes repetitive, the offender is showing her sadistic side, and the relationship has ceased to be healthy for the victim.

10. **I WILL REFUSE TO HAVE ANYTHING TO DO WITH ANYONE WHO IS JEALOUS OR ENVIOUS OF ME.** Healthy relationships cannot exist where there is jealousy or envy. If something nice happens to you, the people who love you will be happy for you, not resentful or jealous. If you have a talent or happen to be good at something, the people who love you will support you and compliment you, not compete with you. If you have worked hard for something and you finally get it, your true friends will rejoice with you, not be envious or competitive or try to undermine you. If someone has your best interests at heart, then she is a good person for you to have in your life. If she is hoping that you will stumble, fail, or endure some misfortune so that she can feel better about herself, then she is not a good person. People who love each other are able to support each other during tough times and celebrate one another's joys and successes. Jealous people are dangerous people.

11. **I WILL NOT GET INVOLVED WITH DRAMA QUEENS.** It is extremely stressful and almost impossible to have a healthy relationship with a drama queen. Some people thrive on constant turmoil and crisis, and if nothing is happening at the moment for them to get all worked up over, they will create something. This addiction to drama can be very nerve-wracking for the rest of us. Drama queens are a subspecies of narcissist. They can be fun and exciting to be around at first, but after a while they are draining, time-consuming, exhausting and high-maintenance. They are best taken in small doses. Becoming involved in a relationship with one is too big of a commitment for a healthy person.

12. **I WILL AVOID RELATIONSHIPS WITH PEOPLE WHO THINK THEY ARE "SPECIAL" OR MORE IMPORTANT THAN ME OR ANYONE ELSE.** People who have an exaggerated sense of entitlement are not relationship material. They are spoiled, selfish and demanding. Nobody is entitled to special treatment. Nobody is entitled to be treated any better than they are willing to treat other people. In a healthy relationship, everyone is *equal.* There cannot be an "equal" relationship if one person believes they are somehow better or more special than the other person.

13. **I WILL REFUSE TO BE IN A RELATIONSHIP THAT FREQUENTLY CAUSES ME PAIN, STRESS OR AGGRAVATION.** Probably the best gauge of whether a relationship is healthy for you or not is how it makes you feel. If you are at peace in the relationship and find joy in being with the other person, if you feel loved and valued, then it is probably a healthy relationship for you. However, if you feel devalued, degraded, frustrated, aggravated, taken advantage of, uncared for and unloved, then it is not healthy. If you

are stressed, depressed, nervous, anxious, upset, angry, hurt or in pain, it's time to cut your losses and run. This is what defines abuse. When you are consistently made to feel bad, then you are in an abusive relationship.

14. **I WILL NOT HAVE A RELATIONSHIP WITH SOMEONE WHO DOESN'T LOVE ME.** Healthy relationships have, at their core, one common element~ *love*. It is simply not healthy for you to love someone who doesn't love you back. What kind of relationship can you have with your sister, for instance, *when **both** of you love **her**, and **neither** of you love **you?*** In a healthy relationship, we do not have to *earn* the love of the other person by doing what she wants us to do or being what she dictates we should be. We are loved for ourselves, just as our Father created us, unconditionally. As survivors of birth family abuse, we have been brainwashed into thinking that we don't deserve to have our needs met, and we don't deserve to be loved. But as children of God, we know that we *are* worthy of being loved. Our birth-families and our church families are not greater than God. If God himself can love us as much as he does, then who are our abusive relatives or toxic church members to make us feel unworthy of their measly, paltry little love? Their love is completely insignificant compared to our Heavenly Father's. If *he* loves us, then surely they should, too. And if they truly love us, then they will never abuse us. Love and abuse are mutually exclusive.

I WILL PRAISE THEE; FOR I AM FEARFULLY AND WONDERFULLY MADE: MARVELLOUS ARE THY WORKS; AND THAT MY SOUL KNOWETH RIGHT WELL...Psalm 139:14 KJV.

CHAPTER 37

WHEN WE START CHANGING

"And there came from the barnyard a great uproar, a mighty racket~ indignant cackling and enormous squawks of protest~ as the eagle rose up into the sky, and left the chickens behind"...
...Sister Renee Pittelli

When we start changing, we might lose a lot of our old friends.

A certain type of person attracts narcissists, and that type of person is *us*~ the type of person who was brainwashed from birth to believe that nasty narcissistic behavior is acceptable, or even normal, and to overlook it. We send out a certain vibe of tolerance and patience to narcissists, and we also have a natural tendency to cater to them and give them narcissistic supply in the form of attention, admiration, sympathy and favors. It is also human nature to be attracted to the familiar, even if it's cruel and destructive, so we tend to be drawn to people who remind us of our narcissistic birth-relatives, until we have progressed far enough along in our healing process to replace that natural attraction with aversion. Hence, a lot of our relationships will be with narcissists, and a lot of our "friends" will happen to be narcissists.

But when we start changing, recognizing narcissism faster, exposing it, avoiding it, not being as accessible to it or as easy of a mark, and even starting to feel repulsed by it, we start sending out a different vibe. Speaking for myself, I know my reaction to most narcissistic characteristics and behavior nowadays is a feeling of strong revulsion. It's repulsive, sickening and distasteful to me when someone is fishing for attention, sympathy, compliments, admiration, respect, or other narcissistic supply. These are things that narcissists actively seek instead of letting them come naturally, because they don't really deserve any admiration, sympathy or respect, and might never get it otherwise.

Little narcissistic "tells," like some blowhard pontificating on the other side of the room who keeps glancing around to make sure other people are listening to him, trigger my self-protective instinct to make no eye contact and to turn my back. When that little bell goes off in my head telling me that someone is fishing for narcissistic supply, I automatically shut down. I get completely turned off, and feel very uncomfortable until I can get away and put some distance between myself and the narcissist. I ignore narcissists and make myself scarce. I've been known to excuse myself and walk away from them in mid-sentence. I never give them supply, or any other excuse to seek me out or approach me. I'm not always aware of doing it intentionally, but my aversion to them is a conditioned reflex at this point in my life.

Normal people don't trigger this reaction in me, and I don't trigger it in them, so nice, normal conversations and relationships can develop between them and me. But because of my reaction, or more precisely, *non*-reaction, to narcissists, most of the new ones I meet either immediately don't like me and are wary of me, or skip over me and move on to other targets who will pay attention to them and give them what they want.

I've noticed that when we begin to change, we start repelling the narcissists just like they are starting to repel us. They feel uncomfortable around us because they can't get the reactions they're looking for and have always easily manipulated other people into giving them. Not being able to work their "charms" on us confuses them and throws them off their game. They feel even *more* uncomfortable around us when they realize we're someone who lives in the truth, who can see through them and figure out what they are, and who might expose them by pointing out their abuse and letting other people know about it. Narcissists typically stay as far away as possible from people who can see through them.

When we start having higher standards for our friendships, then we begin to attract a higher caliber of people. Little by little, we find that the relationships we now have are with healthy, normal folks instead of toxic, draining, attention-hogs. It's a weeding process. We need to reject and discard abusive and potentially abusive people, and keep empty space available in our lives to fill with quality relationships. We need to make room in our lives and refuse to nurture the ugliness, so only the pretty flowers can grow.

WE ARE *NOT* FRIENDS

Note to Narcissists~ Just because you know me and I know you, it doesn't mean we are friends. Occasionally being in the same room together, having an acquaintance or two in common, or having a few conversations (all about you!) does not make you my friend. I have quite a different idea of friendship and people who are friendship material than you do. Your presumptuousness and pushiness and over-familiarity do not work to force me to warm up to you. They make me uncomfortable and turn me off. Thanks to a lifetime of dealing with people like you, I now have actual standards for the relationships I allow myself to get involved in and the people I allow to get close, and you set off all my narcissist alarm bells. You repulse me. So quit following me around, pretending you know me well and we're best buds, and go dig up your own kind to hang out with. My friends are blessings from God, and you are not worthy to be counted among them. You just don't make the cut. (P.S.) And don't even *think* about asking for my phone number, because you're not going to get it.

CHAPTER 38

NO CONTACT: THE ONLY ROAD TO PERMANENT PEACE

There is nothing we can do to make a relationship with a narcissist good. They never truly change. There is simply no such thing. We might be able to get them to modify their behavior a bit, but they will always be looking for yet another way to abuse us, because they never change in their *hearts*. They will always be selfish, manipulative, crazy-making, volatile, lying abusers. Nothing we try works~ not pacifying them, not walking on eggshells, not trying to please them. We can never stop their abuse, we can never improve things for more than a few weeks at a time, we can never be happy with them in our lives, and we can never have peace. It simply isn't in our control. It's all in the narcissist's control. *Narcissists do not want to live in peace with us.* They want to dominate and use us, they want to upset us and hurt us. They have all the power in the relationship, and we have none.

But wait. There *is* one thing, and *only* one thing, we *can* do that will work, and that is totally, completely, one-hundred percent in *our* control. *Going No Contact.* The instant we do that, we have completely changed the game. We have taken all the power away from the narcissists and placed it all in our own hands. Now there is nothing *they* can do. They are as helpless as we were before. The parameters of our relationship are no longer theirs to set, all the choices are no longer theirs to make. We have taken over the decision-making process and rendered them completely impotent. They cannot bully us anymore, they cannot manipulate us anymore, they cannot even talk to us anymore. No Contact ends the abuse when nothing else can. It is empowering, it is freedom, it is courage, it is protection, it is peace. Viva la Revolucion!

WHEREFORE COME OUT FROM AMONG THEM, AND BE YE SEPARATE, SAITH THE LORD, AND TOUCH NOT THE UNCLEAN THING; AND I WILL RECEIVE YOU, AND WILL BE A FATHER UNTO YOU, AND YE SHALL BE MY SONS AND DAUGHTERS, SAITH THE LORD ALMIGHTY...
2 Corinthians 6:17-18 KJV.

CHAPTER 39

LUKE 17:3 MINISTRIES' ABUSER FAQ

YOU, DEAR CHILDREN, ARE FROM GOD AND HAVE OVERCOME THEM, BECAUSE THE ONE WHO IS IN YOU IS GREATER THAN THE ONE WHO IS IN THE WORLD. THEY ARE FROM THE WORLD AND THEREFORE SPEAK FROM THE VIEWPOINT OF THE WORLD, AND THE WORLD LISTENS TO THEM. WE ARE FROM GOD, AND WHOEVER KNOWS GOD LISTENS TO US; BUT WHOEVER IS NOT FROM GOD DOES NOT LISTEN TO US. THIS IS HOW WE RECOGNIZE THE SPIRIT OF TRUTH AND THE SPIRIT OF FALSEHOOD

...I John 4:4-6 NIV.

These are the answers to the most frequent questions I get in e-mails to Luke 17:3 Ministries' website and our social networking pages about abusers, narcissists, and psychopathic family members and church family members:

1. Yes, they know what they're doing.
2. Yes, they know they're hurting you.
3. Yes, they're doing it on purpose.
4. Yes, they can control it. They do whenever they want to impress someone.
5. Yes, they could stop if they wanted to.
6. No, they don't love you, even if they say they do. Actions speak louder than words. They do not feel love, empathy, compassion or remorse. Your relationship is not about love.

It's about control, dominance, power, attention, "respect," admiration and subservience.

7. No, you cannot change them. You can only change yourself.
8. Yes, there is something you can do. *Get out.* I know that's not what you want to hear, but that's the answer. If it takes you years to accept this, you will always regret those lost years that you could have spent living a joyful life.

EPILOGUE

WAR AND NONSENSE STATEMENTS

AND IF THE HOUSE BE WORTHY, LET YOUR PEACE COME UPON IT: BUT IF IT BE NOT WORTHY, LET YOUR PEACE RETURN TO YOU. AND WHOSOEVER SHALL NOT RECEIVE YOU, NOR HEAR YOUR WORDS, WHEN YE DEPART OUT OF THAT HOUSE OR CITY, SHAKE OFF THE DUST OF YOUR FEET. VERILY I SAY UNTO YOU, IT SHALL BE MORE TOLERABLE FOR THE LAND OF SODOM AND GOMORRHA IN THE DAY OF JUDGMENT, THAN FOR THAT CITY. BEHOLD, I SEND YOU FORTH AS SHEEP IN THE MIDST OF WOLVES: BE YE THEREFORE WISE AS SERPENTS, AND HARMLESS AS DOVES.....Matthew 10:13-16 KJV.

This book has been about battle strategies~ the strategies that abusive narcissists both at home and in church use to remain in control and win the never-ending battle for dominance in all their relationships. These strategies are many, and by no means have they all been covered here. It is my hope, instead, to present the bigger picture, to get you thinking when something doesn't add up, to help you recognize when something is going on behind the scenes, to help you realize when you're being stonewalled, to make you just a little suspicious of how things might appear, so that you look beneath the surface for the *real* game plan.

We tend to trust our families and our church-families, and it's hard to break the habit of taking what our abusers say at face value and start taking it with a grain of salt. Things are not always as they seem to be, especially when a clever narcissist or psychopath decides to cover up his true motives, present the negative in a positive light, lay on the phony guilt trip, drag out the pity ploy, manipulate behind the scenes, or get passive-aggressive instead of being honest and forthright. I pray that by studying these few examples you were able to learn a little bit about how they think. And that by better understanding how they operate, you'll be better able to anticipate their moves and prepare yourself to counteract them.

Does this sound a little like a war? Well, that's because it is. A war with many battles~ the battle for control, the battle for dominance, the battle for attention, the battle for power, the battle for admiration and yes, idol-worship, the battle for the freedom to do or say whatever one wants to without having to answer to anyone else, the battle for all the advantages and perks of being in a relationship without any of the responsibilities or effort. There is constant jockeying for position, and any challenge to the Alpha abuser~ real or imagined~ any sign of independence, growth or personal boundaries, has to be put down before it starts a revolution.

Ridiculous, isn't it? In church, we are all supposed to be children of God, but then it turns out that some of us are children of Satan, the wolves in sheep's clothing that Jesus warned us about (Matthew 7:15). In both our personal and church lives, we are supposed to be in a *family,* not a war. But narcissists and psychopaths are at war in *all* their relationships. To them, this is what a family *is.* Life is always a competition, always a battle. Normal people recognize this as crazy, but narcissists don't. If you have gotten to the point where you can see the absurdity and insanity here, I congratulate you. You are healing. You are re-learning all the dysfunctional brainwashing you were raised with. You are on your way to normal. And you are going to leave *them* behind.

Just so you know, they hate it when you get healthy. And you can expect them to do whatever they can to impede your progress. In the introduction to this book, I gave some examples of the inane responses and lame excuses abusers use when we tell them they are hurting us and start setting limits. I like to call these responses and others like them "Nonsense Statements." They are Nonsense Statements because they do not make any sense. They do not resolve anything, they accomplish absolutely nothing, and they don't even directly address our complaints.

When you say, "Mom, I don't want you to tell my personal business to the rest of the family," and she responds with, "After all I've done for you, you shouldn't talk to me like that," that is a Nonsense Statement. It doesn't make sense because it doesn't address what you said. Your complaint never got answered. Whatever your mother might have done for you in the past has nothing to do with you not wanting her to gossip about you in the present or in the future. What she should be saying is, "You're right. I apologize. It won't happen again."

When you say, "Dad, I want you to stop picking fights and ruining every family get-together," and he responds with, "Listen, I'm getting old. That's just how I am," then your complaint never got addressed, and you have no hope that family get-togethers will ever improve. *After all, he is only going to get* ***older.*** *So by* ***his*** *reasoning, his behavior is only going to get* ***worse.*** Where does that leave you? The fact that your father may or may not be getting older doesn't have anything to do with his refusal to control himself and his temper at family gatherings. What you need to hear is, "I'm really sorry. I don't want to ruin everyone else's good time. I promise I'll be more careful from now on."

When you say, "Sister, I don't want you to mention my weight again. I'm tired of your criticism," the proper response is, "I'm so sorry. You're right, I won't mention it again." *Not* "I'm just telling you for your own good." Whether or not your sister thinks it would do you good to lose weight isn't the point. The fact is, you just asked her to keep her opinions to herself. *That* is the point. Her motivation doesn't matter. Whatever supposedly benevolent rationale she claims to have behind her unwelcome comments does not excuse her disrespecting your boundaries. It is simply not her place to decide what is and what is not for *your* "own good." Every thought in her head doesn't have to come out of her mouth.

You're not asking anything so terrible. And you're not asking anything so difficult. All you're asking is for the hurtful behavior to *stop*, and for you to be treated politely, if not kindly. How simple it would be, really, to just say, "Sorry, I won't do it again." That's it. Problem solved, end of story, and everybody's happy. But, noooooo.......

Whenever your abuser coughs up a Nonsense Statement, it's the same as saying, "I deserve to continue abusing you because______," or, "You should let me abuse you as much as I want to because_________."

Abusers automatically defy and resist any boundaries you try to set, because it's really all about power. If you dare to ask for even a small concession, their first instinct is to defy you. Whenever she offended someone and they protested, my borderline grandmother would stridently rant, "Nobody is going to shut *me* up!" Psychopathic Daddy Darling's usual response to perfectly reasonable complaints about his abuse was, "*You* don't tell *me* how to act!" Narcissists and psychopaths don't see relationships as cooperative and mutually beneficial. *They* are the only ones who can benefit from a relationship, and everyone else is just there to be used by them. They see relationships as competitive and adversarial, and they have to *win*. You can't tell them what to do. That would make you their *boss*, when what they really think is that you're just dirt under their feet. No way are they going to let you get too big for your britches.

Nonsense Statements are strategies often used to put *you* on the defensive, with an implied or stated accusation that *you* are mistreating your abuser, that *you* are the one who is being unreasonable, or that *you* have some kind of mental problem. You will then find yourself answering your abuser's insinuations and defending yourself to half the family, sometimes including your own spouse and children, instead of having your abuser answer *your* rebuke.

Nonsense Statements are used to avoid accountability. They are used to avoid committing to a change in behavior. In fact, they are used to avoid the entire issue. They are a way of changing the subject and twisting it around. They divert you onto another track and leave whatever you originally said hanging there, ignored and unanswered, as if you never said it in the first place. They deflect everyone's attention away from what *the abuser* is doing, and onto what *you* are supposedly doing. *You're* hurting your abuser's feelings, *you're* ungrateful, *you're* unforgiving, *you're* uncaring, *you* expect too much, *you're* a bad Christian, *you* misunderstand everything, *you're* making your abuser sick, *you're* wrong. *You* are the one with the problem, *not him.*

Sisters and Brothers, when your abuser or his Silent Partners and Flying Monkeys try to change the subject, don't let them. Ignore their diversionary tactics, stick to your guns, and repeat your request until you get a sensible answer. When you rebuke your abuser, you deserve a response to your rebuke, not some comment out of left field that has nothing to do with anything you just said. When you make a direct statement of complaint to your abuser, you have the right to expect a direct answer to your complaint~ *meaning an acknowledgement that your abuser heard you, that he understands what you said, and that he will stop doing whatever it is that's upsetting you.*

Without this, you have no hope. You can never look forward to a better relationship. Nothing will ever change, nothing will ever get resolved, the abuse and control will continue, and so will your stress, sorrow and pain. You will go around in circles with your abuser for the rest of your life, trying your best to have a mutually respectful and pleasant relationship, while she makes a mockery out of every protest you voice and steamrolls right over you with her preposterous excuses for abusing you. You will be left with only two choices~ to live with it forever, or to end it and walk away, knowing that at least you tried.

What our abusers don't realize when they employ these strategies is that they are forcing our hand. They are leaving us no choice but to disown them in order to live healthy lives, and to protect our spouses and children from being exposed to their abuse and contaminated by their poison. Our attempts to resolve these issues come from a sincere desire to be able to continue being a family or church family, and also to have a nice, pleasant, mutually beneficial relationship with one another. When our rebukes are met with brick walls, and our abusers even go so far as to *plan ahead for future confrontations* by neutralizing our spouses or anyone else who cares for us by turning them against us, then we can have no doubt that they fully intend to continue their abuse and control forever, as long as we remain available as a target.

It is my prayer that this book will present you with some strategies of your own. Don't let your abusers ruin your friendships, your marriage, your family, and your life. Above all, don't let the children of Satan who masquerade as fellow believers in your church family cause you discouragement and disillusionment and ruin your relationship with our loving Heavenly Father. Believe me when I tell you that God is on *your* side, *not theirs*, and he does *not* approve of what they are saying and doing. I pray that being forewarned about the endless variety of lame excuses your relatives and demonic church members will use for abusing you will enable you to arm yourself with your own clear boundaries and be ready to enforce them. You are on the road to recovery. Don't let anyone stand in your way. This *is* war, the war for your mental, emotional, physical and spiritual health, your loved ones, your future, your peace, your freedom and your happiness. We don't want it to be that way, but that's how it is. Understand your "enemies" and their wiles. Understand The Enemy and *his* wiles. Put on the full armor of God, and prepare for battle. You *will* win this war, by the grace of God. May our heavenly Father bless you and hold you forever safe in the palm of his hand.

FINALLY, MY BRETHREN, BE STRONG IN THE LORD, AND IN THE POWER OF HIS MIGHT. PUT ON THE WHOLE ARMOUR OF GOD, THAT YE MAY BE ABLE TO STAND AGAINST THE WILES OF THE DEVIL. FOR WE WRESTLE NOT AGAINST FLESH AND BLOOD, BUT AGAINST PRINCIPALITIES, AGAINST POWERS, AGAINST THE RULERS OF THE DARKNESS OF THIS WORLD, AGAINST SPIRITUAL WICKEDNESS IN HIGH PLACES. WHEREFORE TAKE UNTO YOU THE WHOLE ARMOUR OF GOD, THAT YE MAY BE ABLE TO WITHSTAND IN THE EVIL DAY, AND HAVING DONE ALL, TO STAND. STAND THEREFORE, HAVING YOUR LOINS GIRT ABOUT WITH TRUTH, AND HAVING ON THE BREASTPLATE OF RIGHTEOUSNESS; AND YOUR FEET SHOD WITH THE PREPARATION OF THE GOSPEL OF PEACE; ABOVE ALL, TAKING THE SHIELD OF FAITH, WHEREWITH YE SHALL BE ABLE TO QUENCH ALL THE FIERY DARTS OF THE WICKED. AND TAKE THE HELMET OF SALVATION, AND THE

SWORD OF THE SPIRIT, WHICH IS THE WORD OF GOD: PRAYING ALWAYS WITH ALL PRAYER AND SUPPLICATION IN THE SPIRIT, AND WATCHING THEREUNTO WITH ALL PERSEVERANCE AND SUPPLICATION FOR ALL SAINTS; AND FOR ME, THAT UTTERANCE MAY BE GIVEN UNTO ME, THAT I MAY OPEN MY MOUTH BOLDLY, TO MAKE KNOWN THE MYSTERY OF THE GOSPEL, FOR WHICH I AM AN AMBASSADOR IN BONDS: THAT THEREIN I MAY SPEAK BOLDLY, AS I OUGHT TO SPEAK......Ephesians 6:10-20 KJV.

ALSO BY SISTER RENEE PITTELLI

THE FAMILY FREELOADER

Is there a freeloader in your family? Are you tired of being constantly hit up for money, invitations, and favors? Are you fed up with always being the host and never the guest? Do your family members think they're entitled to your help, but don't think they need to show any appreciation, pay you back, or return the favor? Are you worried about not being a "good" Christian if you say "No" to a freeloader's request? Written with humor, wisdom, and a healthy dose of common sense, The Family Freeloader is just what you need! In this book, Sister Renee Pittelli will:

- Help you recognize the various ploys that freeloaders use to get money and favors from us.

- Explain how con-artist relatives observe and test you, and what personality traits might make you seem like easy prey.

- Systematically debunk many of the most common sob-stories and surprisingly sneaky tactics used by our family freeloaders.

- Teach you 21 Ways to Spot A Con.

- Offer a step-by-step guide of effective strategies for turning down requests for money and favors, and deflecting the hard-luck stories, scams, pressure, and guilt-trips in your freeloader's bag of tricks.

- Include an analysis of what the Bible really says about giving to the poor and needy versus giving to the idle and malingerers, with relevant Scripture verses.

The Family Freeloader is an invaluable lesson for all kind-hearted, generous people-pleasers, who love their families, on how to avoid being taken advantage of by the unscrupulous among us.

ALSO BY SISTER RENEE PITTELLI

NARCISSISTIC PREDICAMENTS

Adult Children of narcissistic families often find themselves stuck in predicaments that people with normal families never have to face. Featuring The 21 Rules of No Contact and 102 Questions to Ask Yourself When Deciding Whether to End an Abusive Relationship, Narcissistic Predicaments has the answers you've been looking for.

When you try to set boundaries, do your abusive relatives accuse you of not being a "good Christian" because:

- You are not honoring your father and mother?
- You have to "forgive and forget," even though your abusers have not apologized or agreed to stop their abuse?
- You must forgive unrepentant evildoers because Jesus said "Father forgive them, for they know not what they do"?
- You are taking revenge by enforcing consequences, and vengeance is supposed to be the Lord's?
- The Bible says "Love your enemies"?

In this book, you will learn effective strategies for protecting yourself and find out what the Bible really says about dilemmas such as:

- Should you let your estranged relatives have contact with your children?
- Dealing with the family meddler who tries to intervene between you and your abusive relative
- Working in the family business with narcissists and sociopaths
- What to expect when you rock the boat and get married
- What to do about holidays, parties, and family celebrations, including Mother's Day and Father's Day
- Does your abuser's apology automatically cover the other relatives who took his side?
- What to expect from estranged relatives who want to drag you back into their web
- Reconciling on your terms, not theirs
- If you don't stick around, who will take care of your abusive parents in their old age?
- Visiting a dying abuser
- When your abuser or estranged relative dies- condolences, funerals, and obituaries

God does not want you to "live in peace" with evil people. A breath of fresh air for Adult Children of abusive families, this compelling book will help you find the peace our heavenly Father promised you, because you are His beloved child.

Learn more at: www.outskirtspress.com/narcissisticpredicaments

ALSO BY SISTER RENEE PITTELLI

BREAKING THE BONDS OF ADULT CHILD ABUSE

ADULT CHILD ABUSE *The Only Form of Abuse still tolerated, accepted and condoned in our society. *The Only Form Of Abuse in which it is considered okay for a competent adult to be controlled, exploited, or damaged by someone else. *The Only Form of Abuse in which the victim is expected to continue suffering indefinitely, criticized for trying to protect herself, judged for escaping from her abuser, and openly discouraged from standing up for herself, talking about it, or revealing the abuse to others. Where do folks get the idea that Christians have to be meek and mild, silently enduring mistreatment, tolerating anything anybody else does, and timidly standing by while abusers trample all over them and other innocent victims? Since when is it a sin to take a stand and speak out against evil? This is what our abusers want us to believe, and it is nothing but misconceptions and lies. Do you know that God wants us to confront people who do evil? That he tells us to have nothing further to do with those who will not listen to rebuke? That there is no biblical requirement to forgive the unrepentant? In this book, you will learn about family abusers and their Silent Partners, why they abuse us and why we let them, setting and enforcing limits, godly confrontation, The Law of Sowing and Reaping and letting abusers suffer the Natural Consequences of their own behavior, how to tell if a comment is really a criticism, family jealousy and how to detect if a relative is jealous of you, recognizing and cutting ties with reprobates, improving your family holidays, how to forgive and what forgiveness really means, and what Jesus would REALLY do. Filled with helpful dialogue, this book offers many valuable lessons, including: *107 Examples of abusive behavior and betrayal *6 Major No-Nos for mature, independent adults *26 Reasons why they abuse us, and 55 questions to help us understand why we allow it *27 Ways to respond to a critic *35 Empowering Statements for declaring your boundaries and enforcing consequences *10 Simple Steps for learning to say no and 8 responses for those who aren't happy about it *40 Off-Limits Subjects *38 Signs of a meaningless apology and 17 signs of a meaningful one *The 21 Rules of No Contact *102 Questions to ask yourself when you're trying to decide if you should end a toxic relationship *5 Strategies for more pleasant holidays with your relatives *The 7 Biblical Duties of a proper parent *11 Steps for getting over a lost relationship. Written with empathy, wisdom and understanding, and loaded with scriptural references, this book is an eye-opener that will help you claim your freedom and change your life.

CPSIA information can be obtained at www.ICGtesting.com
Printed in the USA
BVOW05s2011170116

433173BV00002B/69/P

9 781478 707073